Public Sector Organizations

Series Editors
B. Guy Peters
Department of Political Science
University of Pittsburgh
Pittsburgh, PA, USA

Geert Bouckaert
Public Management Institute
Katholieke Universiteit Leuven, Belgium

Organizations are the building blocks of governments. The role of organizations, formal and informal, is most readily apparent in public bureaucracy, but all the institutions of the public sector are comprised of organizations, or have some organizational characteristics that affect their performance. Therefore, if scholars want to understand how governments work, a very good place to start is at the level of organizations involved in delivering services. Likewise, if practitioners want to understand how to be effective in the public sector, they would be well-advised to consider examining the role of organizations and how to make organizations more effective. This series publishes research-based books concerned with organizations in the public sector and covers such issues as: the autonomy of public sector organizations; networks and network analysis; bureaucratic politics; organizational change and leadership; and methodology for studying organizations.

More information about this series at
http://www.palgrave.com/gp/series/14525

Evrim Tan

Decentralization and Governance Capacity

The Case of Turkey

Evrim Tan
University of Leuven
Leuven, Belgium

Public Sector Organizations
ISBN 978-3-030-02046-0   ISBN 978-3-030-02047-7   (eBook)
https://doi.org/10.1007/978-3-030-02047-7

Library of Congress Control Number: 2018962047

© The Editor(s) (if applicable) and The Author(s), under exclusive license to Springer
Nature Switzerland AG, part of Springer Nature 2019
This work is subject to copyright. All rights are solely and exclusively licensed by the
Publisher, whether the whole or part of the material is concerned, specifically the rights
of translation, reprinting, reuse of illustrations, recitation, broadcasting, reproduction
on microfilms or in any other physical way, and transmission or information storage and
retrieval, electronic adaptation, computer software, or by similar or dissimilar methodology
now known or hereafter developed.
The use of general descriptive names, registered names, trademarks, service marks, etc. in this
publication does not imply, even in the absence of a specific statement, that such names are
exempt from the relevant protective laws and regulations and therefore free for general use.
The publisher, the authors and the editors are safe to assume that the advice and
information in this book are believed to be true and accurate at the date of publication.
Neither the publisher nor the authors or the editors give a warranty, express or implied,
with respect to the material contained herein or for any errors or omissions that may have
been made. The publisher remains neutral with regard to jurisdictional claims in published
maps and institutional affiliations.

This Palgrave Macmillan imprint is published by the registered company Springer Nature
Switzerland AG
The registered company address is: Gewerbestrasse 11, 6330 Cham, Switzerland

*This book is dedicated
to
Vjosa Musliu and Nora Tan.*

ACKNOWLEDGEMENTS

I would like to thank all the people who have supported me in writing this book.

I am grateful to Geert Bouckaert, for his support and academic guidance for the past 9 years. I have been amazingly fortunate to work with him.

I would also like to thank Rahmi Göktaş, Furkan Tanrıverdi, Ozan Korhan Ağbaş, Umut Oran, and valuable experts in Union of Municipalities of Turkey for their support on the field research.

Most of all, I am grateful and thankful to my wife Vjosa Musliu and my family, who unconditionally supported me all these years, and I am grateful for their love, care, and encouragement.

Contents

1 Introduction — 1
Decentralization and Capacity. A Chicken and the Egg Situation? — 1
Theoretical Premises and Promises of Decentralization — 5
When Does Decentralization Lead to Better Governance? — 10
Outline of the Book — 13
References — 15

2 Decentralization and Capacity in Public Governance — 21
What Is the Governance Perspective? — 22
Is There a Theory of Public Governance? — 27
Actors in Public Governance — 33
Decentralization in Public Governance — 37
   Administrative Decentralization — 40
   Political Decentralization — 41
   Fiscal Decentralization — 42
A Theory of Decentralization in Public Governance and Determinants of Success — 43
Governance Capacity — 50
Capacity as a Black Box Concept — 52
Theories of Governance Capacity — 56
   Governance Capacity from a Managerial Perspective — 57

ix

Governance Capacity from an Organizational Perspective	60
Governance Capacity from an Institutional Perspective	63
An Analytical Model for Governance Capacity	66
Research Hypotheses About the Relationship Between Decentralization and Governance Capacity	69
References	71

3 Turkey's Local Government Reform Process — 79

An Overview of the Turkish Local Government	79
The Historical Evolution of the Turkish Local Government	82
The Local Government Reform Process During AKP Government	88
A More Decentralized Public Governance?	98
Central Government's Discretion over Local Governance	103
Administrative Discretion of Central Government	103
Political Discretion of Central Government	108
Fiscal Discretion of Central Government	111
Non-state Actors in Local Governance	113
Citizen Participation	113
Private Sector Organizations	116
Civil Society Organizations	118
Some Final Remarks About Local Government Reforms	121
References	124

4 Local Governance Capacities in Turkey — 127

Financial Capabilities	128
Material Capabilities	132
Communication Capabilities	136
Planning Capabilities	143
Managerial Capabilities	147
Human Resources Capabilities	150
Conclusion	153
References	156

5 What Is the Relationship Between Governance Capacity and Decentralization? — 159

Research Design and Data	159
Research Variables	165

| | CONTENTS | xi |

Decentralization	166
Local Capacity	167
Mobilization Capacity	167
Decision-Making Capacity	169
Implementation Capacity	170
Control Variables	172
Overview of the Field Research	173
Data Preparation and Screening	177
Data Analysis	178
Regression Models	181
Interpretation of Findings	186
Conclusion	189
References	191

6 Conclusion: Toward an Asymmetrical Decentralization Design — 193

Decentralization and Development—Precarious Relationship? — 194

Asymmetrical Decentralization for Better Governance — 203

  Asymmetric Decentralization — 203

  Comparison of Symmetric and Asymmetric Decentralization Designs — 215

Conclusion and Final Remarks — 221

References — 223

Appendices — 229

Index — 265

ABBREVIATIONS

AKP	Justice and Development Party
BDP	Peace and Democracy Party
CHP	People's Republican Party
CSO	Civil Society Organization
EC	European Commission
EU	The European Union
HDP	People's Democratic Party
HR	Human Resource
HRM	Human Resource Management
ICT	Information and Communication Technologies
IMF	International Monetary Fund
LAR II	Local Administration Reform in Turkey Phase II
MDG	Millennium Development Goals
MHP	Nationalist People Party
NGO	Non-Governmental Organization
NPG	New Public Governance
NPM	New Public Management
NUTS	Nomenclature of Territorial Units for Statistics
OECD	Organization for Economic Co-operation and Development
SDG	Sustainable Development Goals
SEE	State Economic Enterprises
SIGMA	Support for Improvement in Governance and Management
SPA	Special Provincial Administrations
SPO	State Planning Organization
TSE	Total Survey Error
UNDP	United Nations Development Program
WTO	World Trade Organization

LIST OF FIGURES

Fig. 2.1	An analytical framework for theories of governance capacity (*Source* Author)	57
Fig. 2.2	An analytical model for capacities in local governance	68
Fig. 3.1	Public bodies according to 'decentralization principle' (*Source* TODAIE [2007: 13])	82
Fig. 3.2	Fiscal trends in public sector (2004–2018) (*Data Source* Republic of Turkey—Ministry of Finance)	100
Fig. 3.3	Trends in public sector employment (*Source* Ministry of Finance-General Directorate of Budget and Fiscal Control)	101
Fig. 3.4	Trends in expenditure (2004–2018) (*Data Source* Ministry of Finance)	102
Fig. 3.5	Importance of central administration in local governance	110
Fig. 3.6	Access to public managers	115
Fig. 4.1	Information structure	139
Fig. 4.2	Structure of participation in strategic planning	145
Fig. 4.3	Staff motivation and performance	149
Fig. 5.1	The relationship between decentralization and governance capacity	188

LIST OF TABLES

Table 2.1	Decentralization typologies	39
Table 3.1	Overview of local administration reform process in Turkey	92
Table 5.1	Survey responses from municipalities	176
Table 5.2	Descriptive statistics	179
Table 5.3	Correlation matrix	180
Table 5.4	OLS regressions	183

CHAPTER 1

Introduction

DECENTRALIZATION AND CAPACITY. A CHICKEN AND THE EGG SITUATION?

In the second half of the twentieth century, the literature on public administration witnessed a rapid transformation in methods and in ways of thinking. This transformation has altered the Weberian state relying on the hierarchical state structure and functioning. Particularly, the embodiment of neoliberal principles in Thatcher and Reagan's public policies paved the way for inclusion of private sector originated principles and techniques into the realm of public administration. New concepts such as deregulation, privatization, and adoption of management principles have occupied the public administration literature, and the field of public management has emerged as a separate branch of public administration. This change in the literature took another turn in the 1990s with the rise of another influential concept, *governance*. Nowadays, governing the society incorporates horizontally public, private, and civil society organizations on the one hand, and vertically local, regional, national, and supranational state organizations on the other into a complex, reticular set of relations. Hence, what used to be a unidimensional relationship between citizen and the state has turned into a multidimensional realm with various interactions among different actors.

Shifting understanding in the way of governing society necessitated local government to incur new roles and responsibilities in public governance. In this juncture, decentralization has become a fundamental

© The Author(s) 2019
E. Tan, *Decentralization and Governance Capacity*, Public Sector
Organizations, https://doi.org/10.1007/978-3-030-02047-7_1

1

2   E. TAN

part of the governance literature. It is widely acknowledged that decentralized governance contributes both to democracy and also to the efficiency and effectiveness of public services. Although decentralization policies and the degree of decentralization vary across country cases, it is expected that decentralized authority and responsibilities provide in return some advantages to governance system, such as effectiveness, efficiency, better service quality, empowerment of different segments of the society, economic growth, democratization, accountability, and even in some cases security (Rodden 2004; Pollitt 2005; Sharma 2006; Treisman 2007). So far, many studies have been conducted to evaluate the effectiveness of decentralization policies in public governance. Yet, the outcomes of decentralization policies are not coherent in each case. Especially, empirical accounts from developing countries showed that decentralization could lead to higher corruption, macroeconomic instabilities, coordination problems, inefficiency, and ineffectiveness on public services (Prud'homme 1995; Litvack et al. 1998; Smoke 2003; Oxhorn 2004). Evidence indicates that decentralization can have a positive effect but only if certain conditions are met (Smoke et al. 2006).

Even though the determinants of effective decentralization policies for public governance are equivocal, one commonly agreed element is an adequate local capacity is necessary for successful implementation of decentralization reforms and for functioning decentralized governance. In that sense, many international donor organizations (e.g., UNDP, World Bank) have undertaken extensive capacity building programs in developing and transition countries to assist them in policy implementation within and after decentralization reforms. Yet, capacity is an elusive concept (Brown et al. 2001) and the question of 'which local capacities are functional for decentralized governance?' remains unresolved.

Indeed, the relationship between capacity and decentralization is mostly unapprehended. Two contradicting views exist about this relationship. One view is that the preceding capacity determines the success of decentralization policies (e.g., Bahl and Linn 1992). An opposite point of view suggests a decentralized government obtains the capacity to govern in time (e.g., Rondinelli et al. 1983). In this regard, the World Bank supports the latter by stating the following;

> Rather than plan and make a large up-front investment in the local capacity building as a prerequisite for devolution of responsibility, there was a broad consensus that it would be quicker and more cost-effective to

begin the process of devolution, to permit learning by doing and to build up capacity through practice. The evidence increasingly shows that local capacity can be built by the process of decentralization, particularly when appropriate programs to increase interaction with the private sector are included in decentralization design[1]

This debate is not only limited to academic circles or international donor organizations but also relevant for policy practitioners and policy makers. For instance, during a technical consultation on decentralization, Fiszbein (1997) gives the following anecdote:

> An interesting illustration of the controversies associated with these questions (i.e. whether the local level has, or can develop quickly enough the necessary capabilities) is the parliamentary debate that took place in Colombia as a new law that would create untied fiscal transfers to local governments was being discussed in the early 1980s. The mainstream opinion in Congress was that no real benefit would be derived from transferring funds and responsibilities to local governments if their lack of capacity would not allow them to manage them effectively in order to improve the quantity and quality of services offered to the population. Interestingly enough, the proponents of the law -that would eventually be passed by Congress- did not try to argue that such capacities indeed existed. Rather, their argument was that only if fiscal resources and responsibilities for service delivery were transferred to local governments would those capabilities develop, as it is only if and when faced with concrete challenges that local institutions would acquire them (Galan [1990]).
>
> In fact, at least for some of the Colombian reformers, the creation of local capacity -- understood as the consolidation of democratic state and civic institutions particularly in more than 800 rural municipios-- was an objective rather than a condition for decentralization. Almost a decade later, Bolivia would follow a similar path, and similar discussions can be found in post-civil war debates in several countries in Central America.

Twenty years after, this debate still remains lively and unabated. The global trend shows that states extensively embrace different forms of decentralization reforms with the aim of improving public governance. It is widely assumed that the relationship between governance capacity

---

[1]Working Group 5 (Institutional Capacity) at the Technical Consultation on Decentralization and Rural Development, FAO, Rome, December 1997.

and decentralization determines the success in governance, but how this relationship function is largely contested. Does decentralization lead to improvement in governance capacities and higher governance capacities bring better governance, or are certain capacities preconditioned for decentralization to lead better governance? As the title of the section suggests, the relationship between governance capacity and decentralization is treated so far as a chicken and the egg situation. In principle, it is difficult to refute any of these arguments, as both can occur concurrently. Yet, this debate boils down to the primary question of 'which capacities are associated with decentralization?'. Addressing this question is not only an academic endeavor, but it is also vital for policy practitioners to design most effective decentralization policies.

An additional level of complexity is that the traditional modes of governance are changing parallel to the overall shift in public management. Now private sector organizations and civil society groups are taking a more tangible role and responsibility in governing the society. In this transitional stage, roles of the state and other actors are re-evaluated in terms of their legitimacy, responsibilities, and function in governance. Inevitably, these new dimensions are expanding the discussion on governance capacities for public organizations. All these systemic changes necessitate reconsidering the implications of decentralization and capacity in the broader sense of governance.

This book aims to reduce the ambiguity surrounding the subject of decentralization and governance capacity by drawing its conclusions from the empirical accounts on the Turkish local government. Turkey, a profound centralized state, has legislated various local administration reform acts since the early 2000s. Functions, roles, and responsibilities of local government have been extended with new legislation. Public services, which used to be under the jurisdiction of the central government, on health, tourism and culture, forest and environment, agriculture and village affairs, social care and children protection, youth and sports, industry, and public works have been devolved to local government. The administrative and financial autonomy of the local government is recognized, and local government is vested discretion in economic activities and fiscal borrowing. The rapid transition of local government has revived the discussions on the topic of capacity enhancement in public governance. These contemporary developments in Turkish public administration present a unique opportunity to explore the dynamics of capacity and decentralization behind better governance.

Theoretical Premises and Promises of Decentralization

Empowering the local versus the center and the vice versa has always been integral in the theoretical debates about governance. There are even authors who perceive the history of governments as a pendulum between centralization and decentralization (see Atasoy 2009; Sanderson 1995). When the term decentralization appeared for the first time in the English language in the mid of nineteenth century, it was used as the binary opposite of centralization which was largely accepted as the panacea of ineffective, bad governance in the post-Napoleonic Europe (see Young 1898). Tocqueville, one of the earliest supporters of decentralization, challenged this idea arguing that decentralization is not only better for democratic principles but also better for efficient and effective governance and thus contesting the key argument of the supporters of centralism. Even though the supporters of decentralization had been marginal until the second part of the twentieth century, both concepts—decentralization and centralization—have prevailed in academic circles. New battlefields were discovered to argue which concept provides the best alternative to democracy building, management, economics, and development. In the second half of the twentieth century, the balance has tipped toward decentralization, and decentralization has taken the upper hand in this long rivalry as the best alternative for governance in the post-nation-state and globalized world system. Once decentralization was acknowledged as the best alternative, the debate on whether decentralization or centralization is better for governance, shifted into the debate of diagnosing the conditions for the best outcomes in decentralized systems.

The theoretical premises of decentralization in public governance have expanded parallel to this conceptual evolution. Cheema and Rondinelli (2007) describe three phases of the evolution of decentralization.

The first phase, in the 1970s and 1980s, was about thinking of decentralization as a form of deconcentrating hierarchical government structures and bureaucracy. After more than two decades of centralization practices following World War II, governments in both developed and less developed countries realized the limits of central economic planning and management governments. Governments started to decentralize their hierarchical structures and shifted part of their competences to local authorities in order to make public service delivery more effective. In the development literature, in the early 1980s, the promotion of administrative decentralization had become part of the development strategies adopted by the aid agencies in developing countries (Cohen and Peterson 1999: 11). Especially, the inability of central governments in Africa to provide public services to local areas (see Kiggundu 1989) and the fall of authoritarian regimes in Latin America fostered the need for decentralization. In this phase, we see that decentralization was acknowledged as a mean to improve the organizational performance in government, preponderated in the organization (see Mintzberg 1980) and development theories.

The second phase took place in the mid-1980s and incorporated new paradigms such as political power sharing and market liberalization. In this period, decentralization was contextualized predominantly within the neo-liberalist discourse. Privatization and market liberalization were embraced by the decentralization literature.

During the third phase of the 1990s, decentralization was seen as a way of governance to wider public participation. Two important discursive developments in governance, the 'New Public Management' movement in the Western countries and the promotion of 'democratic governance' by international organizations, redefined the role of decentralization. The NPM movement defined the efficient government as 'innovative, market-oriented, decentralized and customer oriented' (Osborne and Gaebler 1992), and advocated that the efficiency in public services can only be achieved through the participation of citizens and through the teamwork among the government agencies in a decentralized governance structure. According to NPM, decentralization results in better governance, facilitate the development of more effective and efficient public sector management, increases popular participation in government, allows for better mobilization and use of resources, and encourages market-like responsiveness to the provision and consumption of public services (Hope 2000). Furthermore, 'democratic governance' has become one of the decentralization objectives. This policy has been foremost in the promotion of 'subsidiarity principle' by the EU and in the promotion of 'good governance' by the international organizations including the IMF, World Bank, and UNDP. In overall, decentralization has been embraced by the democratization literature as an essential concept.

Nowadays decentralization in public governance is situated in the midst of enhancing democratic voice and economic efficiency on public services. Although most of the theoretical propositions estimate the positive effect of decentralization on both notions, empirical studies reached contradictory results on backing the theoretical premises.

With regard to the economic efficiency argument, Tiebout posited one of the earliest theoretical applications of decentralization. Tiebout (1956) argued that decentralization would contribute to the economic efficiency of public services by enhancing the competition among local administrations in attracting residents. In the so-called public choice theory, residents of localities are depicted as 'shopping' customers between different municipalities with the flexibility to choose the one with the optimal mixture of taxes and public services. This flexibility in choosing creates a competition among municipalities to provide the best services with the most reasonable amount, thus ensuring the municipalities are not wasting local resources nor overproducing public goods. The most common criticism to public choice theory is that in practice, citizens are not as mobile as the theory predicts and they are not necessarily motivated with rational choices but are bound to their social and local identities. Further theories driven from public choice theory anticipate that in the decentralized or federal systems where the competition is high, local administrations would have abilities to adopt innovative and regenerative systems fostering the economic growth (Feld et al. 2003). Musgrave (1959), on the other hand, pointed to the fact that since local administrations have better information on the needs and demand of localities, decentralization may enable increased efficiency in the distribution of public services. Building on the theses of Tiebout and Musgrave, Oates's (1972) 'decentralization theorem' argues when differences across regions are high and spillover effect is limited, decentralized authority over public goods enforces public responsiveness and brings higher efficiency. In a later account, Brennan and Buchanan's (1980) 'Leviathan hypothesis' assumes decentralization of revenue raising authority would lead to higher efficiencies in public services, and in overall limiting public sector expenditure.[2] So the economic premises of decentralization hinge on the information advantage of local government and the benefit of competition among local governments to bring higher efficiency

---

[2]Cassette and Paty (2010)'s findings on a panel data set of EU 15 countries contest the Leviathan hypothesis on aggregate government expenditures, by showing the tax autonomy tends to increase local government expenditures by a wide margin in the long run despite limiting central government expenditures, and thus leading to higher aggregate government expenditure.

in public services, and through which further theories assume higher return of benefits on macroeconomic stability, economic growth, size of government, income redistribution, innovation, and better quality of governance.

Notwithstanding this wide spectrum of benefits, comparative and empirical studies have failed to verify satisfactorily most of the theoretical assumptions. Especially, the impact of decentralization on economic growth still remains contested. The empirical studies are clustered in two groups in terms of their findings on individual and comparative cases. The first group (see Akai and Sakata 2002; Thiessen 2003; Stansel 2005; Iimi 2005) verified that decentralization has statistically a significant positive impact on economic growth. In opposition, the second group (see Woller and Phillips 1998; Davoodi and Zou 1998; Zhang and Zou 1998; Xie et al. 1999; Jin and Zou 2005; Baskaran and Feld 2009; Rodriguez and Ezcurra 2011) found that the impact of decentralization on economic growth is either statistically insignificant or negative under some certain conditions. The main explanation of contradictory outcomes usually relies on the differences in theoretical approaches and methodological choices.

In contrast to the economic efficiency argument, democratization argument of decentralization stems from political science theories. From the era of Tocqueville and John Stuart Mill, decentralization has often been associated with pluralistic politics and representative government. Decentralization can support democratization by giving citizens, or their representatives, more influence in the formulation and implementation of policies (World Bank 2018). The former appraises decentralization within the traditional forms of representative democracy, and here political decentralization fosters political competition in popular elections through which citizen responsiveness in public governance is enhanced (see Rudebeck et al. 1998; Whitehead 2002; Harris et al. 2004; Grindle 2007). The latter approach treats decentralization in conjunction with deliberative democracy and direct representation. The deliberative democracy theory (see Bessette 1980, 1994) suggests that consultative processes through discussions among various stakeholders are essential to enhance democracy, whereby finding solutions to common problems would be possible with limited resources and constraints (Chambers 2003). For this purpose, local governments should be free from the ties of bureaucracy and then they can be more flexible in consultation and negotiation with local stakeholders. This way, the devised policies will be more responsive to the local needs and will address better to diverse interests in society than those made only by the political authorities (Dahl 1971). In fact, despite their different ontological origins, the democracy argument of decentralization also hinges on the importance of political competition and the information advantage brought about by the inclusion of citizens in improving public governance. The node that binds together both strands of decentralization theories is that local government should be financially and democratically dependent and accountable to local constituents.

Nonetheless, the democratization assumptions of decentralization are empirically contested as well, especially by the studies conducted in developing countries in Asia and Africa (see Smith 1985: 188–191). For instance, Oxhorn et al. (2004) found that decentralization itself does not improve democratic governance, but rather, democratic effects are shaped by (1) motivations of decentralization, (2) historical patterns of state-society relations, and (3) institutional arrangements. Other studies point out the risk of decentralization on the political capture of decision-making procedures by local elites or enforcing practices of exclusions toward certain parts of communities (see Pal and Roy 2010; Shah and Thompson 2004; Bardhan and Mookherjee 2000). Especially, in the cases where civic participation in local government is low and large inequalities in land ownership exist, interest groups and local elites may grasp the power in local governments and direct resources toward their own priorities rather than improving the provision of local public goods and poverty alleviation (Shah and Thompson 2004).

Nevertheless, the motivation of decentralization is not only limited to its structural benefits for democracy and economy outcomes. Shah and Thompson (2004) underline that short-term political considerations have been more decisive in initiating decentralization reforms rather than long-term structural benefits. As widely observed in Central and Eastern European countries, aspirations for the EU membership were substantial to implement wide-range of decentralization reforms. Also, in some other developing countries, political and fiscal crises (e.g., Indonesia, Pakistan, and Turkey) or political calculations to sideline oppositions (e.g., Poland, Peru, and Pakistan) were substantial for decentralization reforms. In relation to the political motivation of decentralization, Eaton (2001) gives three possible cases:

10   E. TAN

i. Decentralization might be a voluntary choice of politicians—it can increase political stability and economic growth in a way that compensates politicians for any loss of power they may experience in the short run (see also Manor 1999).

ii. Decentralization may result from political pressures exerted by sub-national politicians. If sub-national politicians can influence the political careers of their representatives in the national assembly, these legislators may be coerced into supporting decentralization (according to Willis et al. 1999).

iii. Decentralization may reflect short-term gains for politicians since politicians usually discount future gains heavily. When the government is divided, the party in control of the legislature may promote decentralization as a way to constrain the executive branch.

Decentralization reforms are also motivated by the external influences through globalization and information revolution (Shah and Thompson 2004). The globalization perspective relies on that nation-states are 'too small to tackle large things in life and too large to address small things'. Besides, international organizations such as WTO, UNDP, and other specialized institutions in global governance are taking profound roles in regulating the information technologies, international financial transactions, and macroeconomic management. The EU's policies and principles on subsidiarity, fiscal harmonization, and structural funds have also a direct impact not only on candidate countries but also on developing and transition economies.

When Does Decentralization Lead to Better Governance?

Today, decentralization is not only promoted as the way to reach good governance objectives but also decentralized governance is an ideal state within the governance framework (see Osborn and Gaebler 1992). This relationship between decentralization and governance can best be described as symbiotic. In other words, public governance requires decentralizing central functions to lower tiers of government as well as to non-state actors while decentralization is also associated with good governance objectives.

Therefore, it is no surprise; decentralization reforms have been implemented with the aim to develop public governance. Different theoretical and empirical studies have proposed various hypotheses and propositions about the circumstances, which relay decentralization to better governance (see Crook and Manor 1998; Turner 1999; Campbell 2003; Olowu and Wunsch 2004; Oxhorn 2004; Saito 2005; Grindle 2007). It is evident, that empirical and theoretical studies fall short to verify all prospects of decentralization about better governance. Nevertheless, the following assumptions can be deduced on the relationship between decentralization and public governance:

1. Theories suggesting that decentralization leads to better governance anticipate a codependent relationship between citizens and local governments, where the local government relies on finance and information sources in the locality and has the discretion to act on it (Musgrave 1959; Osborn and Gaebler 1992). Residents involved in the governance process as shareholders either directly or through proxy organizations, thereby enhance the accountability, efficiency, and effectiveness in public services. Furthermore, the legitimacy of public governance is created by the mutual interaction between citizens and local government.

2. Arguments suggesting that higher decentralization indicates always better governance are far too optimistic. A more reasonable argument would suggest that both centralization and decentralization have their aptitudes for better governance (Saito 2005). From the state perspective, decentralization and centralization can be a trade-off where the former can enable more flexibility and efficiency on government services whereas the latter is important to ensure social equality and coordination among institutions. Furthermore, the effectiveness of decentralization in the provision of public goods with spillover effect can be enhanced with the presence of strong parties (see Riker 1964) or centralized political parties (see Ponce-Rodríguez et al. 2018). Yet, less party institutionalization in local government can foster the effect of decentralization in advancing participatory governance (Goldfrank 2007).

3. Decentralization serves for better engagement in governance by bringing the government services closer to citizens and promoting grassroots democracy in localities. However, in the cases of a local elite capture or a lack of civil awareness to supervise government actions, decentralization can adversely affect local governance (Prud'homme 1995; Shah and Thomson 2004). In this regard,

a certain level of social capital is imperative to ensure the monitoring of local government's action and tax revenues. Furthermore, local governance can depend on the degree of public sector modernization in the form of new techniques, and digital technologies to improve capacity and local government efficiency (see Grindle 2007; Dunleavy et al. 2005).

4. Decentralization can foster competition in public services horizontally and vertically, which is important for the quality of governance. Yet, it also entails the danger of losing coordination and creating social inequality (Kodras 1997; Prud'homme 1995), and leading to inefficiencies in public service provisions through localization of corruption, vested interests, and provincial protectionism (Tanzi 1995; Bardhan 2002; Fan et al. 2009). Many studies suggest that the presence of central authority assures the equity in service provision and macroeconomic stability (Boyne 1996; Stohr 2001). However, increased influence of central authority can impede the development of endogenous capacities at the local level for better governance. Therefore, better governance would most likely rely on a 'pareto optimum' between the central and local governments in terms of responsibilities and competencies.

5. However, the level of this 'pareto optimum' is dependent on some underlying factors. These underlying factors comprise capacities of governing organizations, socio-economic and sociocultural conditions as well as the regulatory framework (Saito 2001, 2005; Olowu and Wunsch 2004). Especially, certain organizational capacities in governing organizations are deemed necessary for the success of decentralization policies. Among others, a sufficient human capital, the means of collecting information, financial capacity, capacity to ensure proper policy design and implementation have been underscored imperative to reap the benefits of decentralization (Nannyonjo and Okot 2012; Sharma 2014). Additionally, findings suggest that sociocultural conditions and social cleavages arising from ethnic and minority-related issues are also influential on adjusting the share of responsibilities between central and local authorities (Sorens 2009; Nannyonjo and Okot 2012).

There are still many unresolved subjects about what determines the success of decentralization policies in public governance. For this reason, decentralization can lead to unexpected outcomes, but in the meantime, it has the potential to bring increased efficiency, solidarity, and effectiveness in government services. Under these conditions, it is most important for policy practitioners to be aware of contextual conditions and to be capable to deal with what decentralization can bring. Yet, the questions still remain unsolved, 'how should policymakers decide on the degree of decentralization to ensure the best outcome in public governance?' and 'how do governance capacities affect this outcome?'

Outline of the Book

This book addresses the underlying question of 'when does decentralization lead to better governance?' by focusing on the relationship between decentralization and capacity from a public governance perspective. In the book, I address this question by bringing together diverse theoretical and empirical accounts from different fields such as public administration, public economics, management sciences, political sciences, development studies, with my empirical findings from Turkish case, primarily relying on findings from a comparative analysis in Turkish provincial municipalities. The book draws theoretically novel and policy-relevant conclusions, which would be not only for the interest of area practitioners but also a wider readership from academia, policy makers, and practitioners interested in decentralization reforms, local governance, and capacity building would find an added value in it.

There are three main reasons to consider this research problem worthy of consideration. First of all, as mentioned earlier, there is limited knowledge on the mutual implication of decentralization and capacity. It is unclear, which capacities are required in local government to have successful decentralization outcomes or how decentralization policies affect the existing capacities. It has been an under-researched area and the present literature allows limited 'generalizations' (Fiszbein 1997). Understanding the dynamics between governance capacity and decentralization is fundamental to design more effective decentralization policies and policy interventions to improve governance outcomes. Furthermore, most empirical accounts in decentralization literature rely on cross-national regressions, but country-specific institutional, cultural, and political differences impinge on drawing persuasive conclusions. Rodden (2004) states '*A more promising avenue than cross-country regressions is to approach detailed single country studies from an explicitly comparative perspective*'. Secondly, capacity building programs are taken as subsequent actions following decentralization reforms to improve local capacities. In this respect, this research has the potential to bring new perspectives on capacity building regarding '*when to apply?*' and '*what to apply?*'. Third, this study is conducted with a governance perspective, therefore it does not only take into consideration organizational capacities, as most of the capacity assessment studies do, but it includes the endogenous capacity of locality in the assessment of governance capacities. By analyzing the capacities of local government and locality separately in relation to decentralized governance, the study brings up new insights on effective policy interventions to improve public governance.

On a more practical level, policy makers in Turkey will benefit from the findings of the study in assessing the public management reform performance of Turkey and in deciding on future policy actions. Likewise, policy practitioners in developing and transition countries will find the direct policy implications of the findings, and the recommendations on policy design particularly insightful. Furthermore, both theoretical and empirical accounts of the public management reform in Turkey are limited in English written literature. The international readers interested in the public management reforms in other countries will enjoy reading about the Turkish experience, and also will find it useful for comparative purposes.

The book is structured in four substantive chapters as well as an introduction and conclusion, which serve to contextualize the argument in relation to existing debates in public administration, economics, development, and governance literature. Chapter 2 sets out the theoretical approach, elaborates on the analytical framework, and presents the hypotheses on the relationship between decentralization and governance capacity. Chapter 3 familiarizes the reader with Turkish public administration and elaborates the public management reform process in Turkey by analyzing the reform patterns, underlying characteristics, and its implications on both state and non-state actors. Chapter 4 analyzes the implications of decentralization reforms on local government's capacities by relying on national and international accounts as well as surveys conducted with mayors and deputy mayors in provincial municipalities. Chapter 5 tests the hypotheses in the case of Turkish local government and presents the statistical findings to address the question of 'what is the relationship between decentralization and governance capacity?'. The conclusion reflects on the generalizability of the findings and discusses the applicability of asymmetrical decentralization policies to improve public governance.

REFERENCES

Akai, N., & Masayo, S. (2002). Fiscal Decentralization Contributes to Economic Growth: Evidence from State-Level Cross-Section Data for the United States. *Journal of Urban Economics, 52*(1), 93–108.

Atasoy, Y. (2009). *Hegemonic Transitions, the State and Crisis in Neoliberal Capitalism*. New York: Taylor & Francis.

Bahl, R. W., & Linn, J. F. (1992). *Urban Public Finance in Developing Countries*. New York: Oxford University Press.

Bardhan, P. (2002). Decentralization of Governance and Development. *Journal of Economic Perspective, 16*(4), 185–205.

Bardhan, P., & Mookherjee, D. (2000). Capture and Governance at Local and National Levels. *American Economic Review, 90*, 135–139.

Baskaran, T., & Feld, L. P. (2009). *Fiscal Decentralization and Economic Growth in OECD Countries: Is There a Relationship?* (CESifo Working Paper Series No. 2721).

Bessette, J. (1980). Deliberative Democracy: The Majority Principle in the Republican Government. In R. A. Goldwin & W. A. Schambra (Eds.), *How Democratic Is the Constitution?* (pp. 102–116). Washington, DC: AEI Press.

Bessette, J. (1994). *The Mild Voice of Reason: Deliberative Democracy and American National Government*. Chicago: University of Chicago Press.

Boyne, G. A. (1996). Competition and Local Government: A Public Choice Perspective. *Urban Studies, 33*(4–5), 703–721.

Brennan, G., & Buchanan, J. (1980). *The Power to Tax: Analytical Foundations of a Fiscal Constitution*. New York: Cambridge University Press.

Brown, L., LaFond, A., & Macintyre, K. (2001). *Measuring Capacity Building*. Chapel Hill, NC: Carolina Population Center.

Campbell, T. (2003). *The Quiet Revolution: Decentralization and the Rise of Political Participation in Latin American Cities*. Pittsburg: University of Pittsburg Press.

Cassette, A., & Paty, S. (2010). Fiscal Decentralization and the Size of Government: A European Country Empirical Analysis. *Public Choice, 143*, 173–189.

Chambers, S. (2003). Deliberative Democratic Theory. *Annual Review of Political Science, 6*, 307–326.

Cheema, G. S., & Rondinelli, D. A. (2007). From Government Decentralization to Decentralized Governance. In G. S. Cheema & D. A. Rondinelli (Eds.),

16   E. TAN

Decentralizing Governance: Emerging Concepts and Practices (pp. 1–20). Washington, DC: Brooking Institution Press.

Cohen, J. M., & Peterson, S. B. (1999). *Administrative Decentralization: Strategies for Developing Countries.* West Hartford, CT: Kumarian Press.

Crook, R. C., & Manor, J. (1998). *Democracy and Decentralisation in South Asia and West Africa: Participation, Accountability, and Performance.* Cambridge: Cambridge University Press.

Dahl, R. (1971). *Polyarchy: Participation and Opposition.* New Haven: Yale University Press.

Davoodi, H., & Zou, H.-F. (1998). Fiscal Decentralization and Economic Growth: A Cross-Country Study. *Journal of Urban Economics, 43*(2), 244–257.

Dunleavy, P., Margetts, P., Bastow, S., & Tinkler, J. (2005). New Public Management Is Dead—Long Live Digital-Era Governance. *Journal of Public Administration Research and Theory, 16,* 467–494.

Eaton, K. (2001). Political Obstacles to Decentralization: Evidence from Argentina and the Philippines. *Development and Change, 32*(1), 101–127.

Fan, C. S., Lin, C., & Treisman, D. (2009). Political Decentralization and Corruption: Evidence from Around the World. *Journal of Public Economics, 93*(1–2), 14–34.

Feld, L., Zimmermann, H., & Döring, T. (2003). Föderalismus, Dezentralität and Wirtschaftswachstum. *Vierteljahreshefte zur Wirtschaftsforschung, 72,* 361–377.

Fiszbein, A. (1997). *Decentralization and Local Capacity: Some Thoughts on a Controversial Relationship.* Rome: Economic Development Institute—The World Bank.

Goldfrank, B. (2007). The Politics of Deepening Local Democracy: Decentralization, Party Institutionalization, and Participation. *Comparative Politics, 39*(2), 147–168.

Grindle, M. S. (2007). *Going Local: Decentralization, Democracy and the Promise of Good Governance.* Princeton: Princeton University Press.

Harris, J., Kristian, S., & Olle, T. (2004). *Politicising Democracy: Local Politics and Democratization in Developing Countries.* London: Palgrave Macmillan.

Hope, K. R., Sr. (2000). Corruption and Development in Africa. In K. R. Hope, Sr. & B. C. Chikulo (Eds.), *Corruption and Development in Africa.* New York: St Martin's Press.

Iimi, A. (2005). Decentralization and Economic Growth Revisited: An Empirical Note. *Journal of Urban Economics, 57*(3), 449–461.

Jin, J., & Zou, H. (2005). Fiscal Decentralization, Revenue and Expenditure Assignments, and Growth in China. *Journal of Asian Economics, 16*(6), 1047–1064.

Kiggundu, M. (1989). *Managing Organizations in Developing Countries: An Operational and Strategic Approach.* West Hartford: Kumarian Press.

Kodras, J. (1997). Restructuring the State: Devolution, Privatization, and the Geographic Redistribution of Power and Capacity in Governance. In L. Staeheli, J. Kodras, & C. Flint (Eds.), *State Devolution in America: Implications for a Diverse Society* (pp. 79–96). Thousand Oaks, CA: Sage.

Litvack, J., Ahmad, J., & Bird, R. (1998). *Rethinking Decentralization in Developing Countries.* Washington, DC: The World Bank.

Manor, J. (1999). *The Political Economy of Democratic Decentralization.* Washington, DC: The World Bank.

Mintzberg, H. (1980). Structure in 5s: A Synthesis of the Research on Organization Design. *Management Science, 26*(3), 322–341.

Musgrave, R. A. (1959). *The Theory of Public Finance.* New York: McGraw Hill.

Nannyonjo, J., & Okot, N. (2012). *Decentralization, Local Government Capacity and Efficiency of Health Service Delivery in Uganda.* Nairobi, Kenya: African Economic Research Consortium.

Oates, W. (1972). *Fiscal Federalism.* New York: Harcourt.

Olowu, D., & Wunsch, J. S. (2004). *Local Governance in Africa: The Challenges of Democratic Decentralization.* London: Lynne Rienner.

Osborne, D., & Gaebler, T. (1992). *Reinventing Government: How the Entrepreneurial Spirit Is Transforming the Public Sector.* New York: Addison-Wesley Publ. Co.

Oxhorn, P. (2004). Unraveling the Puzzle of Decentralization. In P. Oxhorn, J. S. Tulchin, & A. D. Seele (Eds.), *Decentralization, Democratic Governance and Civil Society in Comparative Perspective.* Washington, DC: Woodrow Wilson Center Press.

Oxhorn, P., Tulchin, J. S., & Seele, A. D. (2004). *Decentralization, Democratic Governance and Civil Society in Comparative Perspective.* Washington, DC: Woodrow Wilson Center Press.

Pal, S., & Roy, J. (2010). *Fiscal Decentralization and Development: How Crucial is Local Politics?* (Discussion Paper 5286). IZA.

Pollitt, C. (2005). Decentralization: A Central Concept in Contemporary Public Management. In E. Ferlie, L. E. Lynn Jr., & C. Pollitt (Eds.), *The Oxford Handbook of Public Management* (pp. 371–397). Oxford: Oxford University Press.

Ponce-Rodríguez, R. A., Hankla, C. R., Martinez-Vazquez, J., & Heredia-Ortiz, E. (2018). Rethinking the Political Economy of Decentralization: How Elections and Parties Shape the Provision of Local Public Goods. *Publius: The Journal of Federalism.* https://doi.org/10.1093/publius/pjy003.

Prud'homme, R. (1995). The Dangers of Decentralization. *The World Bank Research Observer, 10*(2), 201–221.

18   E. TAN

Riker, W. H. (1964). *Federalism: Origin, Operation, Significance*. Boston: Little Brown.

Rodden, J. (2004). Comparative Federalism and Decentralization: On Meaning and Measurement. *Comparative Politics, 36*(4), 481–500.

Rodriguez-Pose, A., & Ezcurra, R. (2011). Is Fiscal Decentralization Harmful for Economic Growth? Evidence from the OECD Countries. *Journal of Economic Geography, 11*, 619–643.

Rondinelli, D., Nellis, J., & Cheema, G. (1983). *Decentralization in Developing Countries: A Review of Recent Experience*. Washington, DC: The World Bank.

Rudebeck, L., Törnquist, O., & Rojas, V. (1998). *Democratization in the Third World: Concrete Cases in Comparative Perspective*. London: Macmillan.

Saito, F. (2001). *Decentralization Theories Revisited: Lessons from Uganda*. Ryukoku: RISS Bulletin.

Saito, F. (2005). *Foundations for Local Governance: Decentralization in Comparative Perspectives*. Germany: Physica Verlag.

Sanderson, S. K. (1995). *Civilizations and World Systems: Studying World-Historical Change*. Lanham: Rowman & Littlefield.

Shah, A., & Thompson, T. (2004). *Implementing Decentralized Local Governance: A Treacherous Road with Potholes, Detours, and Road Closures*. World Bank Policy Research (Working Paper 3353). Washington, DC: The World Bank.

Sharma, C. K. (2006). Decentralization Dilemma: Measuring the Degree and Evaluating the Outcomes. *The Indian Journal of Political Science, 67*(1), 49–64.

Sharma, C. K. (2014). *Governance, Governmentality, and Governability: Constraints and Possibilities of Decentralization in South Asia. Keynote Address, International Conference on Local Representation of Power in South Asia*. Lahore: Department of Political Science, GC University.

Smith, B. C. (1985). *Decentralization: The Territorial Dimension of the State*. London: George Allen & Unwin.

Smoke, P. (2003). Decentralisation in Africa: Goals, Dimensions, Myths, and Challenges. *Public Administration and Development, 23*(1), 7–16.

Smoke, P. J., Gómez, E. J., & Peterson, G. E. (2006). *Decentralization in Asia and Latin America*. Cheltenham: Edward Elgar.

Sorens, J. (2009). The Partisan Logic of Decentralization in Europe. *Regional & Federal Studies, 19*(2), 255–272.

Stansel, D. (2005). Local Decentralisation and Local Economic Growth: A Cross-Sectional Examination of US Metropolitan Areas. *Journal of Urban Economics, 57*(1), 55–72.

Stohr, W. (2001). Introduction. In W. Stohr, J. Edralin, & D. Mani (Eds.), *New Regional Development Paradigms: Decentralization, Governance and the New Planning for Local-Level Development*. Westport, CT: Greenwood Press.

Tanzi, V. (1995). *Fiscal Federalism and Decentralization: A Review of Some Efficiency and Macroeconomic Aspects.* Annual World Bank Conference on Development Economics (pp. 295–316). Washington, DC: World Bank.

Thiessen, U. (2003). Fiscal Decentralisation and Economic Growth in High-Income OECD Countries. *Fiscal Studies, 24*(3), 237–274.

Tiebout, C. M. (1956). A Pure Theory of Local Expenditures. *Journal of Political Economy, 64*(5), 416–424.

Tocqueville, A., Mansfield, H. C., & Winthrop, D. (2000). *Democracy in America.* Chicago: University of Chicago Press.

Treisman, D. (2007). *The Architecture of Government: Rethinking Political Decentralisation.* London: Cambridge University Press.

Turner, M. (1999). Central-Local Relations: Themes and Issues. In M. Turner (Ed.), *Central-Local Relations in Asia-Pacific: Convergence or Divergence?* London: Macmillan.

Whitehead, L. (2002). *Emerging Market Democracies: East Asia and Latin America.* Baltimore: John Hopkins University Press.

Willis, E., Garman, C. B., & Haggard, S. (1999). The Politics of Decentralization in Latin America. *Latin American Research Review, 34*(1), 7–46.

Woller, G. M., & Phillips, K. (1998). Fiscal Decentralization and LDC Econometric Growth: An empirical Investigation. *Journal of Development Studies, 34*(4), 139–148.

World Bank. (2018). World Bank Group. Retrieved July 16, 2018, from World Bank Web Site: www.worldbank.org/en/topic/communitydrivendevelopment/brief/Decentralization.

Xie, D., Zou, H., & Davoodi, H. (1999). Fiscal Decentralization and Economic Growth in the United States. *Journal of Urban Economics, 45*(2), 228–239.

Young, J. T. (1898). Administrative Centralization and Decentralization in France. *The Annals of the American Academy of Political and Social Science, 11,* 24–43.

Zhang, T., & Zou, H. (1998). Fiscal Decentralization, Public Spending, and Economic Growth. *Journal of Public Economics, 67*(2), 221–240.

CHAPTER 2

Decentralization and Capacity in Public Governance

A core assumption linking decentralization to public governance is that better public governance relies on the accountability, effectiveness, and efficiency in public service delivery and responsiveness on citizen expectations, and this can only be attained effectively if the local government is financially dependent on local resources and has the discretion to act on its own decisions on public services. Nonetheless, empirical findings so far brought up a variety of factors, which undermined the reliability of this assumption. We know now country-specific factors, regulative framework, or capacity conditions at organizational and community levels determine the outcome of this presumed relationship between decentralization and governance.

A part of the problem with conflicting accounts on decentralization is, researchers usually don't pay enough attention to the conceptual and methodological underpinnings of empirical applications while reaching broader conclusions through case studies or comparative studies. Indeed, concepts such as governance, decentralization, and capacity have multiple meanings, which do not necessarily complement each other.

Keeping this in mind, this chapter outlines the theoretical and conceptual dimensions of governance, decentralization, and capacity. Laying out the usage of decentralization and capacity from a public governance perspective, the main aim of this chapter is to connect the disparate literature of governance, decentralization, and capacity in a functional way

© The Author(s) 2019

E. Tan, *Decentralization and Governance Capacity*, Public Sector Organizations, https://doi.org/10.1007/978-3-030-02047-7_2

21

What Is the Governance Perspective?

Since the 1990s, governance has become overwhelmingly popular in political sciences. Despite its popularity, the application of the term in public management is often not precise and equivocal. Rhodes (1996) highlights six different usages of governance in the literature: the minimal state; corporate governance; the new public management (NPM); 'good governance'; socio-cybernetics systems; and self-organizing networks. The ambiguity surrounding the term is not limited to its applications in the literature but it pertains to the semantics as well. While in earliest usages, the term was predominantly a synonym for the government, the contemporary ones may refer to the rules, to the practices, or to the system of governing itself. Considering these conceptual weaknesses, it is noteworthy to ask why 'governance' has turned into such a prevailing concept in political sciences. Pierre and Peters (2000) answer this question by underlining 'its capacity to cover the whole range of institutions and relationships involved in the process of governing'. Therefore, it is no surprise that different scholars have highlighted different attributes of governance in their studies and studied the term from their point of view.

The definition made by Rhodes (1996) has become salient in the contemporary usage of governance as networks. Accordingly, governance is 'self-organizing, interorganizational networks' which complement markets and hierarchies as governing structures in authoritatively allocating resources, and exercising control and coordination. Rhodes portrays a transformation in the ways of governing the society where the traditional roles of state institutions on public service delivery are replaced by compelling 'self-organizing networks'. These networks created by governmental and societal actors propel the state to a systematic change where 'no sovereign actor is able to steer or regulate' (Rhodes 1996: 15). In Rhodes' view, governance is an adversary concept against the government where the government is obliged to cooperate with these networks to govern the society.

Another prominent scholar, Gerry Stoker, adopts a more comprehensive approach toward the concept. In Stoker's definition, governance refers not only to networks but also to governing institutions, mechanisms, and styles as well. Accordingly, Stoker describes five propositions on different aspects of governance:

1) Governance refers to set of institutions and actors that are drawn from but also beyond government.
2) Governance defines the blurring of boundaries and responsibilities for tackling social and economic issues.
3) Governance identifies the power dependence involved in the relationships between institutions involved in collective action.
4) Governance is about autonomous self-governing networks of actors.
5) Governance recognizes the capacity to get things done which does not rest on the power of government to command or use its authority. It sees government as able to use new tools and techniques to steer and guide. (Stoker 2008)

Although in Stoker's approach, governance lacks the distinct boundaries to enable a theoretical framework, it envisages a map to identify the key trends and developments in the changing world of government. In this approach, governance is a 'set of practices' for collective decision-making and something independent from the control of any actor, including the state.

Another distinct usage of governance is described by Pierre and Peters (2000). In reference to the etymological roots[1] of the concept, Pierre and Peters prioritize the 'steering' notion on their definition. From their point of view, governance is not a substitute to traditional institutional links between public organization and society, but rather an adaptation of more informal channels to enhance resource mobilization through coordination with key actors inside the society. Here, the state is not depicted as a passive and incapable actor unable to exercise control over emerging networks but instead, it exercises a deliberate policy preference. In their governance definition, the state is the *primus inter pares* and the only potential actor with the ability to mobilize other societal actors for its purposes. Unlike the conventional state perspective, in this governance approach, the strong states are those which incorporate entrepreneurial skills, political zeal, and brokerage abilities, and thus able to coordinate and get the priorities on various joint public–private projects.

---

[1] In its Greek origin, 'governance' refers to 'steering'.

These three distinctive approaches establish broadly the governance perspective. Hence, governance can be perceived as a specific type of governing style (e.g., Rhodes), as the compilation of various attributes to governing (e.g., Stoker), or it can be a generic term to define the style of governing in a setting (e.g., Pierre and Peters). In a cognitive way, governance can correspond to 'one of them', 'all of them', or 'each one of them'. Most of the definitions in the literature approximate to either of these categories. Regardless of the definition adopted, there is a consensus that the prevalence of governance is attributed to the changes in domestic and international dynamics governing the society. Therefore, it is not easy to contextualize governance without stating the causes that led to the changes.

The utmost exogenous factor that has been influential on governance is globalization. Globalization infers that with the internationalization of markets (Hirst and Thompson 1999) and increasing speed on economic transactions among countries, multinational companies have freed themselves from the national boundaries and political control of nation-states (Baylis and Smith 1997). The severe economic competition among multinational companies affected not only the capital markets but also the political institutions regulating the markets. Securing the competitiveness of the business has urged the private sector to be more involved in public decisions and to be influential on the political agenda. Particularly, private actors have become most interested in local politics to safeguard the needed labor force for their business and the efficiency of transport links (John 2001: 13). On the other hand, local and regional governments have taken the disposition of private sector to public service provision as an alternative to state investments for economic development (Parkinson et al. 1992; John 2001: 11). Besides, globalization also influenced the sociocultural segments of the society, thus eventually leading to the creation of complex networks among social, private, and political actors.

Globalization brought along new policy challenges and changes on the citizens' expectations from political institutions. The complexity of newly emergent policy areas such as environmental issues, the upsurge of immigrants and the aging population in the developed world required the involvement of various levels of government and non-government actors in finding solutions. Moreover, the global economic crisis in the 1970s incited an overall citizen dissatisfaction with government policies in the Western world (John 2001: 13). The trust of people in traditional government policies had fallen and the turnout rates decreased gradually. The unconventional forms of political behavior through associations and new interest groups have become popular. The changes in political behaviors encouraged both academicians and politicians to seek new ways to determine public policies. Most prominently, the neoliberal policies pioneered by Thatcher in the UK and Reagan in the USA introduced marketization of public services and the deregulation of government. Privatization, deregulation, cutbacks in public spending, tax cuts, adoption of market-originated practices and philosophies on public service production and delivery have been the hallmark of a new era in public administration (PA), which was later branded as NPM (Hood 1991; Pierre and Peters 2000: 2). Alongside the marketization of public policies, the accountability of the democratic government and the legitimacy of non-governmental organizations have become ambivalent in the context of public governance.

At a more macro-political level, the institutional evolution of the EU contributed tremendously to the role of subnational and supranational bodies in public governance. First, setting the NUTS regions as a precondition of structural funds and adoption of the 'subsidiarity' principle as a constitutive element of the European public governance elevated the status of regional and local governments. Second, the subnational entities found new international platforms, such as the Committee of Regions, to exchange ideas and to interact with other organizations to empower their policies. Third, the Single Market boosted the competition among regional and local governments to attract the international investment. Fourth, the EU framework encouraged the Member States to implement bolder policies on granting political and administrative rights to the historically and ethnically demarcated regions. Fifth, the invention of the 'multi-level governance' to define the functioning of the EU brought a new chapter to the governance literature. Thus, public policy making in the EU has turned into the interplay between subnational, national, and supranational entities. Besides the EU, other international institutions such as the OECD and the IMF have expanded the scope of the governance in the development discourse, by creating and promoting international standards for better governing. The so-called good governance principles set the normative basis for the public organizations in developing countries in conducting their public affairs and managing public resources.

Today, governing the society encompasses horizontally public, private, and civil society organizations on the one hand, and vertically local, regional, national, and supranational state organizations on the other, into a complex, reticular set of relations. What it used to be a bilateral relation between citizen and state turned into a multilateral realm among different actors with competing demands in public governance.

This paradigm shift in public governance compels policy practitioners to reflect upon 'what does good governance mean?' Good governance, despite its popularity in international development literature, is not a well-established concept (Fukuyama 2013). As Bouckaert and Van de Walle (2003) point out, good governance has two distinct ways of conceptualization: (1) good governance as a value with a number of pre-established universal values and (2) good governance as an expression of acceptance of the process and system of governing by the citizens and stakeholders.

Good governance, as a normative concept, is a deductive process. Here, good governance addresses the question of 'how should public governance look like?' This conceptualization of good governance is largely embraced by the development agencies and international donor organizations, as it allows 'yardstick' measurement of governance and benchmarking performances through comparison. The attractiveness of this approach is self-evident in the number of indices and methodologies developed by various organizations to measure governance. For instance, the online portal DataGob initiated by Inter-American Development Bank claims access to 400 different governance indices from 30 different sources in academia, non-governmental organizations, private organizations, and multilateral agencies (IDB 2007). Lately, we observe an increase in popularity of certain indexes with larger data pool (e.g., Worldwide Governance Index) in macro- and meta-level comparison of governance. However, this convergence is largely demand-driven rather than one particular model is superior to other.

The second conceptualization of good governance is, on the other hand, an inductive process. Good governance relies on the citizens' preferences and 'good' is the extent to which a government meets citizens' demands. Good government should monitor the citizen's needs; integrate them in the governance process; and act on citizen's expectations. Here, good governance is the reflection of the citizen satisfaction with the public services and public affairs in general. The challenge that the political scientists are facing today is to adopt a comprehensive theoretical framework to incorporate the normative dimensions of public governance and the subjective expectations of citizens into a comprehensive theory of public governance.

Is There a Theory of Public Governance?

Even though there is a discernible global trend on changing traditional roles between state and society, it is difficult to argue a unifying theory of public governance. Instead, theoretical premises of governance are entrenched in disparate literature. Public governance can carry different objectives such as empowering citizens, contributing to community development, or improving the quality of services. In this part, I will look into salient theoretical expectations from public organizations in governing the society and the means of it.

Until the 1990s, the general consensus was that the state is responsible for steering the society. However, this notion has become contested in time with enhancement of policy networks and emergence of NPM. The state is portrayed as an overly extensive, bureaucratic body, which is ineffective and inefficient in comparison with the private sector. This perception was consolidated during the Thatcher and Reagan eras, and state as an actor in public service delivery was delegitimized. In this period, the foremost studies in the US literature debated the role of informal networks between market and public sector organizations, such as *regimes* (see Stone 1989), as best available practices for local governments to compete in the global market economy. Nonetheless, the scope of regimes remained limited to public decisions concerning market functions rather than wider public governance decisions.

In the European literature, on the other hand, the emphasis was mostly on the policy networks created by societal and international actors and their functions on public governance (see Kooiman 1993). For instance, Kooiman describes governing as 'all activities of social, political and administrative actors that can be seen as purposeful efforts to steer, guide, control or manage societies', whereas governance is 'the patterns that emerge from governing activities of social, political and administrative actors' (Kooiman 1993: 2). Later, Rhodes takes this argument further and strips the mantle of governance from the state. Rhodes (1994) first declared that the state has 'hollowed out' his capabilities to international and national networks of private and societal actors, and thus lost its ability to steer the society. Next, Rhodes (1997) stated the governance of society is 'about managing networks', which have both the capacity and the influence to steer the society and the only way to steer the society is for the government to cooperate with them as an equal actor on public sector management. In this setup, the state is the collection of inter-organizational networks composed of governing actors and society as a whole, in which all actors are interdependent and equal in terms of sovereignty. All actors are motivated by their own interests and the networks are independently organized. The distinction among the public, private, and civil society is no longer important; only the networks created by these organization are at the heart of governance (Rhodes 1997).

This way, networks were acknowledged as the new means of public service delivery and public policy implementation. In this understanding, networks are described as the 'stable patterns of social relations between interdependent actors which take shape around policy problems and/or policy programs' (Kickert et al. 1999: 6). The promotion of networks as the means in public governance brought up further questions such as 'how to manage networks?' and 'how to rationalize the cooperation of actors?' Hence, network governance is introduced in public governance, and the government assumed the role of a network manager. Kickert et al. (1999) describe three varieties of activities in network management: actions concerning a pattern of relations, consensus building, and problem-solving. In relation to these, network managers adopt certain tasks within a network: network activation (initiating an interaction process), organizing interactions (defining the rules and procedures), setting up contacts (linking problems, solutions, and actors), facilitation (putting in place effective conditions for interaction), and mediation and arbitration (conflict solving). In the case of an insolvable situation, the network manager, which is the government, can seek to restructure the network by changing the rules of composition. Moreover, the government can use regulations, financial resources, and communication tools to influence actors to ensure they meet the expectations as best as possible.

The premises of network governance are not exempt from criticism. Since the assumption rests on those actors in the network are interdependent and have the same legitimacy, even though government achieves compromises among network actors, it is not certain the outcome will be in the public interest. The success in sustaining the common interest is too dependent on personal skills of the network manager, and therefore, the collective well-being and public interest can be put in question in cases when a compromise approximates to the interests of private sector actors (Giguère 2008: 48). Furthermore, limitations on democratic participation and the accountability of actors are other challenges faced by networks.

Nonetheless, the prevalence of networks enabled new means in public service delivery, namely public–private partnerships (PPPs) or ad hoc partnerships among public, private, and civil society actors. These partnerships become esteemed on their ability to channel local actors into local development and bringing lessons learned from local to national political level. First cases of local partnerships took place in Ireland in 1991 with the purpose of contributing to local employment and economic development (Giguère 2008: 49). Today, partnerships are widely embraced for public services in developed countries. OECD (2001) identifies the roles of partnerships in public governance as follows: (1) pursuing a general objective such as stimulating economic development, promoting social cohesion, and improving the quality of life; (2) endeavoring to achieve that objective mainly by increasing the degree of coordination between policies and programs via the different services and levels of government, and by adapting them to the local context; (3) when the outcome of improved coordination is insufficient, setting up new projects and services; and (4) working at the local level to involve local actors, and especially civil society, in identifying priorities in project development, and to harness local resources and skills.

Other scholars conceive public governance in terms of structures and processes rather than networks. Pierre and Peters (2000: 22) underline the structural view is essential as it provides a perspective for state and other actors for the roles to play within the framework of public governance. The process-based approach looks into the interactions among structures in 'steering' and 'coordination' and focuses on the degree of inclusion and influence among actors. The process perspective evaluates governance as a dynamic outcome of social and political actors, and thus enables the study of changes in governance structures over time.

Pierre and Peters (2000: 15) identify four modes of governance in political and economic institutions from a structural view: hierarchy, market, network, and community-based governance. Each mode with different strengths and weaknesses has a distinct approach in governing the society and economy.

Hierarchical governance embodies the Weberian public administration, where public services are delivered through vertically integrated bureaucratic institutions that are regulated by law. Here, the state reifies collective interest and by doing so separates itself from the society, and all institutions in the state apparatus function in a hierarchical order through command and control. Subnational governments are embedded in the state hierarchy and the legal authority of the state impinges on their autonomy. Hierarchy does not only regulate the interorganizational relations but it also regulates relations with society. This mode of governance is also called as traditional or 'old', because legal and constitutional institutions buttressing the modern state are created following the hierarchical modes of governance; therefore, it still prevails despite all substantial changes in time.

Market governance refers to both the market actors cooperating together to resolve common problems and also the market principles of supply and demand to govern the public service delivery. The idea is that the justest and most efficient way of resource allocation on public services relies on citizen's choices, not to elected officials, which may or may not be responsive to their constituencies.

Network governance, carried by the networks, represents the organized interests of state and non-state actors on ad hoc policy areas. The relationships among actors are less informal compared to market and hierarchy-based structures, and the coordination mechanism is formed through cooperation and negotiation among equal partners instead of formal rules. The strength of networks is that they enable the diffusion of private sector expertise in the policy process. Their weakness is that their accountability and representativeness are questionable.

Communitarian governance presumes that states are too big to resolve the problems of communities, and thus, communities should resolve their common problems through a collective responsibility with minimum intervention of the state (Etzioni 1995, 1998). Here, the civic virtue is the key to governance. The main criticism of communitarian governance is its simplistic view of individuals that are inclined to make personal sacrifices for the common good of the community.

A third theoretical approach toward public governance is possible by taking a neo-institutionalists perspective. The institutions represent structures and systems of norms, beliefs, practices, and routines (see Peters 1999). Pierre (2011: 21) argues that the literature on governance overlooks the significance of the systems of values and norms that give the processes meaning and purpose. Further, he asserts that without studying the purposes, goals, and objectives, public governance cannot be understood and assessed as a process. By bringing in the processes of value generation and purpose, the neo-institutional theory complements the structural view toward public governance.

From an institutional view, Pierre (2011: 25) describes four different models in urban governance: managerial, corporatist, pro-growth, and welfare governance. Each model upholds different governance objectives and strategies for the local institutions.

Managerial governance underscores relaxing political control over city administration and service production. Customer-oriented approaches are expected on political decisions. While public managers employ public decisions with substantive discretion and autonomy, elected officials focus on long-term goals and objectives. The criticism of this model is entrenched in the wider criticism of NPM that the managerialism in public services is inadequate for sustaining accountability and causes a democratic deficiency.

Corporatist governance underlines the value of organized collective interests for local government and embeds the 'third sector' into public service production and delivery. The effective usage of the corporatist model depends on the governability of cities (see Pierce 1993) in which tensions among different segments of the city (such as labor organizations against business organizations) may impede effective cooperation.

Pro-growth governance suggests the economic growth is the overarching objective of the local governance system, and being the 'unitary interest' among all actors, it should be separated from political debates. This model of governance is the least participatory model among four models and posits concerted public–private actions as the engine of the local economy.

The last model, welfare governance, focuses on the governance of industrial cities whose local economy relies traditionally on manufacturing, and they struggle with restructuring their economic setup to comply with international economic forces. In this depiction, these cities have very limited viability and growth in their local economy and depend on the influx of capital through the central government. Therefore, this type of governance tries to reinvigorate the state's involvement in resource mobilization rather than public–private collaborations. The examples of this model are observable largely in formerly prosperous industrial regions in Germany, the USA, the Scandinavian countries, and the UK.

Last but not least, Bouckaert (2015) describes 'spans of governance' in an attempt to merge the structuralist and institutionalists approaches into a holistic theory of governance. Bouckaert identifies five spans of governance, namely corporate governance, holding governance, public service governance, suprastructure governance, and systemic governance.

Corporate governance embodies the transferability of private sector management systems into the public sector. Holding governance broadens the focus of corporate governance and looks into the 'connectedness' of organizations in terms of function, territory, policy field, and so on. Public sector governance incorporates cooperation with private and non-for-profit actors in public service delivery. Suprastructure governance entails the ideological and normative aspects of governance and deals with values, norms, culture, and ideologies that shape governance. Finally, the systemic governance refers to the system design of governance at the state level. For instance, distribution of power, checks and balances, and macro-level decision-making and implementation fall under the scope of suprastructure governance.

To sum up, the theoretical pursue of governance has found reflections in networks, structures, processes, institutions, and even in spans. Yet, none of these theoretical approaches posit a grand theory of public governance; rather, they expand the theoretical scope of governance. Therefore, the question is whether public governance constitutes by itself a theoretical framework and if it does, to what extent it differs from PA and public management. The differences and similarities of NPM and governance are worthy of consideration for that matter.

The literature widely acknowledges that the premises of NPM have a kinship with the emerging forms of governance (Peters and Pierre 1998). On contrary to traditional PA, both NPM and governance presume the diminished role of elected officials in public services, the diffusion between the public and private sector and perceive competition as positive for public service delivery. Moreover, both perspectives underline the importance of results and output controls and disregard input control as a control mechanism. Output control can either be implemented through customer satisfaction charts and performance indicators like NPM suggests, or it can be generated by bringing members of the private and voluntary sector into public service production and delivery as governance perspective suggests. They also share similar weaknesses in sustaining accountability while replacing the legitimacy of the legal mandate or elected office with alternative forms of leadership. The difference in both approaches is that while governance literature proposes 'stakeholderism' as the alternative to legalistic accountability, NPM has little concern about the accountability by presuming that consumer choice can ensure the integrity of service production and delivery without necessarily the involvement of elected representatives (Peters and Pierre 1998).

The main differences between NPM and governance rest on their theoretical underpinnings. First of all, governance is derived from political sciences unlike the business administration origins of NPM. Inherently, governance anticipates efficiency while maintaining some political control over public services; NPM just seeks to transform the public sector organizations into efficient organizations whose only difference from the private sector is the nature of the product they deliver (Peters and Pierre 1998). Second, NPM focuses on the intra-organizational relations and management techniques to enhance customer satisfaction and efficiency. Governance is, on the contrary, largely about interorganizational relations. Third, NPM presumes a cultural shift in the production of public goods, whereas governance does not require a similar cultural shift.

At this juncture, Osborne (2010: 7) asserts that governance once an element within PA and NPM regimes turned into a distinct regime in itself, which is called now as new public governance (NPG). Osborne argues NPG differs theoretically and practically from PA and NPM regimes. Theoretically, NPG is situated within institutional and network theories and posits 'both a plural state, where multiple interdependent actors contribute to the delivery of public services and a pluralist state, where multiple processes inform the policy-making system' (Osborne 2010: 9). In practice, NPG focuses on organizational relationships and governance of processes and stresses service effectiveness and outcomes in the interaction of public sector organizations with their environment. NGM positions inter-organizational networks at the center for resource allocation and accountability and the latter occurs by negotiations at an interorganizational and interpersonal level within these networks (Osborne 1997).

ACTORS IN PUBLIC GOVERNANCE

The expansion of governance theories did not only alter the traditional roles of public sector organizations but also assign new roles and responsibilities to all stakeholders of public governance. Therefore, it is imperative to elaborate the shifting roles of actors and the expectation from them in public governance.

The first and foremost actor in public governance is the local government. Local governments are democratically elected authorities that exercise political choices within denoted boundaries (John 2001: 34). However, depending on traditional and historical status, there is a great variation among local governments across country cases in terms of size, structure, and discretionary powers. This variety does not only reflect on the functions of local government but also on the expectation of the position.

In his classical work '*Considerations of Representative Government*', John Stuart Mill describes two important functions to local government. First, local government is the keystone of the democratic system as it enables the political participation of local citizens through elections. Second, local government is the means of providing effective and efficient public services as they contain the local knowledge, interest, and expertise, especially compared to the distant central authority. This view of local government has been tremendously influential in the British school (see the works of L. J. Sharpe, K. Joung, and J. Steward). The American school, on the other hand, associates local government usually with pluralism and individual sovereignty (Andrew and Goldsmith 1998; Wolman 1996). In continental Europe, the practices of local government vary across northern and southern countries. According to Page (1991), the northern group of Scandinavian countries, the UK, and Netherlands preserve a form of 'legal localism' accentuating the values of local self-government and decentralization. Here, the local government has the utmost legitimacy to provide public services. Furthermore, there is a clear distinction between local politics and central politics. The southern group (Belgium, France, Spain, Italy, and Greece), on the other hand, emphasizes territorial representation of local interests at the national level, what Page defines as 'political localism'. Dissimilar to the northern group, there is a sense of commonality and unity between the center and local government. It is also common clientelistic practices in southern countries. Page and Goldsmith (1987) draw another distinction between political culture between northern and southern countries reflecting the dichotomy between the Catholic south and Protestant north. They argue because of this dichotomy southern secular states administer the education services centrally, while in northern cases these services are decentralized to the local government institutions. Furthermore, among northern countries, there are few levels of government, smaller numbers of local authorities, and larger average size of local authority compared to southern cases, and while welfare services are provided by local authorities in the north, regional, and central authorities are responsible in the south (John 2001: 36–37).

There are other taxonomies of European local governments (see Bennett 1993; Hesse and Sharpe 1991) that add other patterns next to north and south dichotomy. Among them, it is common to differentiate the UK from the rest of the Nordic group as the local government in the UK has a weak constitutional status, unlike the Scandinavian countries. Furthermore, Germany, Netherlands, and Austria, preserving both local government traditions like in Scandinavian countries and deconcentrated state administrations of Napoleonic countries are forming a unique cluster in some studies. Kuhlman and Wollmann (2014) add one more category to the list of PA models in Europe, namely Central Eastern European Model referring to the post-communist Eastern European countries that are now part of the European Union. They identify two subgroups under Central East European Model according to the administrative traditions of formerly ruling historical empires of Habsburgs, Ottomans, Prussians, and Tsarist Russians. The first group, which used to be part of the realm of Habsburgs or Prussia, adopt decentralized constitutional and administrative model in local government. The second group, which used to be part of the realm of Ottomans or Tsarist Russia, has centrally dependent, weak local administrations.

The local government traditions are not only relevant for comparative purposes but they somewhat determine the transition of local government toward governance. The governments are adopting similar practices to deal with the emerging challenges, but in the meantime, path dependency to traditional institutions determines the course of actions. As John (2001: 23) puts it, the institutional transformation is only one side of the story. The transition in local governance reveals similarities in different country cases but preserves differences inherent in administrative traditions.

The second emergent actor in public governance is the private sector organization and businesses. Looking back to the nineteenth century and early twentieth century, the involvement of local business leaders to local politics is not something new. However, changes in production systems and political development removed big production facilities outside of urban areas and local businesses drifted apart from local politics (Harding 1994). Yet, globalization turned the tides and opened local markets to international competition. Local politicians have become more eager to increase the competitiveness of local businesses and to attract private investment. Social policies affecting the labor market and investment in transport services attracted foremost the interest of private businesses. The widespread decentralization practices empowered the discretion of local government on the planning of local services, which in return motivated the private businesses, even more, to partake in local politics. As an outcome, PPPs have become popular means to realize costly investments for local development projects. Besides, a business-friendly reputation has become a critical aptitude in local politicians.

Third, alongside with businesses, the expectations of citizens and communities in public governance have transformed as well. Nowadays, citizens are expected to partake in decision-making and even in public service delivery, disparate from their conventional role as receivers of public services. New forms of public service organizations, such as city councils, development agencies, tenant management organizations, or neighborhood initiatives, are replacing the conventional public service agents. The participation of citizens and community representatives in public services through co-production and co-creation anticipates engendering enhanced legitimacy in public policy and also better-informed decisions on citizen's needs. Thus, more and more community representatives are taking place in task forces and board of governance institutions. In the same vein, many local governments have now advisory councils and bodies to exchange ideas with civil society institutions. Although the involvement of citizens in local governance is proliferated in practice, there is still no consensus on what the exact added value of citizens and civil society organizations in governance is. The anticipation is putting a variety of people with different expertise and backgrounds together would create coherent public policies and reduce the transaction costs in public service delivery. Notwithstanding, Goss (2001) points out, in reality, neither community nor local politicians have a civic understanding what responsibilities these governance bodies should carry and what should be their role in public service delivery. Therefore, it is somewhat abstruse for policy planners what to learn from citizens' initiatives and how to incorporate them in public service mechanism.

Last but not least, the position of central authority has shifted alongside with other actors. In many Western countries, the role of central government in public governance is reduced. For instance, central authority loosened its control over local development and investment policies. Central planning agencies are removed from local planning decisions. Financial and administrative competencies, which were formerly held by the agents of central authority, are assigned to local authorities.

This decentralization trend was pervasive even in countries with a strong administrative tradition of central government. France, a notorious statist country, has released the central control over local planning gradually, starting with decentralization reforms in the 1980s. Sweden, a strong proponent of the welfare state, has decentralized the central authority on the planning of welfare functions to local authorities. Another noticeable trend was, regional governments are established as a middle tier between the center and local, to overtake some of the central administration's responsibilities on planning decisions. Through contracting out and privatization of centrally owned enterprises, states have created the milieu for local and regional administrations to compete for both public and private sector resources thus to increase the efficiency of public service delivery. By the same token, industrialized countries set up programs to be implemented either by the local authorities or by other local agencies, sign contracts directly with local suppliers for the provision of services, and set up new autonomous agencies in order to perform specific tasks (Giguère 2008: 47).

The discussion at this stage is whether the central authority still possesses the instruments to control or to retain its former power in local policies. There are two different views in this regard. One perspective postulates an irreversible decrease in state power; thus, the central authority lost for good its leverage to control local decision-making (see Rhodes 1997). The other one draws a less deterministic scenario. Accordingly, state transforms itself to adopt the changes in its environment that do not infer lost of control but a deliberate preference, and thereby, central authority still upholds the means (such as indirect transfers and investments from central authority) to shape local politics (see Pierre and Peters 2000: 92). Moreover, the intense agencification on public service delivery led to coordination problems (see Bouckaert et al. 2010) that triggered a re-centralization of certain functions and gave further room for a central authority to intervene in public governance. Therefore, despite its withdrawal from local decision-making, central authority is still a force to be reckoned with in public governance.

DECENTRALIZATION IN PUBLIC GOVERNANCE

From the governance perspective, decentralization is not only a means to achieve the governance objectives but also an intrinsic characteristic of the governance system. The reason lies in the ontology of the concept,

38   E. TAN

which includes both procedural and systematic elements. In public management literature, the term commonly refers to the dispersion of central power and authority to sub-state and non-state actors. Yet again, decentralization is conceptually not entrenched in a single field but its theoretical premises are spread in different scientific fields such as political science, PA, economics, and development studies. As Macmahon puts it eloquently (1961: 15):

> *It is impossible to standardize the usage of the word decentralization by seeking to give it meanings that would be acceptable universally… It is a word that is not confined to public affairs and to the formal organization in government or business… It must be accepted as a word of innumerable applications. Throughout all of them, however, runs a common idea, which is inherent in the word's Latin roots, meaning "away from the center".* (emphasis his)

Unfortunately, even this considerably thick definition falls short on capturing the concept. This is mainly due to the fact it only apprehends the *dynamic* notions. However, decentralization can refer to the diffusion of power and authority within a closed system, and thus be giving the characteristic of the system. Here, a 'decentralized system' implies an organized set of relations either with limited dependency to an acknowledged center or without an established center. For instance, a market economy is a good example of a functioning decentralized system without an established center. Therefore, the definition of decentralization is also bound to the context in which it is applied.

It is no surprise that decentralization is frequently called as an ambiguous and multifaceted concept (Fesler 1965; Prud'homme 1995: 2; Oxhorn et al. 2004: 4; Dubois and Fattore 2009). The ambiguity with decentralization is partly due to its treatment as a sub-concept under broader discussions rather than being the subject of a deep analysis on its own (Prud'homme 1995; Hales 1999). Therefore, in numerous typologies of decentralization, the same terminology often relates to different meanings. Oxhorn et al. (2004: 4) add two additional reasons why decentralization an ambiguous concept is: First, decentralization processes usually lead to inconsistent outcomes, and second, incongruity among different disciplines impedes the development of persuasive theories of decentralization.

Its multifacetedness, on the other hand, is implicit in being at the crossroad of different disciplines. Decentralization has various applications in different disciplines such as economics, organizational science, political science or development studies, and insulating the concept under one discipline is practically inapplicable given the level of interfusion. Therefore, acknowledging the overlapping definitions and adopting a consistent approach is more important than providing precise definitions.

Having said that, Dubois and Fattore (2009)'s index gives a useful overview of decentralization typologies in the literature (Table 2.1).

As earlier mentioned, the same terminology under separate works usually captures different meanings adhered to the scientific field. For example, while political decentralization refers to the legal transfer of power to autonomous bodies in one study (see Benz 2002), in other, it denotes democratic preferences (see Smoke 2003).

Table 2.1 Decentralization typologies

Typology	References
Economic (industrial, regional economic planning), Administrative (administrative/Internal, administrative/Spatial, administrative/Functional), Political (legislative, corporate, millennial)	Furniss (1974)
Administrative, Political	Porter and Olsen (1976)
Vertical vs. Horizontal, Selective vs. Parallel	Mintzberg (1980)
Deconcentration, Delegation, Devolution, Privatization	Rondinelli et al. (1983)
Inter-governmental/Political, Management	Devas (1997)
Fiscal, Political, Administrative	Litvack et al. (1998)
Functional, Territorial	Bray (1999)
Political, Spatial, Market, Administrative	Cohen and Peterson (1999)
Decentralization by default, Privatization, Deconcentration, Fiscal decentralization, Devolution	Manor (1999)
Structural, Decision, Resource, Electoral, Institutional (Treisman [2002]: Vertical, Decision-Making, Appointment, Electoral, Fiscal, Personnel)	Treisman (2002)
Political decentralization, Administrative decentralization, Administrative deconcentration	Benz (2002)
Fiscal, Institutional (local and intergovernmental), Political	Smoke (2003)
Big push vs. small steps, Bottom up vs. top down, Uniform vs. asymmetric	Shah and Thompson (2004)
Administrative, Fiscal, Political	Falleti (2005)
Political/Administrative, Internal/External, Non-competitive/ Competitive, Basis of division (territory/function/process/target group)	Pollitt (2005)

Source Dubois and Fattore (2009)

40   E. TAN

Noting the nuance, types of decentralization usually fall under the categories of political, administrative, and fiscal aspects. Before moving to the theoretical propositions of decentralization in public governance, let us briefly look into the applications of them in practice.

Administrative Decentralization

The World Bank defines administrative decentralization as 'the transfer of responsibility for the planning, financing, and management of certain public functions from the central government and its agencies to field units of government agencies, subordinate units or levels of government, semi-autonomous public authorities or corporations, or area-wide, regional or functional authorities'. Administrative decentralization contains redistribution of authority, responsibility, and financial resources for providing public services among different levels of government.

There are three salient forms of administrative decentralization: deconcentration, delegation, and devolution.

Deconcentration is often considered as the weakest form of administrative decentralization and it refers to the distribution of decision-making authority, and financial and management responsibilities to lower tiers of central government. This form of decentralization is most common in unitary states.

Delegation occurs when central government transfers its decision-making responsibility and certain management functions to semi-autonomous private organizations that are not controlled by the central government, but ultimately accountable for it. Governments can delegate service provisions to public enterprises or private corporations in areas such as housing services, education services, regional development, transportation, or special project implementation. Typically, private organizations have a great deal of discretion in the decision-making of delegated services. They may be exempt from constraints on regular civil service personnel and may be able to charge users directly for services.

Devolution is considered as the most extensive form of administrative decentralization. Some scholars even consider devolution as part of political decentralization.[2] The act of devolution refers to the transfer

---

[2] Before the governance era, there was a more clear-cut distinction between an administrative branch and political branch of government; therefore, the differences between administrative decentralization and political decentralization were more apparent. For

of authority for decision-making, finance, and management to quasi-autonomous units of local government. Devolution usually takes place with the transfer of service responsibilities to municipalities that independently elect their own mayor and council, raise own revenues, and have independent authority to make investment decisions. According to the World Bank, in a devolved system, local governments have clear and legally recognized geographical boundaries over which they exercise authority and within which they perform public functions.

Political Decentralization

Political decentralization signifies empowering citizens and/or their elected representatives in public decision-making. Political decentralization is frequently linked to federalism. Cheema and Rondinelli (2007) associate the following features with political decentralization: 'organizations and procedures for increasing citizen participation in selecting political representatives and in making public policy; changes in the structure of the government through devolution of powers and authority to local units of government; power-sharing institutions within the state through federalism, constitutional federations, or autonomous regions; and institutions and procedures allowing freedom of association and participation of civil society organizations in public decision-making, providing socially beneficial services, and mobilizing social and financial resources to influence political decision-making'. Political decentralization can be used in two separate meanings in transition and democratic countries. In transition countries (or in developing countries), political decentralization usually refers to the establishment of elected local units (see Treisman 2007). On the other hand, in democratic countries, political decentralization refers to the autonomy of locally elected units in decision-making (see Treisman 2002).

example, in Schmandt (1972), administrative decentralization refers to decentralization toward field agencies (also in Fesler 1965), while political decentralization refers to decentralization toward local government or states.

42   E. TAN

Fiscal Decentralization

There are three distinct usages of fiscal decentralization. The first usage connotes systemic features by referring to the dispersal of public expenditure and revenues between tiers of government. In other words, if the local or regional government has a higher share in public expenditures and revenues than central government, this falls into the category of fiscal decentralization.

The second usage of fiscal decentralization captures fiscal aspects of devolution,[3] concerning revenues, debt incurrence, and expenditures. For example, according to the World Bank, fiscal decentralization embraces self-financing or cost recovery through user charges; co-financing or co-production arrangements through which the users participate in providing services and infrastructure through monetary or labor contributions; expansion of local revenues through property or sales taxes, or indirect charges; intergovernmental transfers that shift general revenues from taxes collected by the central government to local governments for general or specific uses; and authorization of municipal borrowing and the mobilization of either national or local government resources through loan guarantees.

The third meaning of fiscal decentralization emphasizes the fiscal discretion of subnational government in public services or its fiscal autonomy. Here, fiscal decentralization encompasses (1) the range of financed public services; (2) commensurateness of revenues with responsibilities; (3) the freedom in allocating the budget to individual services; and (4) the discretion on determining the rates of owned taxes and charges. In this meaning of fiscal decentralization, fiscal decentralization usually used interchangeably with fiscal federalism. Fiscal federalism refers to the allocation of revenue-raising and expenditure assignments among tiers of government and concerns with the most effective allocation of intergovernmental fiscal responsibilities.

---

[3] Davey (2000) makes certain distinctions between administrative and fiscal decentralization. Accordingly, financial management, budgeting accounting, delegation, procurement, auditing, or other similar processes through which local governments manage their financial affairs are not considered as part of the fiscal decentralization policies.

A Theory of Decentralization in Public Governance and Determinants of Success

Earlier I expressed that decentralization and governance form a symbiosis. Unpacking this sentence is the key to make a just claim on how decentralization can lead to better governance. A decentralized system extrapolates a system without an ultimate center, and thus, its functioning is dependent on the interrelations and compromises of the constituents. A decentralized system innately refers to governance as the system functioning. By the same token, the success of governance is reliant on the effectiveness of interrelations and compromises in producing anticipated outcomes. Here, the efficacy of the system can be enhanced either by empowering one single component as an interlocutor or by empowering each constituent to reach an equilibrium with the optimum outcome. In the same vein, central government or state holds two options to improve public governance through decentralization. Option A is empowering local government as the interlocutor of the governance system or as the *'primus inter pares'*. Option B is empowering and encouraging non-state actors and citizens in partaking in governance to reach an optimum outcome for public governance. The challenge faced by public policy designers is to concoct the right mixture in decentralization policies for an optimum public governance outcome. Typically, the success in outcome adheres to the motive behind reform. But, regardless of the political motive, good governance assumes that local government is autonomous and inclusive enough to sustain its affairs and self-sufficient enough to maintain public service provision. A rule of thumb for the success in decentralization reform is not worsening off the pre-reform standards in public services yet causing a less financial burden to the coffers of central government.

This gives a starting point to construct a congruent relationship between decentralization and public governance. Decentralization in public governance corresponds to, as a process, the release of power and authority from central government either deliberately—through administrative, political, and market decentralization reforms—or circumstantially—through the mechanisms of globalization, to lower tier of government and non-state actors, and later as a systemic outcome, keeping at least the same standards in public services while decentralized authority being administratively and financially less dependent on the central government. Under these conditions, local government, with its physical proximity to citizens and pertaining to its democratic accountability, has a privilege to use its informational advantage over central government to better allocate the public resources according to the citizen expectations. Furthermore, public governance perspective allows inclusion of citizens and other profit and nonprofit societal actors in the production and delivery of public services, thus allowing the local government to more effectively use its resources. In economics, the former refers to the allocative efficiency and the latter to the productive efficiency.

However, we know that success in decentralization policies entails certain conditions in governing organizations and institutional surrounding. In the absence of these conditions, decentralization may engender counteractive side effects (such as elite capture, localization of corruption, free rider effect, soft-budget constraints) increasing transaction costs in public services and/or creating bottlenecks on the diffusion of local information into public governance, thus overturning its advantages in public governance. The problem is the assumptions over these conditions do not give a consistent narrative for each case. The question of how different institutional and organizational underpinnings determine outcomes of decentralization policies is important to tie in decentralization with better public governance. For this, we look into comparative accounts from different country cases.

Beginning with a comparative study among seven sub-Saharan countries, Olowu and Wunsch (2004) observe that in order decentralization reforms to be successful they need to be supported by (1) effective local authority and autonomy, (2) sufficient resources for localities, (3) effective institutions of collective action, and (4) open and accountable local political processes. In opposition to that, Saito (2005: 10) argues in most cases these conditions are not in congruence nor complementary as a change in one is bound to change in other. Therefore, decentralization as such does not lead to improved governance; instead, it relies on case-specific arrangements. For instance, in the case of Uganda, decentralization has been salient in redefining the roles and responsibilities of central government, local government, and non-state actors in public governance, whereby they peruse mutually beneficial outcomes (Saito 2001). In the cases of Sri Lanka and Ghana, capacity enhancement in both central and local governments is recommended instead of decentralizing tasks to local governments (Saito 2005: VII). Their accounts also suggest decentralization is not a technical tool to achieve better governance but decentralization reforms are deeply entangled in the political landscape of countries.

On another account, Kodras (1997) studies devolution and evaluates its pros and cons for governance. She underlines that devolution to local government makes public services more flexible by bringing them closer to people. However, devolution also creates inequalities in service provision as a result of differences in expertise, material and financial resources, infrastructures, and political will. By taking a critical approach, she points out local governments usually lack the capacity to provide services that a higher level of government does. Local government is also less capable to compete in the international market and more susceptible to social injustices it generates, unlike the national government that can provide uniform standards and regulations, and adopt a redistributive fiscal policy to overcome inequalities caused by international competition. About fiscal federalism thesis, Kodras points out it can yield efficiency in public services to an extent, but competition with central government on tax incentives, free lands, cheap labor, and infrastructure investments engenders a zero-sum game, eventually costing more to local government than the financial benefits of investment.

Drawing upon the practical experience from Asia, Africa, Europe, and the Americas, Stöhr et al. (2001) compare the strengths and weaknesses of deconcentration and devolution in local and regional development. Stöhr suggests that deconcentration can exercise better resource allocation than devolution by given the former maintains higher centralized control over decision-making through line ministries. Devolution, by contrast, tends to lead to higher innovation in the creation of PPPs and alternative financing strategies. Yet, Stöhr underlines coordination between government departments and ministries may break down in the case of devolution, which may undermine the effectiveness of policies. In opposition, Saito (2005) construes decentralization undermines hierarchical central control over local and regional bodies but replaces it with new forms of coordination mechanisms through consultative processes.

Nevertheless, similar to Saito et al., Stöhr et al. recommend decentralization should be calibrated with specific needs of each context, and decentralization by itself cannot solve the problems of participation, poverty, and inequality without taking into account the national context. In cases with a history of ethnic conflicts, decentralization risks fragmentation and breakdown of the national polity and civil society. Even in Western countries, Sorens (2009) objects the idea of political decentralization in ethnically demarcated regions reduces secessionist tendencies. Puzzled by the trend of political decentralization in Western European countries with subnationalist challenges, he concludes that political parties with stronger regional basis champion the idea of decentralization, as a political insurance in the winner-take-all electoral systems. He posits monopolization of regional politics by a secessionist or other regional party lowers the prospect of further decentralization, as there won't be any further political incentive for national parties to gain further with decentralization.

In overall, Stöhr et al. call for a formula between decentralized and centralized authority, which can fight better against social inequalities than higher decentralization. In the right balance, central authority can ensure redistribution of resources and overcome inequalities ingrained in local politics. They also identify four types of barriers (i.e., psychological, economic, social, and technical barriers) to overcome, for the empowerment of civil society through decentralization. Overcoming these barriers requires time and institutional adjustments, as well as the support of national and supranational agencies to cultivate a sense of solidarity and common purpose in localities. In another comparative account among 135 countries, Ponce-Rodríguez et al. (2018) assess the influence of decentralization/centralization in party politics (i.e., does political party decide on its local representatives or not) with political decentralization (i.e., are there locally elected subnational governments/or field agencies of central government) to service provision at local level. Their findings suggest that 'mixing democratic decentralization with party centralization' gives the best outcome in local service supplies if other things being equal. Their interpretation is centralized party politics brings additional incentive to locally elected representatives to deliver better public services, especially in areas with high spillover effect such as health and education services.

More about the policy choices of central government, Pierre and Peters (2000: 204) make a distinction between decentralization toward lower tiers of government and semi-public agencies. Accordingly, the state can 'decenter-down' its functions to lower tiers of government or 'decenter-out' to agencies and similar institutions in an 'arms-length'. Decentering-down is a strategy for the state to empower the capacity of subnational governments on resource mobilization to provide public services. Yet, this strategy entails a trade-off for the central authority between coordination of public services and increased capacities in subnational governments. Decentering-down is practical for the central government to share the responsibility on socially defined problems and thus release the tension toward central government. Yet, more independent subnational governments can undercut traditional modes of governance. Therefore, governments need to pursue new policy capabilities to effectively respond to potential policy challenges. On the other hand, decentering out public services to private and semi-private institutions raises competition and thus efficiency in service provisions. But again, marketization of public services can foster social inequalities and downplay the role of citizenry in a democracy. In particular, in systems with strong legalistic tradition, decentering out can cultivate dissatisfaction among citizens.

A fundamental proposition in favor of decentralization is competition among local governments—especially in developed countries—is good for the quality of governance; nonetheless, Warner's study on rural governance in the USA (2003) challenges this hypothesis as well. Many rural governments absent of an adequate revenue base or sufficient professional management capacity and sometimes with uneven and hierarchical social capital lack the necessary conditions to buttress effective decentralization. Here, private markets and privatization are embraced as an alternative to decentralized government, yet in the face of uneven markets, this leads to higher inequality on service provision. As a conclusion, Warner argues in favor of cooperation with other levels of government, as well as with private and civil society actors to get efficiency and equity in service provision instead of relying solely on interjurisdictional competition (see also Warner and Hefetz 2003). About the cooperation argument, Boyne (1996) makes a distinction between traditional and new competition. Traditional competition corresponds to interparty competition which is often ineffective at the local level. New competition, on the other hand, refers to the competition between a council and other organizations in service production and encompasses both geographical and tier-level competition. Boyne underlines three elements which shape the new competition: (1) structures of organizations (i.e., consolidated vs. fragmented), (2) autonomy in setting policies, and (3) finance. Here, Boyne postulates the higher the level of central funding is, the lower the incentive for fiscal movement among regions will be, and thus, the efficiency assumption of 'public choice theory' would be undermined. However, Boyne acknowledges that in order to achieve 'horizontal equity', some central funding is deemed necessary to overcome regional income discrepancies. In that regard, Bird and Smart (2002) discuss the use of capacity equalization practices through horizontal transfers (from richer regions to lower) or shares from common tax bases. They suggest if transfers are based on a formula of the revenue-raising capacity of regions and kept at the margin, they don't create a disincentive for local governments to raise revenues. Yet again, they also raise concern over the difficulty of measuring the revenue-raising capacity of regions, and in case the local government can directly or indirectly manipulate the proxies for measurement, then these efforts can have adverse effects in incentives as well.

Lastly, studies on developing countries underscore how institutional and organizational shortcomings can lead to inefficiencies in recently decentralized systems. In their study on health service delivery in Uganda, Nannyonjo and Okot (2012) account for several occasions where decentralization fails to improve governance. In a nutshell, they draw up the following recommendations: (1) decentralization may increase local monitoring and in return reduce corruption as long as communities possess a certain level of social capital and local awareness of corrupt government practices; (2) the absence of oversight mechanisms and local elite capture of resources for public services can pose challenge for effective decentralization; (3) social capital is also important for local government to collect user's fees and taxes; (4) in case where local communities lack the means of information on local governance services, decentralization can lead to lowering the quality of public services; (5) even in the case where there is a certain level of capacity on receiving information, residents may not be in a position to hold local leaders accountable or the central government may be too weak to monitor local leaders; (6) coordination problems among different public bodies and tiers of governments might impede a direct accountability between citizens and the administration responsible on individual public services; (7) decentralization might fail to achieve efficient service delivery because of poor design; (8) the most important factor of failure in decentralization policies is the lack of institutional capacity and skills in local politicians and bureaucrats especially to levy taxes, to administer resources, and to operate certain public services which require a certain level of technical adequacy; (9) decentralization failures might be a result of the lack of human capital that ensures taxes are diligently collected and channeled into social services; (10) decentralization failures can take place due to challenges on recruiting, motivating, and retaining the staff, lack of resources because of program failures, reduced independence, and complexity in central-local relations; (11) the level of decentralization might be an impediment on the success of decentralization as in the cases of grants allocated by the central government to local governments. If the block grants are conditioned on too many restrictions, the local leaders might claim that they have no authority over public spending. Yet, the grants without any restrictions might lead to local elite capture; and (12) while the ability of localities to raise revenues independently from the central government might increase electoral accountability, it can easily lead to regional imbalances and internal migration toward richer regions resulting in social imbalances.

Similarly, Sharma (2014) summarizes eight preconditions to reap the advantages of decentralization while averting potential dangers: (1) social preparedness and mechanisms to prevent elite capture; (2) strong administrative and technical capacity at the higher levels; (3) strong political commitment at the higher levels; (4) sustained initiatives for capacity-building at the local level; (5) strong legal framework for transparency and accountability; (6) transformation of local government organizations into high-performing organizations; (7) appropriate reasons for decentralization; and (8) effective judicial system, citizens' oversight, and anti-corruption bodies to prevent decentralization of corruption.

What can public policy professionals in both developing and developed countries learn from all these accounts? Decentralization comes with a handful of improvements to governance but also entails many pitfalls that public managers should be aware of. There is no one-size-fits-all in decentralization policies. Decentralization without corresponding regulative and coordinative institutional adjustments is likely to endanger the quality of governance. The 'invisible hand' creating a just outcome for every stakeholder is rather a wishful thinking. Decentralization has the danger of creating social inequities by unveiling subtle rivalries deeply ingrained in the community or exposing local government precipitately to global competition. Decentralization can improve service quality and bring price advantages by incorporating private service providers in public services, but their legitimacy and accountability will be subject to question. Most of all, decentralization calls for new capabilities in problem-solving through cooperation, mitigation, and compromises, so governing institutions become resilient against emergent challenges. In that regard, *governance capacity* is the cumulative ability of government institutions to effectively address these challenges.

50   E. TAN

GOVERNANCE CAPACITY

We have seen so far how the evolution of societies and global economy led to a network-shaped system in public governance, and how governments try to steer this system through empowering actors or the hubs of actors to get better public policy outcomes. What is missing here is the way governance creates public value. So, what qualities do a governance system and its constituents need to produce a public good? Without apprehending the value creation of governance, we cannot tinker with the system in the hope to produce better outcomes.

This brings us to the next key concept in the book, the governance capacity. Capacity and improving capacity are two beloved concepts in the milieu of public policy and development experts. There exists an abundance of governance capacity frameworks either to improve good governance (e.g., World Bank, UNDP) or to address a particular policy challenge (e.g., health, policy capacity, crisis management). Yet, almost each theoretical and empirical account employs a different governance capacity definition compliant with the scope of the work. What seems to be missing in the governance literature is studies particularly focusing on the concept of 'governance capacity', elaborating on its nature and functionality.

Having said that, there are some accounts, which provide workable definitions for governance capacity. For instance, Ingraham and Kneedler (2000) define capacity as 'government's ability to marshal, develop, direct and control its financial, human, physical and information resources'. There are also broader definitions, such as 'a set of attributes that help or enable an organization to fulfill its missions' (Eisinger 2002) or 'the ability to carry out stated objectives' (Goodman et al. 1998). Chaskin (2001) describes capacity even in a more comprehensive manner as 'any quality that can promote or impede successes'.

Morgan (2006) mentions five present different approaches to capacity development in governance: first, treating capacity as human resources, which has something to do with skills, development, and training of people; second, extending capacity into problem-solving abilities and producing results, as 'the means' to improve results and performance; third, taking it as a buzzword that encompasses everything, thus becoming almost impractical. The proponents of this approach are usually skeptical about the function of capacity interventions in performance improvement; fourth, emphasizing the symbolic importance of the term which can incorporate a wide range of issues, such as 'ownership, commitment, innovation, partnership, learning, institutional development, decentralization, public sector reform, knowledge management, change, scaling up, sustainability, participation, training accountability, performance improvement and so forth'. In this perspective, capacity is a flexible concept, which can cover everything from micro- to macro-level. Therefore, any action can be within the pretext of improving capacity; and the last one according to Morgan is a newly emerging way of thinking about capacity, which opposes the former approach. The argument here is the former approach fails to operationalize capacity in a practical manner. As a response, the last perspective advocates seeking some central ideas for capacity, which can guide capacity development. This perspective places the questions of 'how and why capacity emerges' next to the traditional question of 'what types of capacities are needed'.

On the other hand, 'governance capacity' as the synonym of power in governing is hardly present in the literature. The most comprehensive theoretical accounts on that matter are in Dutch literature under the concept of *'bestuurskracht'*, which can be translated as the power of governing. For instance, according to Nielsen et al. (2000), *bestuurskracht* indicates the degree to which the government is successful in solving the problems or in avoiding the problems to occur. Derksen et al. (1987) argue that *bestuurskracht* in local government shows the capability of carrying out the tasks legally and solving the local problems and needs. Maes (1985) associates *bestuurskracht* with the ability to fulfill the daily needs of the citizens, which require the appropriate means (e.g., financial and human resource capacities), self-sufficiency and effectiveness on service delivery, and a democratic and transparent organization. Lastly, Delmartino (1975) suggests that the term infers the capability of local government in governing the local, taking care of both cultural and material needs in the locality and solving the problems in the domain effectively.

In sum, capacity can have 'thin' or 'thick' definitions depending on the scope of the study and on the perspective of the researcher. In this work, capacity will be studied as part of public governance, which entails all theoretical expectations from public sector organizations in terms of better governance. Yet, the theoretical propositions about better governance oblige us to consider expectations both in relation to public sector organization and in relation to its surrounding conditions. However, there is one fundamental issue to address before moving to theoretical propositions about governance capacity, and that is the conceptual properties of capacity.

Capacity as a Black Box Concept

It is easy to abstract the concept of capacity, but it is definitely not an easy task to define capacity. The literature describes capacity as a process and an outcome (see Sowa et al. 2004); as the ends and the means to the ends (see Honadle 1981); as dynamic and multidimensional (see Ingraham et al. 2003); it is given both tangible and intangible, or quantitative and qualitative dimensions (see Kaplan 2000; Christensen and Gazley 2008). Academics, practitioners, and policy analysts attribute different meanings to capacity, and the scope of capacity varies depending on the macro- or micro-visions on the concept (Morgan 2006). This elusiveness complicates defining the concept, and thus, various definitions exist in the literature. However, in almost every definition, capacity is associated with an *ability to perform.*

While this definition is comprehensive enough to avoid potential conceptual shortcomings, it is too abstract to operationalize. In fact, this problem is derived from the nature of capacity. Capacity is, in essence, an ethereal concept. All efforts to define this essence are bound to the material limits of its conceptualization. Nonetheless, we can still identify certain axioms in its abstraction.

First, capacity is not a monolithic concept; it is the collective ability of different components. Each component preserves an aspect of capacity which is separate by itself but at the same time, part of a whole. These components create jointly the capacity of the whole. Thus, capacity is also an outcome of the joint functioning of these components. The literature phrases this feature of capacity as 'the ends and the means to the ends'. As an analogy, there is no doubt Usain Bolt has a high capacity to run fast in short distances, but running fast is in the meantime an outcome of good reaction time[4] and acceleration time.[5]

Second, components of capacity are not necessarily tangible, quantifiable elements. Intangible elements such as 'responsibility, endeavor or team spirit' are as important as skills and resources on capacity assessment. In fact, Kaplan (2000) argues that intangible elements are more important and higher-valued components, since they determine the organizational functioning.

---

[4] The elapsed time to start running.

[5] The required time to reach full speed.

Third, capacity usually exists in a latent state. Through changes in external conditions and/or with external interventions, capacity can reveal better or worse outcomes. In a way, this feature is the underlying rationale for capacity-building practices. For instance, we know that with better training and new skills, capacity can be augmented.

Fourth, despite being latent, capacity is not a static concept. It can increase or decrease over time. The changes in capacity can be a result of exogenous or endogenous factors. This feature is related to, in fact, what called as 'capacity development' in the literature. The exogenous impacts can result from deliberate actions or simply from enabling surrounding conditions. Going back to the runner example, Bolt had probably a good capacity to run fast even when he was a child, but his capacity has developed in time with growing up and having stronger muscles. Furthermore, his capacity has extended even more with good nutrition and training. So, the former refers to an endogenous change, while the latter can be an example of exogenous changes. In addition, Bolt grew up in Jamaica, which is known for its successful sprinters in running competitions. This is a good example of an enabling environment.

Fifth, capacity is a multidimensional concept. Honadle and Howitt (1986: 10) pinpoint five dimensions for organizational capacity. First, capacity entails the ability of an organization to *survive* by being self-sustaining. Second, capacity can refer to the *power* of an organization to achieve its goals. Third, capacity can be regarded *institutionally* as the development and maintenance of the organization. Fourth, capacity as a *system* refers to the ability to convert inputs into desirable outputs. And fifth, capacity can refer to the ability of an organization to carry out self-defined objectives ('inner directedness') or directed objectives from external sources ('other directedness'). Honadle and Howitt (1986: 13) conclude that organizational capacity captures at a minimum all of these dimensions: survival, power, institutions, systems, conforming to local expectations, and external standards.

To sum up, a study of capacity should pay attention to the following aspects: (1) Capacity comprises both the end and the means to the end; (2) capacity contains both tangible and intangible elements; (3) capacity can be in a latent state and change with external interventions; (4) capacity is not a static concept it can change as a result of endogenous and exogenous factors; and (5) capacity is multidimensional. These underpinnings are important to grasp capacity comprehensively.

54   E. TAN

Now, the question is how do you assess capacity? Capacity is not a standalone variable, it needs an adjacent concept to say 'capacity of what?' Second, we cannot observe capacity directly. We observe only outcomes of capacity, e.g., successes, failures, or achievements. Similarly, we cannot observe the change in capacity; we refer to change in outcomes as the change in capacity. Analogous to the transformation of potential energy to kinetic energy, capacity upholds the potential of the object to perform, which can only be assessed by the amount of energy released by moving from potential to kinetic state.

These types of concepts are commonly associated with the well-known 'black box' metaphor. The black box metaphor implies that we can observe something solely in terms of its input, output, and transfer characteristics without any knowledge of its inner mechanism. As a result, measuring capacity requires additional concepts indicating the changes in the input and output stages. Therefore, concepts such as 'capability' or 'performance' are employed to reify the impact of capacity.

Surely, the frequent interchangeable use of capacity with its close synonyms—capability, competence, and performance—is bewildering. Here, Franks (1999) makes a distinction of capacity from competence and capability. While capability denotes 'the knowledge, skills, and attitudes of the individuals or groups and their competence to undertake the responsibilities assigned to them', capacity refers to 'the overall ability of the individual or group to actually perform the responsibilities'. Accordingly, capacities do not only hinge on the capabilities of people but also 'on the overall size of the tasks, the resources which are needed to perform them, and the framework within which they are discharged'.

Peter Morgan (2006) draws a further distinction between capability and competence. He explains that competencies refer to the attributions of individuals, whereas capabilities are collective skills that can be both technical and logistical or 'harder' and 'softer'.[6] From this perspective, capacity is the construct of five core capabilities: the capability to act, the capability to generate development results, the capability to relate, the capability to adapt, and the capability to integrate. Thus, capability encompasses pretty much everything that a system requires to produce a value, while capacity is the ability of the system functioning.

---

[6] Morgan explains 'harder' capabilities such as 'policy analysis or financial management' and 'softer' capabilities as 'the ability to earn legitimacy, to adapt, to create meaning and identity'.

On another note, performance differs from capacity as the latter corresponds to 'the means to achieve performance' (Honadle 1981). Here, performance is the end product of capacity. Similarly, Hou et al. (2003) describe capacity as a prerequisite for performance. They define capacity as the formal rules that 'restrain discretion and direct behavior of both political and administrative actors in a way expected to facilitate the achievement of the performance objective'. Consequently, performance is a key element to work on capacity. Albeit not being part of capacity, performance changes signify changes in capacity.

It is clear that scholars vary on their definitions depending on their research interests. Studies focusing on the impact of capacity emphasize output part and incorporate performance indicators to assess capacities. On the other hand, studies focusing on the capabilities of actors emphasize input dimension in assessing capacities. Yet, a comprehensive capacity assessment should integrate both input and output stages while taking into account the operational framework. For that matter, UNDP (2008) underlines that an appropriate capacity assessment should be 'a structured and analytical process which should include assessment of various dimensions within the broader systems context, as well as the evaluation of specific entities and individuals within the system'.

One last critical aspect is that capacity assessment is contingent on temporal and spatial conditions. Lack of capacity does not necessarily emerge from inadequate resources. Rather, changes in the expectations can cause a capacity gap. The Usain Bolt analogy can assist us here as well. With his physical attributions and training, we would have expected a good result from Usain Bolt even in his earlier runs. If he had failed to achieve good running times despite his attributions (i.e., input), we would have judged that he is not using his full capacity. Yet, we wouldn't have the same expectations about a runner with weaker ascription. Therefore, with expectations, we create different bars of evaluation for the same activity. Our expectations about Bolt have heightened in time because of his phenomenal achievements in consecutive runs. In case of failure or any less fulfilling result in succeeding competitions, he could be judged on not fully using his capacity. And lastly, to visualize the effect of the context, we wouldn't expect the same results from Bolt if he were 40 years old. Even though his timing was not as good as his previous runs, we would still think he is using his full capacity, because our judgment is shifted by the changes in his physical attributions.

To sum up, capacity is not a directly observable phenomenon. In our abstract thinking, we conceptualize capacity with inputs to the entity and with outputs from the entity. Concepts such as capability or performance facilitate the analysis of the inputs and outputs. Moreover, capacity assessment changes over time with changing conditions in the context. In other words, the same abilities could be insufficient in different cases and at different times. Therefore, capacity assessment should incorporate a clear understanding of contextual conditions as well.

THEORIES OF GOVERNANCE CAPACITY

The expansion of governance from the Weberian public administration, first to NPM and later to NPG, extended alongside the scope of governance capacity. Today, governance capacity incorporates individual, organizational, and institutional dimensions, as well as hierarchical, market, and network modes of governance. Yet, our knowledge is rather limited about whether there are particular capacities that fit better to certain modes of governance, and if yes, whether these capacities are complementary or contradictory with each other. For example, capacities that complement hierarchical governance could undermine capacities in network governance. Unfortunately, even hypothetically, it is difficult to isolate the impact of one type of capacity on another, as it would require a controlled environment to test where capacity components are free from contextual restrictions or intangible capacity components are exempt from diffusing with each other. These assumptions would contradict the innate features of capacity.

So, it is important to approach holistically to governance capacity, but in the meantime, it is also necessary to feature the building blocks of the whole—or the components of capacity. The capacity components are derived from the theoretical underpinnings of governance capacity. In that regard, governance capacity is situated amid the organizational theories, system theories, and management theories. Therefore, there are three salient ways to indicate governance capacity. First, 'management' or 'managerial' capacity corresponds at large to the managerial qualities of decision-makers in an organization. Second, 'organizational' capacity reflects the total ability of an organization to produce governance outcomes. Organizational capacity encompasses all processes, resources (e.g., human, financial, technological), and competencies that control the internal and external functioning of the organization. The third approach can be named as 'systemic' or 'institutional', presumes

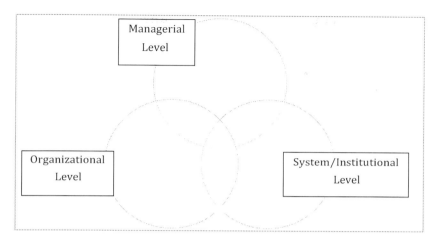

Fig. 2.1 An analytical framework for theories of governance capacity (*Source* Author)

organizational performance is dependent on the surrounding conditions. Commonly, institutional capacity dwells upon how regulations, legal frameworks, and policies affect organizations and denote the impact of coordination on the governance of inter-organizational relations.

They together demarcate three venues, where components of governance capacity locate. Hence, governance capacity reflects (a) capacity of decision-makers (i.e., managers and leaders of the organization), (b) capacity of the organization, and (c) capacity of the institutional milieu. While each venue has distinct features, they are conjoint, and changes in one have profound effects on others as well. Therefore, a comprehensive theoretical framework of governance capacity compounds on all (Fig. 2.1).

By this theoretical approach to governance capacity, in the following parts, I will highlight certain capabilities from each viewpoint, which I will later integrate into my own analytical framework for the analysis of the relationship between governance capacity and decentralization.

Governance Capacity from a Managerial Perspective

Honadle and Howitt (1986) give a variety of abilities comprised by managerial capacity: the ability of identifying problems and developing policies to solve these problems; the ability of conceiving programs for the implementation of the policies; the ability of attracting and absorbing financial, human, material, and informational resources; the ability of managing these resources; and the ability of evaluating the activities for future guidance. In other words, managerial capacity conveys all competences pertained to the manager, which brings the organization into success.

Not all taxonomies of managerial capacity put the weight on the shoulders of the manager. According to Ingraham and Kneedler (2000: 294), the government's managerial capacity relies on 'management subsystems' driving the management of financial, human, material, and informational capital of the organization. These management subsystems rely on environmental factors (e.g., characteristics of constituent populations and socioeconomic conditions) and qualifications of managers such as effective leadership, use of information, allocation of resources, and a 'results focus'. Thus, managerial capacity is an overarching ability of the organization to allocate the necessary resources at the right time into the right place.

On the contrary, Raboca et al. (2010) argue managerial capacities do not rely on the merits of management subsystems alone but also on the way these systems are integrated. They define managerial capacity as 'those competencies, skills, aptitudes possessed by the leading factors in an institution and which are necessary for managing the activities and the internal processes from the institution successfully'. Accordingly, three sources determine managerial capacities of public sector organization: (1) the configuration, the processes, and the activities connected to the managerial subsystems and the link between them; (2) the way the systems are integrated; and (3) a result-oriented whole managerial system.

Altogether, the abilities of manager, the components of management systems (i.e., the act of leading and the processes), the way the management systems are coming together, and an overall vision to produce intended outcomes designate the essentials of managerial capacity. The next step is to ascribe capabilities to these managerial aspects from a governance perspective.

In traditional public administration, regardless of the political configuration, the head of local government is the agent of both central authority and citizens. The primary responsibility of local government is to ensure the public service delivery and assure the satisfaction of both principals. In a way, the manager is the interlocutor of demand and supply relationship between central authority and citizens. Therefore, the managerial capacity is determined alongside the fruitful relationships kept with a central authority. Nonetheless, with emergent modes of governance, the head of local government is expected more and more to be an active, entrepreneurial, and independent actor who can juggle among national, international, and local actors to mobilize the means to satisfy various private, public, and civilian interests.

These new expectations call for new capabilities and skills to become competent. First of all, a new model of leadership is required for public governance. The politically neutral, executive leaders are no longer satisfactory. The fragmented nature of local politics and conflicting interests demand stronger brokerage and linking abilities (Bekkers et al. 2011). Naturally, these new responsibilities require a different set of personality attributions. According to Minnaar and Bekker (2005: 141–142), great organizational leaders hold the following characteristics: a special charisma, self-belief that tends to bother on arrogance at times, the ability to move out a 'comfort zone' in order to shift traditional paradigms, the ability to question the status quo, which makes these people good innovators, an ability to convince others to follow them in pursuit of a new direction. Similarly, a strong leader in public governance is the one who set the vision for others to follow and in addition, builds motivation and trust among shareholders. Furthermore, a strong leader has the necessary skills to face challenges in volatile conditions and to resolve conflicting interests effectively. Many leaders, who lack the ability to empathize and to be imaginative, fail to be successful in their endeavor (Goss 2001: 193).

The reliance on legal and constitutional powers is no longer satisfactory for competency. Therefore, a strong leader is not the one who execute policies by relying on the legislative powers vested in the post, but the one who can create 'safe places' for the organizational and societal interactions. Pierre and Peters (2000: 198) point this out as former bureaucratic powers are replaced with 'entrepreneurial skills', 'political zeal', and 'brokerage abilities'. This situation nonetheless undercuts the legitimacy of bureaucracy. In this sense, Moore (2000) asserts successful public managers build legitimacies for their actions through managing relationships with politicians and the public. Likewise, Goss (2001: 161) states that managers should sponsor innovation, manage risk and legitimacy.

The type of knowledge sought by the managers has also changed. Nowadays, reliance on professional knowledge like financial management, project management, or human resources management is less and less sufficient to determine action. The knowledge on how to extract

60   E. TAN

the resources and capacities of others and channel them into a socially valuable action is becoming more predominant (Goss 2001: 161). Unfortunately, these changes create a pressure on public servants who are used to think in former ways, and they frequently fail to provide the knowledge sought by the managers. Therefore, public managers should also pioneer new education and training activities for their staff to enable self-directedness and self-driven learning (Du Plessis 2008: 134).

Lastly, citizens take an active role in decision-making and implementation of public services, which turn them into active shareholders rather than passive receivers in public affairs. This brings new responsibilities to public managers as network managers. For instance, Osborne (2010: 414) states that 'stakeholder management' is an important duty in new public governance. In a similar vein, Voets and De Rynck (2011: 209) argue 'boundary-scanning' and 'boundary-spanning' activities are imperative to create interrelations among various actors. Public managers should convey the information about their environment to their organization and in the meantime keep other actors informed about their organization. On that regard, Voets and De Rynck distinguish five distinct roles for public managers, whereby they can create the innovative capacity to cope with inter-institutional challenges. These are 'vision keeper', 'creative thinker', 'network promoter', 'network champion', and 'network operator'. A public leader is expected to combine these different features or at least to create the organizational conditions to cover these roles.

Governance Capacity from an Organizational Perspective

Managerial capacities are closely attached and dependent on the capacity of organizations. There are certain characteristics of capable organizations that are similar for all types of organizations. For instance, Honadle (1981) states the organizational capacity of local government comprises 'the ability to forge effective links with other organizations; processes for solving problems; coordination among disparate functions; and mechanisms for institutional learning'. Furthermore, the capacity of an organization is not limited to the inputs such as resources on personnel, revenue, information, or community support, but its real strength lies in its capacity to attract and absorb resources. On community development centers, Glickman and Servon (1998) outline five core components of capacity: resources, effective leadership, an external helping network, specialized skills to undertake housing and development projects, and political resources. Eisinger (2002)'s study on non-charitable organizations underlines five critical components of capacity: resources, effective leadership, skilled and sufficient staff, a certain level of institutionalization, and links to the larger community environment. In another study about nonprofit human service organizations, Austin et al. (2011) attribute five aspects for organizational capacity: normative vision (indicating missions, values, and strategies); societal context (social space); requisite resources (human, financial, information, etc.); actors (institutions, networks, individuals); and functions required (planning, decision-making, etc.).

In overall, a capable organization is well aligned with the overall strategy, has clear and simple tasks for employees, and acquires sufficient resources and effective working systems. Nevertheless, these ubiquitous features of capable organizations are also susceptible to change along with changing expectations on governance. The reclusive, socially detached public sector organizations are no longer deemed as capable organizations. Public sector organizations are expected to generate new means and ways to interact with citizens, to be flexible and capable of responding effectively on rapidly changing conditions. This transformation demands, first of all, a fundamental change in the organizational behavior. Hence, capable public sector organizations are also the ones that hold effective means to organizational learning and acquisition of knowledge.

There are different approaches to organizational learning. One approach to organizational learning derives from individual learning (Goss 2001: 174). Another approach sets collective action as the source of organizational learning (Argyris and Schön 1996). This approach recommends adaptation of rewarding mechanisms to encourage the staff in organizational learning. Another means in organizational learning is promoting the intra-organizational share of knowledge. One caveat here is, if people feel as competing with each other, they will likely withdraw themselves from sharing knowledge and instead use it to achieve supremacy over others.

Another foot of organizational learning is outside of the organization. Recently, advancements in social innovation have brought up new venues where organizational learning can take place. Negotiation workshops, citizen juries, community workshops, interactive conferences, and open-space events are some options where citizens, politicians, and managers can exchange ideas and learn from each other.

In addition to cultivating organizational learning, capable organizations develop new means to extract information and financial resources for public services. Public sector organizations are expected to have the revenue-raising ability in tax collection and in commercial services yet also to attract private investment in public services. In practice, this creates a controversy between modes of governance, as private investment calls for less coercive instruments and less rigid regulative control to be attractive for private investors. If state institutions lay too strict regulatory policy instruments for private capital, private investments can shift into less hostile environments (Pierre and Peters 2000: 204). Furthermore, successful collaborations with private sector organizations necessitate interorganizational and interpersonal trust as a precondition. This entails a new organizational behavior that replaces widespread apathetic organizational culture in bureaucratic organizations.

The information capital connotes the organizational capacity in ICT infrastructure to gather and store information on citizen needs and complaints, but also to oversee partnerships with profit and nonprofit organizations. In addition, public sector organizations need relevant human capital and effective feedback mechanisms. Setting certain quality standards in accountability and transparency engenders the public trust and eventually effective feedbacks into public sector organizations.

Governance perspective also obliges public sector organizations to be capable in managing partnerships. Rhodes (1997: 138–141) lists certain organizational conditions for successful partnerships: 'a clear strategic focus, strategic leadership and support, the importance of trust, organizations, and people in partnerships, capacity for cooperation and mutualism, organizational complementarity, co-location and coterminosity, the value of action and outcome-oriented procedures'. Trafford and Proctor (2006: 120) underscore good communication, openness, effective planning, ethos, and direction in successful partnerships. Specialized training for those partaking in partnerships can improve organizational capacity in effective partnerships. For instance, Mcquaid (2010) recommends joint studies between involving parties to develop a common vocabulary and understanding on how to work together. Actually, governing relations among public, private, and voluntary sector organizations falls under the scope of another thematic field under governance, the 'metagovernance'. Jessop (2000) sets the following rules for better metagovernance: 'Provide the ground rules for governance and the regulatory order in and through which governance partners can pursue their aims; ensure the compatibility or coherence of different governance mechanisms and regimes; act as the primary organizer of the dialogue among policy communities; deploy a relative monopoly of organizational intelligence and information with which to shape cognitive expectations; serve as a 'court of appeal' for disputes arising within and over governance; seek to re-balance power differentials by strengthening weaker forces or systems in the interest of system integration and/or social cohesion; try to modify the self-understanding of identities, strategic capacities, and interests of individual and collective actors in different strategic contexts and hence alter their implications for preferred strategies and tactics'.

Last but not least, capable organizations rely on clear processes of planning, implementation, monitoring, and evaluation of governance services. Only organizations with adequate managerial and technological capabilities can coordinate these processes effectively.

Governance Capacity from an Institutional Perspective

The capable organization is not only about resources, capital, structures, processes but the relations with other organizations are equally important on the performance. From an organizational point of view, institutional capacity can be related to the ability of governance systems to build new institutions to create means of collaborations through formal and informal ways with society (see Matthiesen 2002); to the creation of 'micropolitical processes' within neighborhoods which can annihilate the processes which produce social exclusion (see Allen and Cars 2002); to a style of policy making which relies on negotiation and persuasion which allows mutual learning (see Taylor 2002); or to the capacity or organizations to create new relationships for engaging collective action (see Healey 1998). In overall, the abilities to engage and build relations, abilities to learn and use the knowledge, or the abilities to build a necessary institution to enable collective actions are some dimensions of institutional capacity for public sector organizations. Additionally, the systemic view conveys the relational capacity of other organizations and enabling external conditions into institutional capacity. The governability of society, the formal and informal rules regulating social interactions, political culture, and compatibility of the organization with all these societal conditions are also fundamental in institutional capacity.

64   E. TAN

Similar to organizations, being an active participant in governance seeks a learning process for communities. Yet, learning capacities of communities vary depending on sociocultural premises. Having a culture of participation in politics and trust in institutions facilitates the transition process. More and more, capacity-building programs target community representatives and organizations, to build the necessary skills in negotiation and cooperation in governance through training of staff, facilitators, and community leaders. However, learning is not a linear process. In particular, for communities with nominal culture in participation and cooperation, a process of exploration and testing on participation is required to build self-aware, self-managing communities (Goss 2001: 191). In a similar vein, De Visser (2005: 133) underlines the success of public participation does not depend on formal actions to regulate the system but instead on inculcating a culture of community participation by utilizing innovation and creativity in actions. So, building institutional capacity requires a process of learning for the community, whereby experimenting and informal ways of interactions are necessary to enable sustainable participation.

In addition to community learning and enabling cultural elements, the regulative framework is indispensable to institutional capacity. The regulative framework sets the conditions for reaching an agreement among participants in governance. For instance, the World Governance Survey (WGS) sets six dimensions to assess the regulative framework in public governance: (1) rules that shape the way citizens raise and become aware of public issues (civil society); (2) rules that shape the way issues are combined into policy by political institutions (political society); (3) rules that shape the way policies are made by government institutions (government); (4) rules that shape the way policies are administered and implemented by public servants (bureaucracy); (5) rules that shape the way state and market interact to promote development (economic society); and (6) rules that shape the setting for resolution of disputes and conflicts. Moreover, it is substantial for the governance actors to have recognized and legitimate roles and responsibilities, as well as a clear framework to avoid possible coordination problems, which can undermine the effectiveness of partnerships.

Mutual trust of actors is also substantial for successful collaborations. Kale et al. (2000: 218) point out the 'relational capital'—the level of mutual trust that arises out of close interaction at the individual level between alliance partners—is an important strategic resource to ensure successful partnerships. In particular, considering the high level of failure rates[7] among private-public partnerships, relational capital appears as a reliable resource against such failures. Although trust as a commodity is deeply intermingled with sociocultural factors, informal interactions and 'open networks' are operational to build trustworthy relations in local communities (Bekkers et al. 2011: 211).

Another dimension in institutional capacity is the 'governability' of the community. This dimension of institutional capacity relies on the assumption of certain social structures are fundamental to the governance performance. One core concept in this discussion is the 'social capital', refers to 'the features of social organization, such as trust, norms, and networks that can improve the efficiency of society by facilitating coordinated actions' (Putnam 1994: 167). According to Putnam, societies with limited social capital will likely to perform poorly on democratic governance. Even though we have limited knowledge of how institutions affect the proliferation of social capital (Hooghe and Stolle 2003), many accounts on institutional capacity postulate on social capital. For instance, Cars et al. (2002) define institutional capacity as 'transforming, creating and mobilizing the institutional capital of a place in the collective effort of shaping its future', where 'institutional capital' refers to the social capital in governance. Here, institutional capital links three essential elements for social interactions: 'knowledge resources', 'relational resources', and 'mobilization capacity'. Knowledge resources refer to 'the frames of reference, creativity, and knowledgeability, the conceptions of place and identity relevant to governance'. Relational resources comprise 'the resources of trust and co-operation contained in networks, the nature of bonding elements in them and networks to draw resource, rules, and ideas into the effort of collective action'. Mobilization capacity is the capacity of stakeholders in a locality to mobilize the knowledge and relational resources to act collectively for a common goal.

Lastly, institutional capacity also connotes the external expectations of public governance. For instance, Gargan (1981) explains the capacities of local governments rely on any point in time on the interaction between community expectations, community problems, and community resources. By this token, expectations involve 'perceptions and attitudes on adequate levels of public services, appropriate styles of political

---

[7]Authors give different ratios on the failure of PPPs from 30 to 70% (see Duysters et al. 1999; Park and Ungson 2001; Overby 2006; Klijn 2010: 194).

66   E. TAN

leadership, and accepted ways of conducting public affairs'. Community resources encompass tangible elements such as money, knowledge, administrative skills, private sector associations, neighborhood organizations, and political popularity but they are not limited to these. Problems, on the other hand, refer to the community-specific issues, which entail different preferences in accomplishing governance objectives. Hence, Gargan equates governance capacity to 'the function of expectations, resources and problems'.

An Analytical Model for Governance Capacity

New ways of thinking in governance do not only compel public sector organizations to be capable in public service delivery, but to realize this is a paradigm where rules on legitimacy, roles, and expectations are no longer ubiquitous nor static. What defines a successful organization is not only reliant on organizational performance, but also on the standpoint of other public and non-public actors, which have a distinct role to uphold in governance perspective. Under these circumstances, any analytical model of governance capacity is bound to the limits of contextual conditions in the country case and subjective choices of the researcher.

Nevertheless, many concepts in social sciences are subject to arbitrary choices in measurement. The caveat here is, if the study aims to set the premises of a pervasive model of governance capacity which is applicable in diverse country cases, it is imperative to clarify the way subjective and contextual conditions affect the outcome of the analysis. Therefore, the following parts in the book will pay further attention to contextual conditions and methodological choices in determining the relationship between governance capacity and decentralization, and adjust the model of the study accordingly.

Having said that, in the following parts of this book, public governance will be conceptualized close to Pierre and Peters' definition as 'steering the actors in localities in order to cover the service provision and demands of citizens, whereas the local government is the *primus inter pares*'. However, this theoretical viewpoint toward public governance does not exclude the role of other actors by reducing their functions as passive bystanders but also takes into account their relational position. Thus, our model will incorporate both capacity of local government and the capacity of the surrounding conditions.

About the local government capacity, the first step is to set the expectations in public governance. The governance perspective embarks the local government the responsibility to mobilize the necessary resources (e.g., financial, human resources, information), from the actors in the local domain and channel them wisely to the needs and demands of the residents. This basic algorithm discerns three distinct functions for the local government: (1) mobilizing resources; (2) decision-making; and (3) implementation.

These three functions of local government will set the premises of our model to measure governance capacity. From an output-oriented view, governance capacity indicates the performance of local government in resource mobilization, in decision-making on right policy action, and in the implementation of effective and efficient public services. From an input-oriented view, on the other hand, managerial, organizational, and institutional theories denote various capabilities for the governance capacity. Categorically, governance capacity relies on seven types of capabilities: (1) financial capabilities, (2) material capabilities, (3) communication capabilities, (4) planning capabilities, (5) managerial capabilities, (6) human resource capabilities, and (7) institutional capabilities or local capabilities. Financial capabilities encompass owned financial resources and the means to extract the financial resources. Material capabilities feature the adequacy of equipment and the means of acquisition. Communication capabilities incorporate the means, processes, and systems for the exchange of information between managers, organization, and other actors in governance. Planning capabilities refer to the methods and processes to strategize between actions, goals, and financial means of the local government. Managerial capabilities refer to the leadership qualities of managers, the features of management systems, and the processes for the effective delivery of policy actions. Human resource capabilities pertain to personnel attribution and the means to enhance the necessary skills in personnel. The last category, institutional capabilities reflect the relational capacity existing in the locality indicating the socioeconomic conditions.

The outcome in governance capacity is congruent to the capabilities in governance. Analytically, 'mobilizing the resources' pertains to the financial and material capabilities; 'decision-making' pertains to planning and communication capabilities; and 'implementation' pertains to human resource and managerial capabilities. With the addition of the institutional capabilities, we designate four subcategories to measure

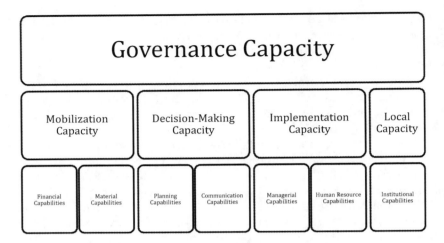

Fig. 2.2 An analytical model for capacities in local governance

governance capacity: (1) mobilization capacity; (2) decision-making capacity; (3) implementation capacity; and (4) local capacity. The first three belong to the local government's capacities, whereas the last one denotes the relational capacity of locality (Fig. 2.2).

The conceptual features of capacity suggest the capacities under governance capacity are separate on their own but at the same time collectively they constitute the governance capacity. Accordingly, mobilization capacity indicates the capacity of the local government in mobilizing essential financial and material resources for services and functions. Mobilization capacity reflects the three stages in mobilizing the resources: (1) the ability in bringing in financial resources for purchasing, (2) the capability in channeling the financial resources for purchasing goods and services, and (3) the adequacy in financial and material means for municipal functions.

Decision-making capacity indicates the capacity of the local government in determining how to allocate and where to allocate resources. The former indicates the planning capabilities in strategizing how to allocate local government's resources to the policy action. On the other hand, the best decision on where to allocate resources demands adequate and effective means for information gathering and processing. Hence, decision-making capacity reflects the effectiveness and efficiency in planning and communication stages.

Implementation capacity indicates the capacity of local government in management and human resources. The managerial dimension incorporates individual skills and abilities of managers, but also management practices to increase organizational performance. Education, experience, collaboration, and initiative taking in management, and management practices for higher performance constitute the managerial dimension. Additionally, successful implementation also relies on the quality and sufficiency of local government's personnel. Quantitative and qualitative features of personnel and practices in employment and personnel formation are some aspects to consider the effectiveness of human resource capabilities.

Local capacity signifies the institutional capabilities in the locality. Institutional capabilities are, *inter alia*, the economic dynamism, social capital, organized community representation, and other qualities with the private sector and voluntary sector organizations. It is difficult to comprise all local elements related to public governance, but socioeconomic development embodies overall local capacity in governance.

RESEARCH HYPOTHESES ABOUT THE RELATIONSHIP BETWEEN DECENTRALIZATION AND GOVERNANCE CAPACITY

We have two research questions to address: (1) How should policy makers decide on the degree of decentralization in order to get the best outcome in public governance? and (2) how does governance capacity affect the outcome of decentralization in public governance? The literature contests the arguments suggesting more decentralization leads to better governance, but instead a right balance between central and local government is anticipated to ensure the best outcome in public governance. The assumption is if the relationship between governance capacity and decentralization can better be understood, an optimal level of decentralization can be designated for better public governance.

With regard to the relationship between decentralization and governance capacity, there are two prevailing positions in the literature. One position is decentralization leads to the formation of the relevant capacities or enhancement in them. The opposing view is some capacities are preconditioned for the success of decentralization. In fact, this debate is to a certain extent linked with the conceptual feature of capacity, as capacity can change in time due to exogenous and endogenous conditions. Therefore, it is difficult to refute any of these arguments, as both can endure concurrently. Yet, this debate boils down to the primary question of 'which capacities are associated with decentralization?' The assumption here is the success in decentralization should be associated with constituting capacities of governance capacity if the contextual conditions (i.e., sociocultural and legal framework) are taken as ceteris paribus. This inevitably necessitates a comparison of local governments operating under the same regulative conditions in the same country case.

Before positing a hypothesis about the relationship between decentralization and governance capacity, it is also imperative to explain what does 'success in decentralization' refer. The governance perspective situates decentralization both as means and an outcome in public governance. However, in order to test the relationship between governance capacity and decentralization, it is important to uphold a static meaning for decentralization. Decentralization as a static concept indicates the autonomy of local government in public governance. Thus, the extent that local government is self-dependent on sustaining the public affairs designates the success in decentralization.

Moreover, the literature emphasizes the importance of socioeconomic conditions on the success of decentralization, but our knowledge is limited to what extent socioeconomic conditions determine the success in decentralization. A basic premise, shared by capacity-building programs, is better capable public sector organizations produce better public policy outcomes. Yet, today public governance is no longer exclusive to the capabilities of local government, and it is possible that the success in decentralization is dependent on the socioeconomic conditions more than the capacities of local government.

Under these assumptions, the following three hypotheses can be deduced on the relationship between governance capacity and decentralization in public governance:

H1: Decentralization is influenced by local government's capacities while the impact of local capacity apart is limited or insignificant.
H2: Decentralization is influenced both by the local government's capacities and local capacity significantly and independently.
H3: Decentralization is influenced by local capacity while the impact of local government's capacities apart is limited or insignificant.

The H1 suggests that there is not a direct relationship between local capacity and decentralization where the impact of local capacity is only effective via its influence on local government's capacity. In H1, local government's capacities constitute an intervening relationship between local capacity and decentralization. Therefore, local capacity influences the local government's capacities but not directly decentralization.

H2 suggests that local capacity has also a direct relationship with decentralization, and in this case, the level of local capacity affects the extent of decentralization independent from any possible influence through local government's capacities.

If H1 represents the reality, a decision on decentralization policies should depend on the assessment of the capacities in local government. In this scenario, higher decentralization can lead to better governance as long as local government upholds ample capacities. However, if H2 represents the reality, the socioeconomic conditions in the surrounding should be a matter of concern on designing decentralization policies.

Nevertheless, the literature does not exclude the possibility that the presumed relationship between local government's capacity and decentralization is shaped by local capacity, and socioeconomic conditions determine the success in decentralization. The H3 suggests the relationship between local government's capacities and decentralization is explained by the degree of local capacity, and the impact of local government's capacities on the outcome of decentralization policies is dependent on the socioeconomic conditions.

This brings us to the end of the theoretical chapter on governance capacity and decentralization. In the next two chapters, I will elaborate on the contextual conditions in Turkey in relation to decentralization and governance capacities. The country-specific conditions in Turkey will provide the context-dependent input to supplement the empirical analysis in Turkish local government.

REFERENCES

Allen, J., & Cars, G. (2002). The Tangled Web—Neighbourhood Governance in a Post-Fordist Era. In G. Cars, P. Healey, A. Madanipour, & C. De Magalhães (Eds.), *Urban Governance, Institutional Capacity and Social Milieux* (pp. 90–106). Hampshire: Ashgate.

Andrew, C., & Goldsmith, M. (1998). From Local Government to Local Governance—And Beyond? *International Political Science Review, 19*(2), 101–117.

Argyris, C., & Schön, D. (1996). *Organizational Learning II: Theory, Method, and Practice*. Reading, MA: Addison-Wesley.

Austin, M. J., Regan, K., Samples, M. W., Schwartz, S. L., & Carnochan, S. (2011). Building Managerial and Organizational Nonprofit Human Service

72 E. TAN

Organizations Through a Leadership Development Program. *Administration in Social Work, 35*(3), 258–281.

Baylis, J., & Smith, S. (1997). *The Globalization of World Politics*. Oxford: Oxford University Press.

Bekkers, V., Edelenbos, J., & Steijn, A. J. (2011). *Innovation in the Public Sector: Linking Capacity and Leadership*. Houndsmills, Basingstoke: Palgrave Macmillan.

Bennett, R. J. (1993). European Local Government Systems. In R. Bennett (Ed.), *Local Government in New Europe* (pp. 28–51). London: Belhaven.

Benz, A. (2002). Die Territoriale Dimension von Verwaltung. In K. König (Ed.), *Deutsche Verwaltung an der Wende zum 21. Jahrhundert* (pp. 207–228). Baden-Baden: Nomos.

Bird, R. M., & Smart, M. (2002). Intergovernmental Fiscal Transfers: International Lessons for Developing Countries. *World Development, 30*(6), 899–912.

Bouckaert, G. (2015). Governance: A Typology and Some Challenges. In A. Massey & K. J. Miller (Eds.), *The International Handbook of Public Administration and Governance* (pp. 35–55). Cheltenham: Edward Elgar.

Bouckaert, G., Peters, B. G., & Verhoest, K. (2010). *The Coordination of Public Sector Organizations: Shifting Patterns of Public Management*. Basingstoke: Palgrave Macmillan.

Bouckaert, G., & Van de Walle, S. (2003). Comparing Measures of Citizen Trust and User Satisfaction as Indicators of 'Good Governance': Difficulties in Linking Trust and Satisfaction Indicators. *International Review of Administrative Sciences, 69*(3), 329–343.

Boyne, G. A. (1996). Competition and Local Government: A Public Choice Perspective. *Urban Studies, 33*(4–5), 703–721.

Bray, M. (1999). Control of Education: Issues and Tensions. In R. Arnove & C. A. Torres (Eds.), *Comparative Education: Dialectic of the Global and the Local*. Boston, MA: Rowman and Littlefield.

Chaskin, R. J. (2001). Building Community Capacity: A Definitional Framework and Case Studies from a Comprehensive Community Initiative. *Urban Affairs Review, 36*(3), 291–323.

Cheema, G. S., & Rondinelli, D. A. (2007). From Government Decentralization to Decentralized Governance. In G. S. Cheema & D. A. Rondinelli (Eds.), *Decentralizing Governance: Emerging Concepts and Practices* (pp. 1–20). Washington, DC: Brooking Institution Press.

Christensen, R. K., & Gazley, B. (2008). Capacity for Public Administration: Analysis of Meaning and Measurement. *Public Administration and Development, 28*(4), 265–279.

Cohen, J. M., & Peterson, S. B. (1999). *Administrative Decentralization: Strategies for Developing Countries*. West Hartford, CT: Kumarian Press.

Davey, K. J. (2000). Fiscal Decentralization. Basic Policy Guidelines for Practitioners. *Local Government Quarterly, 3*, 15–25.

Delmartino, F. (1975). *Schaalvergroting en bestuurskracht. Een beleidsanalytische benadering van de herstructurering van de lokale besturen.* Leuven: Katholieke Universiteit Leuven.

Derksen, W., Van der Drift, J., Giebels, R., & Terbrack, C. (1987). *De bestuurskracht van kleine gemeenten.* Beleidsrapport.

Devas, N. (1997). Indonesia: What Do We Mean by Decentralization? *Public Administration and Development, 17*(3), 351–367.

De Visser, J. (2005). *Developmental Local Government: A Case Study of South Africa.* Oxford: Hart Publishing.

Dubois, H. F., & Fattore, G. (2009). Definitions and Typologies in Public Administration Research: The Case of Decentralization. *International Journal of Public Administration, 32*(8), 704–727.

Du Plessis, M. (2008). What Bars Organizations from Managing Knowledge Successfully? *International Journal of Information Management, 28*(4), 285–292.

Duysters, G., Kok, G., & Vaandranger, M. (1999). Crafting Successful Strategic Technology Partnerships. *R&D Management, 29*(4), 343–351.

Eisinger, P. (2002). Organizational Capacity and Organizational Effectiveness Among Street-Level Food Assistance Programs. *Nonprofit and Voluntary Sector Quarterly, 31*(1), 115–130.

Etzioni, A. (1995). *New Communitarian Thinking: Persons, Virtues, Institutions, and Communities.* Charlottesville: University Press of Virginia.

Etzioni, A. (1998). *The Essential Communitarian Reader.* Lanham, MD: Rowman & Littlefield.

Falleti, T. G. (2005). A Sequential Theory of Decentralization: Latin American Cases in Comparative Perspective. *American Political Science Review, 99* (3), 327–346.

Fesler, J. W. (1965). Approaches to the Understanding of Decentralization. *The Journal of Politics, 27*(3), 536–566.

Franks, T. (1999). Capacity Building and Institutional Development: Reflections on Water. *Public Administration and Development, 19*, 51–61.

Fukuyama, F. (2013). What Is Governance? *Governance, 26*(3), 347–368.

Furniss, N. (1974). The Practical Significance of Decentralization. *The Journal of Politics, 36*(4), 958–982.

Gargan, J. J. (1981). Consideration of Local Government Capacity. *Public Administration Review, 41*(6), 649–658.

Giguére, S. (2008). The Use of Partnerships in Economic and Social Policy: Practice Ahead of Theory. In M. Considine & S. Giguére (Eds.), *The Theory and Practice of Local Governance and Economic Development* (pp. 40–62). New York, NY: Palgrave Macmillan.

74 E. TAN

Glickman, N., & Servon, L. J. (1998). *More Than Bricks and Sticks: Five Components of CDC Capacity*. New Brunswick: Rutgers Center for Urban Policy Research.

Goodman, R. M., Speers, M. A., McLeroy, K., Fawcett, S., Kegler, M., Parker, E., et al. (1998). Identifying and Defining the Dimensions of Community Capacity to Provide a Basis for Measurement. *Health Education & Behavior, 25*(3), 258–278.

Goss, S. (2001). *Making Local Governance Work: Networks, Relationships and the Management of Change*. New York, NY: Palgrave Macmillan.

Hales, C. (1999). Leading Horses to Water? The Impact of Decentralization on Managerial Behaviour. *Journal of Management Studies, 36*(6), 831–851.

Harding, A. (1994). Urban Regimes and Growth Machines: Toward a Cross-National Research Agenda. *Urban Quarterly, 29*(3), 356–382.

Healey, P. (1998). Building Institutional Capacity Through Collaborative Approaches to Urban Planning. *Environment and Planning A: Economy and Space, 30*(9), 1531–1546.

Hesse, J., & Sharpe, L. (1991). Local Government in International Perspective: Some Comparative Observations. In J. Hesse (Ed.), *Local Government and Urban Affairs in International Perspective: Analysis of Twenty Western Industrialized Countries* (pp. 603–621). Baden-Baden: Nomos.

Hirst, P., & Thompson, G. (1999). *Globalisation in Question*. Cambridge: Polity Press.

Honadle, B. W. (1981). A Capacity-Building Framework—A Search for Concept and Purpose. *Public Administration Review, 41*(5), 575–580.

Honadle, B. W., & Howitt, A. M. (1986). *Perspectives on Management Capacity Building*. Albany: State University of New York Press.

Hood, C. (1991). A Public Management for All Seasons? *Public Administration, 69*(1), 3–19.

Hooghe, M., & Stolle, D. (2003). *Generating Social Capital: Civil Society and Institutions in Comparative Perspective*. New York, NY: Palgrave Macmillan.

Hou, Y., Moynihan, D. P., & Ingraham, P. W. (2003). Capacity, Management, and Performance: Exploring the Links. *The American Review of Public Administration, 33*(3), 295–315.

Ingraham, P. W., Joyce, P. G., & Donahue, A. K. (2003). *Government Performance: Why Management Matters*. Baltimore: Johns Hopkins University Press.

Ingraham, P., & Kneedler, D. A. (2000). Dissecting the Black Box Revisited: Characterizing Government Management Capacity. In J. C. Heinrich & L. E. Lynn (Eds.), *Governance and Performance: New Perspectives* (pp. 292–308). Washington, DC: Georgetown University Press.

Inter-American Development Bank. (2007). *IDB Launches Datagob Portal of Governance Indicators*. Available at http://www.iadb.org/en/news/news-releases/2007-04-23/idb-launches-datagob-portal-of-governance-indicators,3807.html.

Jessop, B. (2000). Governance Failure. In G. Stoker (Ed.), *The New Politics of British Local Governance* (pp. 11–34). Basingstoke: Palgrave Macmillan.

John, P. (2001). *Local Governance in Western Europe*. London: Sage.

Kale, P., Singh, H., & Perlmutter, H. (2000). Learning and Protection of Proprietary Assets in Strategic Alliances: Building Relational Capital. *Strategic Management Journal, 21*(3), 217–237.

Kaplan, A. (2000). Capacity Building: Shifting the Paradigms of Practice. *Development in Practice, 10*(3), 517–526.

Kickert, W. J., Klijn, E.-H., & Koppenjan, J. F. (1999). *Managing Complex Networks: Strategies for the Public Sector*. London: Sage.

Klijn, E. H. (2010). Trust in Governance Networks: Looking for Conditions for Innovative Solutions and Outcomes. In S. Osborne (Ed.), *The New Public Governance? Emerging Perspectives on the Theory and Practice of Public Governance* (pp. 303–322). New York, NY: Routledge.

Kodras, J. (1997). Restructuring the State: Devolution, Privatization, and the Geographic Redistribution of Power and Capacity in Governance. In L. Staeheli, J. Kodras, & C. Flint (Eds.), *State Devolution in America: Implications for a Diverse Society* (pp. 79–96). Thousand Oaks, CA: Sage.

Kooiman, J. (1993). *Modern Governance: New Government—Society Interactions*. London: Sage.

Kuhlmann, S., & Wollmann, H. (2014). *Introduction to Comparative Public Administration: Administrative Systems and Reforms in Europe*. Cheltenham: Edward Elgar.

Litvack, J., Ahmad, J., & Bird, R. (1998). *Rethinking Decentralization in Developing Countries*. Washington, DC: The World Bank.

Macmahon, A. W. (1961). *Delegation and Autonomy*. Bombay: Asia Publishing House.

Maes, R. (1985). Naar een principiële openbaarheid en een verdere democratisering van het bestuur. *Gemeente en Provincie*, 8–22.

Manor, J. (1999). *The Political Economy of Democratic Decentralization*. Washington, DC: The World Bank.

Matthiesen, G. U. (2002). Transformational Pathways and Institutional Capacity Building: The Case of the German-Polish Twin City. In G. Cars, P. Healey, A. Madanipour, & C. De Magalhães (Eds.), *Urban Governance, Institutional Capacity and Social Milieux* (pp. 70–90). Hampshire: Ashgate.

Mcquaid, R. W. (2010). Theory of Organizational Partnerships: Partnership Advantages, Disadvantages and Success Factors. In S. Osborne (Ed.), *The New Public Governance? Emerging Perspectives on the Theory and Practice of Public Governance* (pp. 140–162). New York, NY: Routledge.

Mill, J. S. (1861). *Considerations of Representative Government*. London: Parker, Son and Bourn.

Minnaar, F., & Bekker, J. (2005). *Public Management in the Information Age*. Pretoria: Van Schaik.

Mintzberg, H. (1980). Structure in 5s: A Synthesis of the Research on Organization Design. *Management Science, 26*(3), 322–341.

Moore, M. H. (2000). Managing for Value: Organizational Strategy in For-Profit, Nonprofit, and Governmental Organizations. *Nonprofit and Voluntary Sector Quarterly, 29*(1), 183–208.

Morgan, P. (2006). *The Concept of Capacity.* Brussels: European Center for Development Policy Management.

Nannyonjo, J., & Okot, N. (2012). *Decentralization, Local Government Capacity and Efficiency of Health Service Delivery in Uganda.* Nairobi, Kenya: African Economic Research Consortium.

Nielsen, N., Goverde, H., & Gestel, N. V. (2000). *Bestuurlijk vermogen: analyse en beoordeling van nieuwe vormen van besturen.* Bussum: Coutinho.

OECD. (2001). *Local Partnerships for Better Governance.* Paris: OECD Publications.

Olowu, D., & Wunsch, J. S. (2004). *Local Governance in Africa: The Challenges of Democratic Decentralization.* London: Lynne Rienner.

Osborne, S. (1997). Managing the Coordination of Social Services in the Mixed Economy of Welfare: Competition, Cooperation and Common Cause? *British Journal of Management, 8*(4), 317–328.

Osborne, S. (2010). Introduction. In S. Osborne (Ed.), *The New Public Governance? Emerging Perspectives on the Theory and Practice of Public Governance* (pp. 1–17). New York, NY: Routledge.

Overby, M. L. (2006). Public Opinion Regarding Congressional Leaders: Lessons from the 1996 Elections. *Journal of Legislative Studies, 12,* 54–75.

Oxhorn, P. (2004). Unraveling the Puzzle of Decentralization. In P. Oxhorn, J. S. Tulchin, & A. D. Seele (Eds.), *Decentralization, Democratic Governance and Civil Society in Comparative Perspective.* Washington, DC: Woodrow Wilson Center Press.

Page, E. (1991). *Localism and Centralism in Europe.* Oxford: Oxford University Press.

Page, E., & Goldsmith, M. (1987). *Central and Local Government Relations.* Beverly Hills, CA: Sage.

Park, S. H., & Ungson, G. (2001). To Compete or Collaborate: A Conceptual Model of Alliance. *Organizational Studies, 12*(1), 37–53.

Parkinson, M., Bianchini, F. D., Evans, R., & Harding, A. (1992). *Urbanisation and the Functions of Cities in the European Community.* Brussels: European Commission.

Peters, B. G. (1999). *Institutional Theory in Political Science.* London: Pinter.

Peters, B. G., & Pierre, J. (1998). Governance Without Government: Rethinking Public Administration. *Journal of Public Administration Research and Theory, 8*(2), 223–242.

Pierce, N. (1993). *Citistates.* Washington, DC: Seven Locks Press.

Pierre, J. (2011). *The Politics of Urban Governance.* New York, NY: Palgrave Macmillan.

Pierre, J., & Peters, B. G. (2000). *Governance, Politics and the State*. London: Macmillan.

Ponce-Rodríguez, R. A., Hankla, C. R., Martinez-Vazquez, J., & Heredia-Ortiz, E. (2018). Rethinking the Political Economy of Decentralization: How Elections and Parties Shape the Provision of Local Public Goods. *Publius: The Journal of Federalism*, 1–36. https://doi.org/10.1093/publius/pjy003.

Pollitt, C. (2005). Decentralization: A Central Concept in Contemporary Public Management. In E. Ferlie, L. E. Lynn Jr., & C. Pollitt (Eds.), *The Oxford Handbook of Public Management* (pp. 371–397). Oxford: Oxford University Press.

Porter, D. O., & Olsen, E. A. (1976). Some Critical Issues in Government Centralization and Decentralization. *PublicAdministration Review, 36* (1), 72–84.

Prud'homme, R. (1995). The Dangers of Decentralization. *The World Bank Research Observer, 10*(2), 201–221.

Putnam, R. D. (1994). *Making Democracy Work: Civic Traditions in Modern Italy*. Princeton: Princeton University Press.

Raboca, H. M., Lazar, I., Lazar, P. S., & Zagan-Zelter, D. (2010). An Explanatory Analysis of the Management Capacity within the Local Public Administration from Romania. *Transylvanian Review of Administrative Sciences, 31E,* 133–146.

Rhodes, R. (1994). The Hollowing Out of the State: The Changing Nature of the Public Service in Britain. *The Political Quarterly, 65*(2), 138–151.

Rhodes, R. (1996). The New Governance: Governing Without Government. *Political Studies, 44*(4), 652–667.

Rhodes, R. A. (1997). *Understanding Governance: Policy Networks, Governance, Reflexivity, and Accountability*. Buckingham: Open University Press.

Rondinelli, D. A., Nellis, J. R., & Cheema, G. S. (1983). *Decentralization in Developing Countries: A Review of Recent Experience*. World Bank Staff (Working Paper 581). Washington, DC: The World Bank.

Saito, F. (2001). *Decentralization Theories Revisited: Lessons from Uganda*. Ryukoku: RISS Bulletin.

Saito, F. (2005). *Foundations For Local Governance: Decentralization in Comparative Perspectives*. Germany: Physica Verlag.

Schmandt, H. J. (1972). Municipal Decentralization: An Overview. *Public Administration Review, 32* (Special Issue: Curriculum Essays on Citizens, Politics, and Administration in Urban Neighborhoods), 571–588.

Shah, A., & Thompson, T. (2004). *Implementing Decentralized Local Governance: A Treacherous Road with Potholes, Detours, and Road Closures*. World Bank Policy Research (Working Paper 3353). Washington, DC: The World Bank.

Sharma, C. K. (2014). *Governance, Governmentality, and Governability: Constraints and Possibilities of Decentralization in South Asia*. Keynote Address, International Conference on Local Representation of Power in

South Asia. Lahore: Department of Political Science, Government College University.

Smoke, P. (2003). Decentralisation in Africa: Goals, Dimensions, Myths, and Challenges. *Public Administration and Development, 23*, 7–16.

Sorens, J. (2009). The Partisan Logic of Decentralization in Europe. *Regional & Federal Studies, 19*(2), 255–272.

Sowa, J. E., Selden, S. C., & Sandfort, J. R. (2004). No Longer Unmeasurable? A Multidimensional Integrated Model of Nonprofit Organizational Effectiveness. *Nonprofit and Voluntary Sector Quarterly, 33*(4), 711–728.

Stöhr, W. (2001). Introduction. In W. Stöhr, J. Edralin, & D. Mani (Eds.), *New Regional Development Paradigms: Decentralization, Governance and the New Planning for Local-Level Development*. Westport, CT: Greenwood Press.

Stoker, G. (2008). Governance as Theory: Five Propositions. *International Social Science Journal, 50*(155), 17–28.

Stone, C. N. (1989). *Regime Politics: Governing Atlanta, 1946–1988*. Lawrence: University Press of Kansas.

Taylor, M. (2002). Is Partnership Possible? Searching for a New Institutional Settlement. In G. Cars, P. Healey, A. Madanipour, & C. De Magalhães (Eds.), *Urban Governance, Institutional Capacity and Social Milieux* (pp. 106–125). Hampshire: Ashgate.

Trafford, S., & Proctor, T. (2006). Successful Joint Venture Partnerships: Public–Private Partnerships. *International Journal of Public Sector Management, 19*(2), 117–129.

Treisman, D. (2002). *Defining and Measuring Decentralization: A Global Perspective*. Unpublished manuscript.

Treisman, D. (2007). *The Architecture of Government: Rethinking Political Decentralisation*. London: Cambridge University Press.

UNDP. (2008). *Capacity Assessment Practice Note*. New York, NY: UNDP.

Voets, J., & De Rynck, F. (2011). Exploring the Innovative Capacity of Intergovernmental Network Managers: The Art of Boundary Scanning and Boundary Spanning. In V. Bekkers, J. Edelenbos, & B. Steijn (Eds.), *Innovation in the Public Sector: Linking Capacity and Leadership* (pp. 155–175). Basingstoke, Hampshire: Palgrave Macmillan.

Warner, M. E. (2003). Competition, Cooperation, and Local Governance. In D. Brown & L. Swanson (Eds.), *Challenges for Rural America in the Twenty-First Century* (pp. 252–262). University Park, PA: Penn State University Press.

Warner, M. E., & Hefetz, A. (2003). Rural and Urban Differences in Privatization: Limits to the Competitive State. *Environment and Planning C: Government and Policy, 21*(5), 703–771.

Wolman, H. (1996). Theories of Local Democracy in the United States. In D. King & G. Stoker (Eds.), *Rethinking Local Democracy* (pp. 158–163). London: Macmillan.

CHAPTER 3

Turkey's Local Government Reform Process

Previous chapter gives the topography of local governance in Turkish public administration with a particular focus on the roles and positions of state and non-state actors in local governance. This chapter will not only familiarize the reader with the features of local governance in Turkey but also sheds light on country-specific factors, that may exercise an influence on the relationship between decentralization and capacity in public governance. The chapter starts with an overview of the historical evolution of local government in Turkey and proceeds with present legislation on public administration system. A further emphasis is given on public management reforms after 2002, which revamped the Turkish public administration toward a more decentralized, managerial system. The latter sections give a macro-analysis of how decentralization reforms have changed the roles of state and non-state actors in public governance and assess whether they have improved the position of local government in public governance.

An Overview of the Turkish Local Government

The Turkish public administration system is established on the basis of a strong central authority that presides over local administration through a tutelage relationship. This system is usually known in public administration literature as 'Napoleonic' administrative tradition (Peters 2008). Some general features of this administrative model are a highly centralized state structure, dependency on deconcentrated central field

© The Author(s) 2019
E. Tan, *Decentralization and Governance Capacity*, Public Sector
Organizations, https://doi.org/10.1007/978-3-030-02047-7_3

79

80 E. TAN

agencies, and constitutional status of local administration bodies (Hesse and Sharpe 1991).

Turkey is a unitary state and has two tiers of administration; central administration and local administration. In 1999, as part of the EU membership process, regional development agencies (RDAs) were created based on the NUTS system. However, these agencies do not have administrative competencies, and legislatively they are under the jurisdiction of the central authority.

The state administration is allotted into 81 provinces, which are headed by an appointed governor. The governor is the highest ranked representative of the central authority in provinces and its main function is to be a medium between locality and the central authority. Today, the governor has more regulatory power on local issues instead of a decision-making authority.[1] Provinces are subdivided into districts, which are headed by appointed district governors (*kaymakams*). Local governments in provinces are governed by elected authorities. The principal local government is the municipality. There are five categories under municipal administrations; metropolitan, provincial, metropolitan district, district, and town. Other local governments are special provincial administrations (SPAs) and village administrations.

The municipality is the backbone of Turkish local government, and 93.3% of the Turkish population lives in municipalities (Turkish Statistical Institute 2014). Following the municipal amalgamations in 2014, the number of municipalities in Turkey has decreased from 2950 to 1396. Today, there are thirty metropolitan municipalities that have particular jurisdictional powers and structures different from the rest of municipalities. Metropolitan municipalities are established in 1984 for larger urban areas where the population exceeds 750.000 inhabitants. In contrast to other municipalities, metropolitan municipalities have two tiers of administration in which the metropolitan administration (second tier) is vested with the responsibility of coordinating the district

---

[1] Starting in early 2016, and gaining pace with the state of emergency declaration following the coup d'état attempt in July 2016, the central government has appointed governors and district governors as trustees to almost 100 municipalities on account of supporting terrorist groups, replacing the elected representatives of local governments. The majority of municipalities (a total of 94 municipalities as of January 2018) were governed by People's Democratic Party (HDP), the epitome of Kurdish politics. The replaced municipalities include the provincial municipalities of Ağrı, Batman, Hakkari, Tunceli, Mardin, Siirt, Şırnak, Diyarbakır, Van, and Bitlis.

municipalities (first tier). Nonetheless, all municipalities share the same responsibilities on public service provision.

The second type of local government, SPAs are responsible for the provision of services in rural areas outside the jurisdiction of municipalities. SPAs are established following the French *département* system. SPA has an elected provincial council, but the governor is the official head of SPA. Therefore, for many years, the status of SPAs has been contested as a local government due to the central government's direct involvement in the decision-making process. Following the legislative changes in 2003–2005, the governor's discretion in SPA's decision-making processes has decreased and its function evolved rather to an administrative position. Village administrations are another form of local government, established in small communities in rural areas. An elected alderman's council and an elected *muhtar* govern them. Although villages are recognized as public organizations subject to the Law on Villages (issued in 1924), they don't have allocated financial sources to carry out their own services. Therefore, all public services in villages are delivered by SPAs. The legal framework for each consecutive body is defined by separate laws and determined by the general principles on local administrations in the constitution.

In the Turkish constitution, two administrative principles are defined to regulate the local administration system. The first principle, 'integral unity in administration', establishes a strong tutelage relationship between the central authority and the local government. The second principle, 'decentralization', refers to the allocation of power to public bodies on functional and territorial bases (TODAIE 2007: 13). The territorially identified public administrations in local governance are called 'local administrations' or 'local government' and they are established to meet the needs of inhabitants in a geographically defined territory (Gözler 2003: 125). Legislatively, there are four types of local administration; i.e., Special Provincial Administration, Municipality, Metropolitan Municipality and Village. The functionally identified administrations are public corporations established outside of the central hierarchy for specific scientific, economic, trade, social, and technical functions that require a specialized expertise (TODAIE 2007: 13). Here, 'decentralization' corresponds to a service-based allocation. State economic enterprises (SEEs), public universities, social security institutions, and regulatory and supervisory public authorities fall under this category (Fig. 3.1).

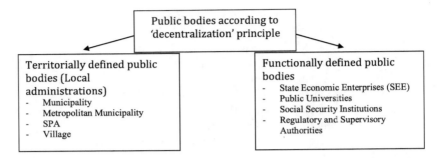

Fig. 3.1 Public bodies according to 'decentralization principle' (*Source* TODAIE [2007: 13])

The Historical Evolution of the Turkish Local Government

The Turkish public administration system is characterized by a strong bureaucratic administrative tradition inherited from the Ottoman era (Ökmen and Yılmaz 2004). The origins of current public administration system go back to the mid-nineteenth century, to the modernization period during the Ottoman Empire.[2] In this period, alongside with the transformation from an absolute to a constitutional monarchy, the local administrations have achieved a legal and constitutional status, which was largely preserved in the new Turkish republic. In the late period of the Ottoman Empire, two schools of thought have emerged within the governing *Ittihat ve Terakki*[3] Party. The first group, headed by Ahmet Riza, was favoring an authoritarian modernization steered by the central authority. The second group, headed by Prince Sabahaddin, was advocating a liberal modernization through the means of political decentralization and market economy. Eventually, the former became prevalent in the ideological scene, and the centralist modernization strategy turned into a state policy.

---

[2] The first municipality is established in 1855 following the Crimean War (Keleş 2011: 136).

[3] Ittihat ve Terakki Party (Committee of Union and Progress) governed the Ottoman Empire from 1908 to 1918.

The modernization of the Ottoman Empire was an autocratic modernization and the primary purpose of the modernization strategy was to prevent the Empire from further dissolution. Consequently, the formation of local administrations was driven by establishing state authority in the locality to safeguard tax collection and public order (Ortaylı 1985). At a time when the Western influence was decisive on the stability of the Empire, the solution of the policy makers was to introduce the European institutions and systems into the traditional administrative system (Ortaylı 1999). The outcome was an amalgam of two different administrative systems, the 'old' customary and the 'new' French system, and the coalescence among the values and norms of these two administrative systems has shaped the bureaucratic evolution (Eryılmaz 2008: 12). In contrary to the European counterparts, the local administrations in the Empire did not have any historical ties with the feudal past. In the old system, the public services were covered by '*qadi*'s[4] and by artisans' guilds (Keleş 2011: 135). Therefore, a grassroots political evolution toward enhanced local or regional rights was absent in the Turkish case, and the local administrations in Turkey have relatively a short institutional past.

Following the establishment of the Republic in 1923 until the end of the World War II, Turkey was ruled as a one-party state. Most of the ruling elite of the time originated from the *Ittihat ve Terakki* Party, and the continuation of the centralist modernization strategy has been present during the first years of the Republic. Alike to the Ottoman time, the local government functions in the new Turkish state continued to be dependent on the discretion of the central authority. This trajectory toward centralization has only changed in the 1930s when special legislation on local administrations was enacted. Although the core functions of local administrations did not change drastically, the municipalities were delegated a certain extent of discretion in public services such as on city planning (Tekeli 1992). The 1930s were also the period when 'étatism' was adopted as part of the development strategy. National state planning was introduced and the SEEs were created to realize the aims of the nation-building and industrialization (Özcan 2000). Overall, this period marks a peak point of centralist tendencies

---

[4]An Islamic judge, who is the highest political authority in local settlements responsible for settling the disputes and overseeing the public services.

84 E. TAN

in Turkish public administration both in terms of policy planning and also in economics.

The general elections in 1950 marked the end of the single-party period, and a new party, the Democrat Party, stayed in power for a decade. The changing conditions of the social, economic, and political environment motivated the new government to initiate a comprehensive structural reform in the existing system. The Democrat Party opposed the *étatism* and advocated the private sector to be freed from statist policies in order for the economy to flourish. Notwithstanding, the SEEs continued to keep their central role on investments throughout the Democrat Party government and the policies toward private sector had largely failed (Heper 1991). The multi-party system has brought the political competition to the local level as well, and through some ostensibly political decisions, the central authority has tried to restrain the local authorities. For instance, some competencies of local administrations were transferred to the newly established field agencies of central authority. Thus, some authors argue during this period the dependency of local administrations on the central authority has even increased (Ökmen 2008: 52). Yet again, the orientation toward free market economy empowered the role of local businessmen and land-owning elites in politics, and the capitalist development prevailed through private entrepreneurship and through the alliance with the West and NATO (Özcan 2000). The Democrat Party government was toppled from power with a military coup d'état in 1960.

Shortly after the coup, the military committee has introduced a new constitution. Remarkably, the 1961 constitution is widely considered as a progressive document with regard to its underlying democratic character. The constitution has recognized the principle of 'decentralization' in public governance and guaranteed the status of local administrations constitutionally. Furthermore, the central government is held accountable for safeguarding the allocation of financial sources to local authorities in compliance with their constitutional responsibilities (Ökmen 2008: 52). It seems that the intention was to protect local administrations from the recurrent interventions of central authority. Yet again, the dependence of municipalities on central authority did not diminish along with enhanced legal rights owing to their limited financial capacities. For some scholars, consecutive governments have exploited this weakness as a control mechanism by confining financial sources to local administrations (Ökmen 2008: 53). For others, the central authority has just failed to cope effectively with increased demands from municipalities driven by rapid urban growth. Nonetheless, the municipalities have remained politically and economically weak (Güler 1992).

In the 1970s, the municipalities have increased their demands for more public participation and political freedom in local government. Especially, the municipalities led by social democrats spearheaded this movement, which has generated a lively political debate between the right-wing parties in control of central government and the social democrats in control of most of the big cities. The shift in rural demographics and the rapid rise in urban population during the 1960s have strengthened the position of municipalities, and as a compromise, the Ministry of Local Administrations has been established for a short period from January 1978 to November 1979. The principal responsibility of the Ministry was to enhance the financial and administrative capacities of municipalities and to reconcile their demands with the central authority. There have been various debates on the purpose and function of the Ministry, but the need to establish a Ministry focusing only on the needs of local administrations verifies the increasing importance of local administrations in Turkish politics (Keleş 2011: 475). Yet, the deteriorating macroeconomic conditions at the end of the decade and the violent clashes between left- and right-wing groups led to hyperinflation, political instability, and street terror, and eventually to another coup d'état in 1980.

Following the coup d'état in 1980, a new constitution came into force in 1982. Despite numerous amendments, this constitution is still the principal legislative document in Turkey. The 1982 constitution is regarded by many as a downgrade for the democratic gains of local government. In terms of local politics, the 1982 constitution has brought the following changes in local government (Keleş 2011: 145–147);

1. The administrative tutelage of central authority over local administrations is constitutionalized. Even though an unofficial administrative tutelage relationship existed beforehand, the 1982 constitution gave it a legal recognition.
2. A special local governance structure is envisaged for bigger municipalities, which eventually led to the formation of metropolitan municipalities.
3. A special right was granted to the Ministry of Interior to discharge the mayor if there is a criminal charge against the mayor or an

86   E. TAN

ongoing prosecution against the municipality. This right has been invoked on some occasions for partisan displacements of mayors, which were in some cases reversed by the court decisions, convicting the act of the Ministry illegal (Keleş 2011: 147).

4. The establishment of the union of municipalities has been conditioned onto the consent of central authority.

Overall, the 1982 constitution was an attempt to re-establish the control of the central authority in local government and more generally in society. Notwithstanding this, the 1980s have witnessed the embracement of liberalism both in economics and politics, which reduced gradually the role of the state in public administration.

First of all, the economic crisis in the early 1980s called for the reassessment of economic policies. The first general elections after the coup d'état had ended up with the landslide victory of Motherlands Party (ANAP), which predominantly advocated liberal economic policies. A radical reorientation took place in state policies including the change from import substitution to export promotion; from interventionism to market forces, and from the promotion of SEEs to the promotion of the private sector. The state's role in the economy was reduced further through the privatization of some SEEs. Notwithstanding, the privatization of SEEs had largely failed as the legal, institutional, and political base for privatization was largely missing (Kjellström 1990). For instance, the block sales of some SEEs were canceled by the court order on the grounds of illegality. Especially, the foreign sales had turned into a contentious political issue.

In 1984, the Metropolitan Municipalities Act was enacted as a response to the increasing pressure from rapid urban growth. Through this act, the roles and responsibilities of small municipalities and districts, and their relationships with metropolitan municipality were redefined. Consequently, the influence of locally elected administrations on policy making has increased. Furthermore, in 1987, Turkey signed the European Charter of Local Self-Government.[5]

---

[5] The Charter was opened for signature by the Council of Europe's member states on October 15, 1985. Turkey signed the charter in 1987, but it became part of the jurisdiction only after 1993. Turkey made reservations for 7 articles in the Chart. These reservations are the following; Article 4.6: 'the manner and timing of consultation should be such that the local authorities have a real possibility to exercise influence'; Article 6.1: 'local authorities must be able to order their own administrative structures to take account of

The biggest change in public policy in this period took place with the devolution of urban planning decisions to municipalities. Municipalities were allowed to issue building permits with a regulation in 1985. Yet, this new function of municipalities raised severe criticisms against the government policies as it led to increasing corruption and misuse in planning. For many, this function has turned into 'an instrument of local patronage and political mediation' (Marcou 2006).

In a nutshell, in the 1980s, decentralization, and privatization policies have gained ground in Turkish politics along with the global trend. Important structural reforms took place in public administration, which shifted the state-led development policy to a more liberal system. Some public services carried by the municipalities have been privatized or encouraged for privatization.

This enthusiasm toward neoliberal transformation of the public administration has declined gradually as moving to the 1990s, largely driven by three dynamics; (1) the lack of political stability and instability among coalition governments; (2) the armed conflict with PKK[6] had reached its climax and underpinned centralist tendencies, and (3) relations with the EU had lost momentum in the aftermaths of Turkey's full membership application in 1987. The impact of the EU was relatively limited until the Helsinki Conference in 1999 where Turkey was granted candidate status.

In the late 1990s and early 2000s, the trajectory has changed parallel to the changes in the abovementioned factors. The official recognition of the EU candidate status, military achievements against PKK, and probably most importantly the 1999 and 2001 economic and political

---

local circumstances and administrative efficiency'; Article 7.3: 'disqualification from the holding of local elective office should only be based on objective legal criteria and not on ad hoc decisions'; Article 8.3: 'according to the principle of proportionality, the controlling authority, in exercising its prerogatives, is obliged to use the method which affects local autonomy the least'; Article 9.4, 9.6, and 9.7 'the rules and conditions on the allocation of financial resources to local authorities'; Article 10.2 and 10.3; 'rules and conditions on forming associations between local authorities'; Article 11.1: 'access by a local authority to a properly constituted court of law'.

[6]PKK is an internationally recognized terrorist organization, which has been involved in an armed conflict with the Turkish state since the 1980s with the initial aim to create a Kurdish state, that later evolved to Kurdish autonomy following the capture of the head of the organization, Abdullah Öcalan.

crises gave impetus to reform the public administration system. Thence, two bills in 1999 and 2001 were drafted as part of a comprehensive plan to restructure the public administration system. For instance, the 1999 draft bill foresaw an enhanced administrative and fiscal decentralization in local services (Ökmen 2008). This document proclaimed new responsibilities and competencies for local administrations and an increase in the share of local administration from 15 to 35% in overall public expenditures. The revised version in 2001 detailed the issues of reallocation of responsibilities, competencies, and financial sources between the center and local administrations. Most importantly, the subsidiarity principle was recognized as the basis of the public service delivery.

Nonetheless, the political turmoil in the aftermaths of the severe political crisis in 2001 impeded the coalition government to enact the bills. The coalition government was replaced in November 2002, by the one-party government of Justice and Development Party (AKP).

Almost after 15 years of coalition governments, AKP came to power at a time when the candidate status of Turkey for the EU membership had already been proclaimed, the devastating PKK threat was at the lowest level since the 1980s and after the serious economic crisis in 1999, the signals for an upward trend on the economic growth were evident. These convenient conditions consolidated with a strong discourse for the EU membership facilitated a swift reform process until the start of the EU membership negotiations in September 2005.

The Local Government Reform Process During AKP Government

The Justice and Development Party (AKP) announced its 'Urgent Action Plan' shortly after winning the elections in 2002 to initiate the economic and social transformation of the country. In compliance with the plan, the official reform program was introduced in March 2003. The aim of the reform process is set to 'efficient, participative, decentralized and transparent public management system'.

A threefold reform strategy has been designed; (1) changing the principles of the public administration system, (2) changing the local administration laws, and (3) changing the public personnel regime (Erdoğdu 2003). Accordingly, in December 2003, the draft act on 'Law on Basic Principles and Reorganization of Public Administration'-or more simply the Public Administration Basic Law, was brought to the parliament.

The act was formulated to set the principles of the new public administration system and the legal basis for the subsequent reforms. The bill has identified the anticipated system as follows;

- Performance-based system and strategy planning will be set as essential for all public administration bodies.
- Local administrations will be responsible for all local areas where the jurisdiction is not specified in the constitution.
- Duties and competencies regarding the services on health, tourism and culture, forest and environment, agriculture and village affairs, social care and children protection, youth and sports, industry, and public works will be transferred from the provincial organizations of ministries to municipalities, and to SPAs for the areas outside of the municipal borders. The provincial administrations of the respective ministries will be abolished.
- State enterprises in the areas where private enterprises are already present will be privatized or shut down.
- Further changes in public personnel regime, working procedures of local assemblies and regional development agencies will take place in future acts.

Some provisions in the draft act have been subject to change following the revision in the parliamentary commissions. The most significant revision took place on the devolution of education services. In the revised bill, the devolution of education services to SPAs has been removed because of their lack of capacity to deliver the services. The revised bill was approved by the parliament in July 2004. However, the bill was partially vetoed by the president arguing that some provisions were conflicting with the 'integral unity in administration' principle, and the president sent it back to the parliament for review. According to the constitution, the parliament has the right to return the bill without any changes. In that case, the president has two choices, either to promulgate the act or to litigate in the Constitutional Court. However, the parliament did not send the bill back to the president, and the bill has been put aside ever since despite the change of the president later to a pro-government name.[7]

---

[7] The president Abdullah Gül was a former minister in the AKP government.

The bill on 'Public Administration Basic Law' was a roadmap for public management reform rather than a detailed reform act. The initial strategy was creating a legal framework on the principles of the NPM system to be complemented by additional laws such as the rules on allocation of resources between central and local administration or auditing of local administrations. Nevertheless, the reform strategy of the government has changed following the veto of the president, and instead of a comprehensive piece of legislation, separate laws on 'Special Provincial Administration Law', 'Municipality Law', 'Metropolitan Municipality Law', 'Law on Unions of Local Governments', 'Public Financial Management and Control Law', and 'Law on the Establishment, Coordination and Duties of Development Agencies' were enacted subsequently in following three years.

In June 2006, the deputy Prime Minister, Mehmet A. Şahin assessed the reform performance of the government by underlining that '32 out of 45 targeted reforms in the Urgent Action Plan' has been realized. Reforms on 'redefining liabilities and competencies of central authority', 'empowering financial structure of local administrations', 'empowering human resources of local administrations', 'transferring some provincial organizations and their personnel to provincial administrations', are mentioned as non-accomplished objectives related to public management. In the same assessment, the veto of the President on the Public Administration Basic Law has mentioned as the reason why the rest of the anticipated laws were not enacted. However, the stagnation of the reform process even after the election of a new president contests the reliability of the argument.

The pace of reform process has declined after 2005. There appears to be a variety of reasons for this ostensible change. The year 2007 was the election year, and public management reform was not a priority in the run-up to the public vote. In 2006, security had become a pressing issue in domestic politics. The assaults of PKK began to ramp up following relatively peaceful years after the capture of the head of the organization in 1999. Given the concentrated Kurdish population in the southeastern and eastern Turkey, the already heated political discussions around the fear of segregation made the government even more reluctant to take further political action toward decentralization. Moreover, the EU membership process stands out as another influential factor. The peak of public administration reform process in 2002–2005 has been marked with the aim of starting the full membership negotiation process, which eventually commenced in September 2005.

Nevertheless, the public administration reform process continued at a slowing pace. Ultimately, new laws were enacted to fix the emergent contradictions following the structural reforms in 2003–2005. Capacity problems, redundant administrations, overlapping competencies between local-local or central-local administrations, and coordination problems have become pressing issues. In response to the challenges, new laws regulating the intergovernmental transfer shares, public employment regime and most significantly a new law on metropolitan municipalities are enacted. A new law on the metropolitan municipalities in 2014 has expanded the metropolitan municipal borders to the provincial borders and created 14 new metropolitan municipalities. By expanding the metropolitan municipal border to the provincial border, the SPAs within the provincial borders are abolished, and the town municipalities are transformed into district municipalities.

Table 3.1 gives the overview of the reforms during the AKP government and highlights the identifying characteristics of two stages in the reform process. Structural changes on the local government and on the rules of public management are salient at the first phase of the reforms from 2003 to 2005. This *structural* phase was about reforming the public administration system according to the contemporary trends in public management. The second phase of the reform process was about restoring the contradictions and backlashes emerged in the public management system as a result of the initial reform phase.

Each piece of legislation, and how it affected the local governance is elaborated further below.

(a) *5018 n^o Public Financial Management and Control Law*

The law was enacted in December 2003. It regulates the rules, norms, and the institutions in public financial management. The law brought the following changes;

- The rules on budgeting, accounting, reporting of financial transactions and financial control are reorganized.
- Financial transparency, accountability, effective acquisition and efficient use of public resources are acknowledged as the operating principles in public financial management.
- The periodic publication of the local government financial statistics is regulated.

Table 3.1 Overview of local administration reform process in Turkey

	1st Phase: Structural reforms (2003–2005)	2nd Phase: Revisions and adaptations (2006 onwards)
Legislation	• Public Financial Management and Control Law (2003) • Metropolitan Municipality Law (2004) • Special Provincial Administration Law (2005) • Municipality Law (2005) • Law on Unions of Local Governments (2005)	• Law on the Establishment, Coordination, and Duties of Development Agencies (2006) • Law on Allocation of Intergovernmental Transfer Shares across Special Provincial Administrations and Municipalities (2008) • Law on Establishment of District Municipalities within the Metropolitan Municipal Borders (2008) • Law on Employment of Contracted Personnel in Permanent Position (2013) • Law on the New Metropolitan Municipalities (2014)
Characteristics	• Structural Change in Public Administration System • Increased financial and administrative autonomy for local government • Transfer of service responsibilities from central authority to local government • New management practices and values (e.g., performance-based budget planning, strategic plans, ex-ante control and ex-post auditing, financial transparency, effectiveness, efficiency, and accountability) • From tutelage to coordination between central and local authority	• Fixing the contradictions in the post-reform area. (e.g., capacity problems, overlapping competencies, redundant administrations, coordination problems…) • More streamlined and larger metropolitan municipalities • Less number of municipalities with larger economies of scales • Abolishment of redundant local administrations such as first-tier municipalities or SPAs in metropolitan municipalities

Source Tan (2018)

- The internal control system for financial management is established. Ex-ante control and ex-post auditing are introduced for public institutions.
- All public bodies are expected to prepare strategic plans and adopt performance-based budgeting in public finance management.

(b) 5393 n° Municipality Law (the revived 5272-coded law)

The initial 5272-coded bill on municipal administration was enacted by the parliament in 2003, but the Constitutional Court annulled the bill on the procedural grounds. The revised bill was ratified by the President and came into force in July 2005. Yet, the President brought a lawsuit to the Constitutional Court to remove the provision about the pre-elementary schools. The Court judged on the annulment of the provision in 2007.

The 5393-coded law introduced the following changes in municipal management;

- A municipality is redefined as "a public entity having administrative and financial autonomy which is established to meet common local needs of inhabitants of a town whose decision-making body is elected by voters'"[8] With this definition, the administrative and financial autonomy of municipalities is constitutionalized.
- The minimum population to establish a municipality is increased from 2000 to 5000 residents. Moreover, the meeting obligation of the municipal council has been rearranged from three times per year to once per month.
- The neighborhood administrations, *mahalles*, have become part of the municipal jurisdiction from provincial jurisdiction. In return, municipalities have become responsible for the delivery of public services in *mahalles*.
- Municipal services are expanded to include services in the management of the geographic and urban information systems, environment and environmental health, forestry, parks and green areas, culture and artworks, tourism, youth and sport activities, social services and social aid, vocational and skills training, and economic and

[8] Translation is taken from www.lawsturkey.com.

94   E. TAN

commercial development.[9] Accordingly, provincial agencies of some ministries have been abolished and transferred to municipalities. Unlike the previous legislation, the law did not specify any prioritization in the delivery of public services, and thence the discretion of the municipalities on public services has improved (Eryılmaz 2008).

- Efficiency and effectiveness of personnel management, output- and performance-based supervision of public services, and participation of non-state actors to the specialized committee meetings are introduced as new processes in public governance.

(c) *5216 nº Metropolitan Municipality Law*

The law came into force in July 2004. The opposition party, Republican People's Party (CHP), brought lawsuits to the Constitutional Court for the annulment but only minor changes took place in the revised law. The law brought the following changes to the metropolitan municipalities;

- Alongside with all municipalities, the administrative and financial autonomy of the metropolitan municipalities is constitutionalized.
- The discretion of the metropolitan municipalities over district municipalities has extended over certain areas such as investment programs, budget, planning authority, police services, and business permits. The responsibilities of the first-tier municipalities are constrained with the local land use planning, programming on specific activities and management of service delivery in their districts (Marcou 2006).
- Instead of a tutelage relationship with first-tier municipalities,[10] a coordinative role is assumed for metropolitan municipalities.

---

[9] In the initial version, 'opening and operating of pre-elementary schools' is mentioned as part of the municipal services. The Constitutional Court has annulled this provision with the decree in 2007. The Court justified its decision on 'acknowledging pre-elementary education part of the national education, thus it cannot be a local demand, and as a local authority municipality cannot be in charge of these services'.

[10] First-tier municipalities are established inside the metropolitan municipal borders and they have the same competencies as the district municipalities. Their difference from district municipalities is that the first-tier municipalities cannot have territories outside the metropolitan municipal borders. First-tier municipalities are abolished after the enactment of the new metropolitan law in 2012.

The indirect financial control of lower-tier municipalities is reduced by the removal of the input-based budget auditing (Kaplan 2005). However, the supervisory power of the metropolitan municipality over district municipalities, especially in planning activities, has been extended (Marcou 2006).

- Metropolitan municipalities are authorized to establish companies in line with their duties and services. They are allowed to contract out the operation of municipality-owned kiosks, tea gardens, and car parks to other companies or private individuals without being subject to the provisions of the law on public procurement.

(d) 5302 n° Special Provincial Administration Law

The initial bill was vetoed partially by the President on the basis of 'integral unity in administration' principle. The revised draft was enacted in February 2005. It was brought once again by the President to the Constitutional Court, which decreed in 2007 that the law is not unconstitutional by underlining the ex-ante control presumes the 'integral unity in administration' principle. The law brings the following changes;

- The governor has been divested of the decision-maker position. Formally, being the head of administration, the governor held the position of the final decision-maker in the former legislation. Given that the governor is not an elected figure but an appointed one, the status of SPAs as local governments had been subjected to dispute (Güler 2003). With the new legislation, the governor is divested of the position as chairman of the provincial council. The council is expected to elect its own chairman, and some of the former obligations of the governor are devolved to the elected chairman. Yet again, the governor kept its executive position as upholding the chair of the executive committee. The financial and administrative autonomy of the SPA has been guaranteed by the public law along with other local administrations. In overall, the direct control of the central authority on the SPA has reduced.
- Their duties and responsibilities of the public services have expanded along with other local administrations, but their role in education services is reduced. The empowerment of the SPAs as a local government has removed the direct control of the Ministry

of Education on the delivery of the education services. The state elite in bureaucracy and the secular parts of the society has strongly objected to the devolution of the education services to local administrations during the reform process because of the fear of undermining the secular public education. In the final legislation, SPAs retained only the duties on the construction and maintenance of elementary and secondary schools.

- The meeting schedule of the provincial council is reorganized as once a month instead of twice a year. The governor is permitted to delegate some of his responsibilities and powers to district governors in district municipalities, and deputies or other officials within the SPAs. The executive committee members are allowed to suggest agenda items, which was only performed by the governor in the former legislation. In short, a more inclusive governance system is designed for the management.
- Norm cadre system, performance auditing, transparency and more flexibility in management have become part of the SPA's management.

(e) *5355 n⁰ Unions of Local Governments Law*

The opposition party brought a lawsuit for the annulment of some provisions of this law. The Court rejected all annulment requests and the law was enacted in May 2005. The law defines the unions of local governments as public entities formed by local administrations to perform certain services for which they are responsible. The most important novelty of the law is that the union of local government is recognized under the public law. The union of local governments can carry out certain functions, which are delegated to them by member municipalities. There is not a certain list of functions that the unions are allowed to carry out, but the law obliges the local governments to form a union or participate to an existing one for cross-border projects relating to ecological protection, waste and water management. The formation of a union is subject to the authorization of the Council of Ministers, but membership to an existing union does not require any formal approval from the central authority. Outside of these formal provisions, the law does not bring any revisions to the administrative autonomy or duties of the unions.

(f) 5449 n⁰ Law on the Establishment, Coordination and Duties of Development Agencies

The law came into force in January 2006. The opposition party brought a lawsuit for the annulment claiming that the law assumes a new tier (i.e., regional level) in public administration system, which is not identified in the Constitution. The Court rejected all annulment requests decreeing that the agencies are on functionally defined public administration status.

In fact, the RDAs were established in 2002 as part of the pre-EU membership obligations in order to implement development strategies in regional scale according to the NUTS system. The law has only granted a functional public administration status to RDAs with the initial purpose of introducing a sustainable regional growth on a competitive basis. Although RDAs were expected to operate under the supervision of the State Planning Agency, some critics argued that the law broke the monopoly of the Agency on the planning and management of the development strategies (Bağlı 2009: 205). Once the State Planning Agency transformed into the Ministry of Development in 2011, the relationship of the Ministry with the RDAs has been rearranged as development agencies transformed to local agencies of the Ministry. Hence, the disputed administrative status of development agencies is solved for good as being formally part of the central government structure.

(g) 5779 n⁰ Law on Allocation of Intergovernmental Transfer Shares Across Special Provincial Administrations and Municipalities

The law came into force in July 2008 to improve the deteriorating financial situation of local administrations and to better match with their new functional responsibilities. The law introduced a new formula on the intergovernmental shares from the central budget. Formerly, the intergovernmental transfer system was based only on the population criterion. The legislation has changed the transfer formula for SPAs by reducing the weight of population criterion to 50% and introducing additional criteria: geographic size (10%), number of villages (10%), rural population (15%), and development index (15%). For municipalities, the weight of the population is reduced to 80% and the development index (20%) is added to the transfer formula. The law was effective in closing the fiscal deficits in local administrations by improving the local administrations' revenues by about 30%.

(h) *5747 nº Law on Establishment of District Municipalities Within the Metropolitan Municipal Borders*

The law is enacted in March 2008. With this law, first-tier municipalities were abolished and municipalities with a population less than 2000 residents were downgraded to *mahalles* in urban areas or villages in rural areas. The law streamlined the local government system by removing the overlapping jurisdictions between first-tier and district municipalities and abolishing small municipalities lacking economies of scale and capacities to provide municipal services.

(i) *6360 nº Law on Establishment of 13 New Metropolitan Municipalities and 26 District Municipalities*

The law is enacted in November 2012. Thirteen provincial municipalities with a population above 750.000 residents were upgraded to the metropolitan municipality status. Furthermore, the municipal borders of metropolitan municipalities were adjusted to the provincial borders, and thus all municipalities inside the provincial borders but outside the metropolitan municipality borders turned into district municipalities. In the former law, the borders of the metropolitan municipalities were designated according to the urban size varying in each case. For instance, in Istanbul and Kocaeli, the metropolitan municipal borders were already been equal to the provincial borders. By removing the administrative difference between the urban and provincial borders, the SPAs have become obsolete and they are abolished in the metropolitan areas. Replacing the SPAs, new administrative units called 'Unit of Monitoring Investment and Coordination' were established as provincial agents of the central government under the jurisdiction of the Ministry of Interior.

A More Decentralized Public Governance?

After a decade-long reform process, the public administration in Turkey has been overhauled toward a more decentralized system. The field agencies of many ministries have devolved their functions to local administrations, and they are abolished. The financial and administrative autonomy of local administrations has been guaranteed by law. Moreover, the legal status of new public bodies in local level such as development agencies and unions of municipalities has been recognized.

Nevertheless, it is important to acknowledge the reform process as a structural transformation of the state apparatus toward a more efficient, regulatory state rather than the mere empowerment of the local government (Tan 2014). The 'Public Financial Management and Control Law' has introduced managerial responsibilities and instruments such as strategic planning, ex-ante control and ex-post auditing, performance-based budgeting to all public administrations. The overall assessment of the reform agenda indicates the aim to transform the administrative state to a managerial state in line with New Public Management (NPM) principles.

In order to better assess whether the reform process has empowered the local government's position in public governance in comparison to the central government, it is important to analyze the trends and changes in the public finances and public employment following the reform process.

Figure 3.2 displays the evolution of the budget balance, revenues, and expenditures in local government after the initial reforms. Right after the implementation of first local administration laws, we observe a steady deterioration in local government budget balance until 2009. In 2009, the 'Law on the allocation of intergovernmental transfer shares across special provincial administrations and municipalities' has come into force. The law was enacted to improve the financial situation in local government in order to better match with new public service responsibilities. The graph indicates that the legislation was effective in improving the local government budget outlook. 2009 was also the year when the global financial crisis was at its peak, and its impact on the general budget balance is distinct. By 2013, the central and local budget balance coincide around 100% implying that both tiers of government become successful in managing a balanced budget. Yet, from 2015 onwards, budget balances of both central and local government start to deteriorate, which is more salient at local government. The graph also includes the changes in local revenues and expenditures according to the GDP. The trend on the revenues and expenditures at the local level do not point out any drastic change, suggesting that the local administration reforms did not alter significantly the importance of local government in public sector finances.

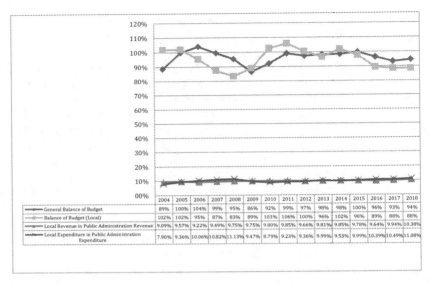

Fig. 3.2 Fiscal trends in public sector (2004–2018) (*Data Source* Republic of Turkey—Ministry of Finance)

Figure 3.3 shows three employment patterns in local government. The dotted line, indicating the share of local government in overall public employment, shows a slight downward trend. The share of local government in public employment from 2007 to 2018 decreases close 2%. The second line, the dashed line, shows the share of employment in municipal enterprises to overall municipal employment. Here, we observe an upward trend from 5 to 10% until 2015, and after 2015 a sharp spike up to 47% in 2017. Municipal enterprises operate under the corporate law with an independent budget and in time they have become popular means for municipal employment in time, as their corporate status allows them more flexible rules in the recruitment and dismissal of employees. The sharp increase after 2015, however, results from two legislative changes in 2014. First, the personnel of the abolished first-tier municipalities and SPAs within metropolitan municipal borders were transferred to municipal enterprises. Secondly, a new legislation came into force in 2014, which granted the subcontracted personnel of municipalities a permanent status in municipal enterprises. The employment status of subcontracted personnel in municipalities was a standing issue

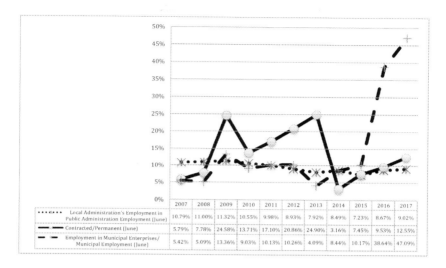

Fig. 3.3 Trends in public sector employment (*Source* Ministry of Finance-General Directorate of Budget and Fiscal Control)

for a long time, and this legislative change allowed them to have permanent contracts but they were exempted from public worker status. The third line reflects the ratio of contracted personnel to permanent personnel in local government. This line shows characteristics of the sawtooth pattern, and two peak points are discernible in 2009 and 2013. The stark declines in the pattern after each respective year occurs as a result of specific legislative changes. First, in 2009, a new legislation on the employment of contracted personnel is enacted. The law introduced new quotas and regulations on the employment of contracted personnel at the local level. Secondly, in 2013, a subsequent law allowed the contracted personnel to apply for permanent positions. It is no coincidence that the years of acts coincide with the local elections in Turkey. Both regulations were implemented to improve the status of contracted personnel in local government. Yet, the upward trend in contracted personnel appears to be still strong despite the regulative changes.[11]

---

[11] A small parenthesis is needed here. After the 2016 coup-d'état attempt, Turkey has declared a state of emergency. This allowed the government to enact draft decrees only with President's approval without going through the parliamentary process. Under decrees

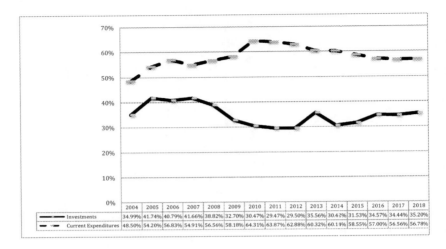

Fig. 3.4 Trends in expenditure (2004–2018) (*Data Source* Ministry of Finance)

The changes in the employment patterns together display a structural change in the public sector employment. Municipalities are employing less but more contracted personnel, and they employ the new personnel in municipal enterprises, which operate under the corporate law. Furthermore, the opposite trends in the employment of contracted personnel and in the employment in municipal enterprises after 2013 suggest that the decrease in the percentage of contracted personnel did not necessarily occur because of the growing employment in permanent positions. It rather shows a shift toward the employment in municipal enterprises. The trends in public personnel employment indicate that the municipal enterprises, with their flexibility in personnel employment and public procurement, have become popular means in service provisions.

The final graph focuses on the changes in public service expenditure. Figure 3.4 shows the changes in current expenditures and investments

issued during the state of emergency, as of December 2017, 113 102 civil servants have been dismissed, among them, 4022 were dismissed from local administrations. So, not only the number of contracted personnel has increased but also the number of permanent personnel has decreased. https://memurunyeri.com/memur/manset-haber/17023-29-aralik-2017-itibariyle-kurumlara-gore-toplam-ihrac-ve-iade-sayilari.html.

from 2004 to 2018. The dashed line indicates that there has been about a 10% increase in the share of current expenditures in the overall expenditures. In the meantime, the share of investments in the local expenditures remains roughly the same. The increase in current expenditures despite the decrease in the number of public employees in the same period points out the average expenditure on public personnel has increased. As the current expenditures are extensively about the salaries and performance payments, the data do not suggest an increase in the efficiency of public personnel employment. Additionally, the decrease in the share of investment in expenditures signifies a decrease in the effectiveness of public spending in local government. This finding challenges significantly the success of the reform process with regard to a more efficient and effective public sector management at the local level. Despite the reduction in the number of municipalities and the enlargement of the metropolitan municipal borders after 2014, the data from 2014 and 2018 do not point out a significant improvement in the overall trend as well.

CENTRAL GOVERNMENT'S DISCRETION OVER LOCAL GOVERNANCE

The macro data in the public sector do not suggest a significant change in the position of local government in public governance. However, the projected reforms, despite some drawbacks and minor revisions, were largely realized, and the local government's responsibilities in local governance have expanded. The question is now to what extent the central government is still influential in local governance, and through which means that the central government can exercise its influence. In this section, we will look at how the reforms have changed in practice the central government's discretion on administrative, political, and financial dimensions of local governance.

Administrative Discretion of Central Government

There are three articles in the constitution, which regulate the administrative basis of relations between central and local government, namely Article 123, 126, and 127. These articles constitute the principles by which the public sector organizations operate.

The Article 123 states that: 'The administration forms a whole with regard to its structure and functions, and shall be regulated by law. The organization and functions of the administration are based on the principles of *centralization* and *local administration*.[12] Public corporate bodies shall be established only by law, or by the authority expressly granted by law'. This sentence needs some clarification. These principles refer to the source of administration. In other words, there are two types of public administrations in Turkey, and these are the central and local administrations. The relation between the central and local administrative bodies is described in detail in Article 127.

The Article 126 describes the foundation of the central administrative structure in local level; 'In terms of central administrative structure, Turkey is divided into provinces on the basis of geographical situation and economic conditions, and public service requirements; provinces are further divided into lower levels of administrative districts. The administration of the provinces is based on the principle of deconcentration.[13] Central administrative organizations comprising several provinces may be established to ensure efficiency and coordination of public services. The functions and powers of these organizations shall be regulated by law'. The important point of this article is that 'deconcentration' constitutes the relation between the provincial organizations and central administrations.

Article 127 describes the functioning of the local administrations and sets the relationship between central and local government:

> Local administrative bodies are public corporate entities established to meet the common local needs of the inhabitants of provinces, municipal districts, and villages, whose decision making organs are elected by the electorate described in law, and whose principles of the structure are also determined by law. The formation, duties, and powers of the local authorities shall be regulated by law in accordance with the principle of decentralization...The central administration has the power of administrative trusteeship over the local governments in the framework of principles and

---

[12] The translation is taken from the official Web site of the constitution, www.anayasa. gov.tr. The principle of 'centralization' refers to the 'integral unity in administration' and 'local administration' refers to the principle of 'decentralization'.

[13] The original term '*yetki genişliği*' is translated in the English version as the 'devolution of wider powers', but terminologically 'deconcentration' should be the right choice of word.

> procedures set forth by law with the objective of ensuring the functioning of local services in conformity with the principle of the integral unity of the administration, securing uniform public service, safeguarding the public interest and meeting local needs, in an appropriate manner. The formation of local administrative bodies into a union with the permission of the Council of Ministers for the purpose of performing specific public services; and the functions, powers, financial and security arrangements of these unions, and their reciprocal ties and relations with the central administration, shall be regulated by law. These administrative bodies shall be allocated financial resources in proportion to their functions.

In a nutshell, the Turkish constitution describes the public governance as a holistic, unified act allowing the devolution of powers and responsibilities to local government through specific legislation but upholds the superior position of central government to ensure public services are carried out uniformly and appropriately. Clearly, this restrictive description of public governance is contradicting with the theoretical premises of NPM and good governance on decentralization, which relate the effectiveness and efficiency of public services with the closeness of local government to local constituents and its convenience to mobilize local resources and act on local needs.

As formerly mentioned, the tutelage relationship described in the constitution has been brought up by opponents on several occasions to rescind the legislation. Especially, the clause on the "integral unity in administration" (Art. 127) has been instrumental in the cases brought to the Turkish Constitutional Court. The Court overruled most of the opposing arguments by stating that the "integral unity in administration" implies the center can delegate some of its responsibilities to the local administration as long as the "administrative tutelage" is preserved. In other words, the administrative and financial autonomy allocated to local administration is evaluated not as devolution but as delegation. However, this perception contradicts with the philosophy of the anticipated system, as the center preserves actual decision-making authority notwithstanding local administration's administrative and financial autonomy. On the other hand, the European Charter on Local Self-Government, which was ratified by Turkey in 1993, acknowledges the subsidiarity principle in local governance (Art. 4). The subsidiarity principle mentioned in the Public Administration Basic Law as the basis of public service delivery. In the ruling, the Constitutional Court interpreted the subsidiarity principle in the public service delivery as

106   E. TAN

unconstitutional and contrary to the tutelage relationship between central and local government. Since international laws are binding and cannot be taken to the Constitutional Court, this creates a legal contradiction according to some scholars (Keleş 2011: 511). Consequently, the legal framework—and primarily the constitution—remains an important source of contradiction.

Nonetheless, the administrative discretion of central government over local administration has been notably reduced with new legislation. The most striking change occurred on the role of the appointed governor over local government. The final decision-making authority of the governor over administrative and financial issues has been replaced with a regulatory role. According to the new municipal law, the central authority upholds the administrative discretion in the following circumstances;

- The municipalities require the consent of the governor on territorial changes regarding the borders of municipalities and neighborhood administrations (mahalles).
- The veto power of the governor on municipal decisions, including the general budget, has been abolished with the new law. Yet, all municipal decisions require being sent to the governor in seven days to become valid. The governor also has the right to litigate the case to an administrative court within ten days following the decision.
- In case of serious disturbances in public services, and if the mayor is not able to overcome the problems, the Ministry of Interior delegates the responsibility to the governor to re-establish the order.
- To appoint the general secretary in the metropolitan municipalities, the consent of the Ministry of Interior is required.
- The mayor can be removed from the post by the decision of the Council of State. Additionally, the Article 127 of the constitution allows the Ministry of Interior to remove the elected members of municipalities based on the tutelage relationship (Keleş 2011: 402).

Furthermore, the supervision and control mechanisms of the central administration over local government have changed. In the previous system, the ex-ante approval of the governor was required for the municipal council's deliberations and the municipal budget. The new system replaces this control mechanism with modern auditing practices. This system foresees an internal audit by the municipal council or by the private auditors, and an external audit by the Court of Accounts and the Ministry of Interior. The Ministry oversees the administrative unity of activities. The Court of Accounts, on the other hand, controls the financial accounts and supervises performance management of local administrations.

There are some critics arguing that the new provisions supplement the discretion of the Ministry of Interior over local government. For instance, Marcou (2006) argues that according to Article 30(b) of the new municipal law, the Ministry of Interior can request the Council of State to dissolve the municipal council without a need of investigation or prosecution, if the latter 'has taken decisions on political issues not related to the functions conferred on the municipality'. In that case, the Council of State shall decide on the fate of the municipal council within one month from the request. Moreover, the Ministry of Interior can ask the Council of State to postpone any new meeting of the municipal council until the final decision. Based on that, Marcou claims the new provision can be an instrument for the Minister to apply pressure upon local governments.

The Ministry of Interior holds more direct intervention means to be evoked in the case of corruption charges. The municipality law bestows the Ministry of Interior to suspend the mayors from their post in case an investigation or prosecution is initiated on account of an offense connected with the duties. According to the 4737-coded parliamentary question, in the following 3 years after 2009 local elections, a total number of 1097 prosecutions were opened against mayors predominantly on the basis of corruption and fight against terrorism. The distribution of charges among the political parties in percentage has been as follows; 42.39 AKP, 27.99 CHP, 14.31 MHP, 5.47 BDP, and 9.85 others. These numbers largely correspond to the distribution of electoral votes among the political parties in the 2009 local elections. However, the distribution of suspended mayors according to the political parties is generally unbalanced. According to the same parliamentary question, a total of 36 mayors have been suspended during the investigation process. Their distribution among political parties has been as follows; 8 AKP, 6 CHP, 2 MHP, 15 BDP, and 4 others. Yet, the number of mayors and elected local representatives that are incarcerated or prosecuted has multiplied following the coup d'état attempt in July 2016 and the subsequent declaration of the state of emergency. During the state of emergency, the decree-law number 674 has passed which vested the Ministry of Interior to replace the local elected representatives with an appointee by the

108   E. TAN

central government. This decree-law supersedes the rules of suspension described in the municipality law, which declares the deposed mayor should be replaced with a candidate elected by the municipal assembly. Based on the decree-law number 674 and a broad interpretation of the 3713-coded Law to Fight Terrorism, several executive orders were issued in 2016 to remove the elected mayors and councilors in 82 municipalities, a majority of them governed by the BDP.[14] The deposed mayors are replaced with appointees by the central government basically suspending the function of local government in a majority of the Kurdish populated regions. This also creates another layer of legal contradiction on Turkey's international commitments under the European Charter on Local Self-Government contradicting with the Art.3 and Art.7, which clearly state that local government should be governed by freely elected local representative organs.[15]

Political Discretion of Central Government

The political importance of municipalities has grown in time and controlling the municipalities have become critical objectives for political parties. There are several reasons for it. First, municipalities have a better reach to a majority of electorates as over 93%[16] of the overall population is living in municipal jurisdictions. Secondly, most of the political parties in Turkey, assign their candidates for municipal elections through a top-down process by the decision of the executive board. Therefore, the mayors are closely attached to the party politics for their future political career. This direct control of political parties on the municipal candidates affects the voting behaviors on the general elections as well. For instance, the poor performance of social democrats in Istanbul metropolitan municipality in the early 1990s was punished in the next general

[14] Following 2014 local elections, BDP created a joint structure with the People's Democratic Party (HDP), and since then HDP runs in general and local elections largely representing Kurdish voters.

[15] For further information, see the Report CG32 (2017) prepared by the fact-finding mission of the Council of Europe.

[16] According to 2015 data of Turkish Statistical Institute.

elections by the drop-off in their votes.[17] On the other hand, effective social aid programs organized by the municipalities governed by the Welfare Party (Refah Partisi) were instrumental in their general election victory in 1995. Thirdly, the municipalities are usually perceived by the politicians as a showcase to promote their own political career. The current president Recep T. Erdoğan, for instance, was the mayor of Istanbul from 1994 to 1998 and his acclaimed performance prepared the ground for his future political career.

The post-reform system empowers the position of the elected central and local politicians while reducing the discretion of appointed bureaucrats in public administration. However, this shift brings the political competition in central government even closer to the local government. For instance, pork-barrel politics in investment decisions and social services have been extensively used by AKP to promote their candidates in local elections (Çınar 2016; Buğra and Candaş 2011). For instance, Buğra and Candaş (2011) give the example of the Social Solidarity Foundation, a special state fund for social assistance, has tripled the amount of in-kind contribution to poor in municipalities, which conventionally vote for Kurdish parties, before 2009 local elections. When the Turkish Electoral Council has intervened to stop the distribution of social aid, on the ground of it hinders the fairness of elections, the governor did not implement the decision of the Council, and later Erdoğan, the prime minister at that time, backed the governor by stating that 'Charity is legitimate in our culture'. Similarly, Celbis et al. (2014) point out political bias in public investment decisions of regional transportation and communication in Turkey.

Evidently, the competition among political parties constitutes an important dimension of relations between central and local administrations. However, it seems that municipalities maintain a working relationship with the central government regardless of their political affiliation. In my field study in Turkey, I have asked the mayors of provincial municipalities to assess the importance of central authority in local governance. The responses of the mayors showed that the central authority plays an important role in municipal decisions. Two most popular choices after the municipal assembly have been the governorate and the agents of the

---

[17] In the general elections of 1991, the Social Democrat Public Party (SDHP) won 21% of the votes. In the following elections in 1995, only 11% of votes were gained by the Republican People's Party (CHP), which succeeded SDHP.

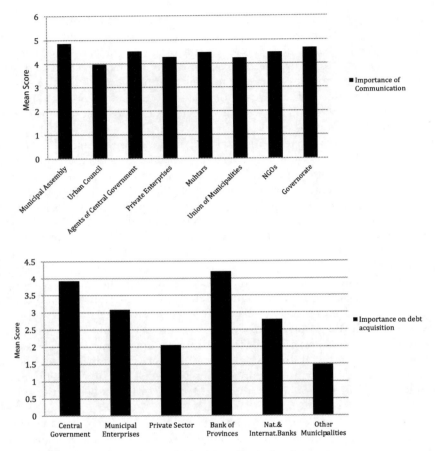

Fig. 3.5 Importance of central administration in local governance

central government (see Fig. 3.5). The graph implies that for the mayors, the communication with the central administration is more important than the local actors, such as NGOs, Urban Councils, muhtars, and private enterprises. Both of these graphs point out that central government maintains a strong position in local governance despite the financial and administrative decentralization process. In a follow-up question, the mayors are asked the most preferred way of communication with central government. Accordingly, mayors primarily prefer personal contact with the central government (94.2%), followed by 'through associated political parties' (72.4%), and with a slight difference by 'through provincial agencies of the central government' (54.8%) and 'through a union of municipalities' (51.6%). These findings suggest that mayors have generally a direct access to central government and they prefer a direct communication with the central government about their affairs.

More on the contemporary political level, the AKP government or more precisely the former prime minister and current president Erdoğan, has displayed staggering authoritarian tendencies in state administration over the years, reaching to its pinnacle in 2017. Before the April 2017 constitutional referendum, which has replaced the parliamentary system of the government toward a presidential system, the presidential position was expected to be politically neutral. Although Erdoğan had maintained his de facto leadership of AKP even before, the referendum formalized his position as the head of the party and switched the role of the president to an executive one. The most imminent impact of this change was on the forced resignations of the mayors from the AKP at the end of 2017. Along with 10 other mayors, the mayors of Ankara and Istanbul have been compelled to resign from their positions following the informal request of Erdoğan ostensibly due to their failure in securing the majority of in favor votes during the referendum. This example demonstrates once again that the local politics are closely intermingled with the central government politics.

Fiscal Discretion of Central Government

There are different means for the central authority to exert financial control over local administrations. First, local administrations are highly dependent on the general budget. Among the OECD countries, Turkey has one of the lowest ratios of the local tax revenue to the GDP, and local administrations have limited taxation autonomy. According to 2011 data, 78% of local taxes are based on tax sharing in which the revenue sharing can be changed unilaterally by the central government, and for the rest of the local taxes, the central government sets the rate and the base of the local tax (see OECD Tax Autonomy statistics). Among seven taxes assigned to municipalities (i.e., environment cleaning, advertising, communication, electricity and liquid petroleum gas consumption, fire insurance, entertainment, and property taxes), only in property tax, the municipalities have the discretion on setting the tax level. SPAs, on the other hand, do not have any taxation authority; they receive only a share of the real estate tax.

Secondly, Turkey is one of the few OECD countries where the central government has a high discretion over intergovernmental transfer shares. According to the 2010 data, 58% of earmarked transfer shares from the general budget are categorized as discretionary and non-matching, and the rest of intergovernmental shares are categorized as not earmarked and discretionary (see OECD statistics on Intergovernmental Grants by Type-percentage of total grants revenue).

The central administration has also the discretion over local debts and aids. Municipalities and affiliated corporations, whose half of the capital is controlled by the municipality, require the consent of the Ministry of Interior to take domestic loans exceeding 10% of their budgets. For the loans from external sources, municipalities require the approval of the Treasury. On the other hand, financial aids are allocated on the basis of conditionality. These aids are not subject to objective criteria and cannot be utilized outside the allocation purposes.

Given that, some experts argue that the financial control remains an effective control mechanism on municipalities, especially for those with limited financial resources. In my field study, I asked mayors to evaluate the importance of different financial sources on their preferences with debt acquisition, in order to see to what extent central administration is influential on their local finances. Their responses showed that the Bank of Provinces (a state-owned development and investment bank) and the Central Government are two primary sources of debt acquisition (see Fig. 3.5). Since a primary function of the Bank of Provinces is to provide interest-free loans to municipalities, it is understandable why the Bank has been a popular choice. Yet, the central government is the second most preferred choice ahead of other national and international private and public sources. Remarkably, the responses do not carry a bias in terms of party affiliations. This once again indicates, despite the distinct political polarization in Turkey, local governments sustain a working relationship with the central government.

An interesting outcome of the study is that the mayors' expectations from the central government differ in local governance. Two opposing positions were noticeable in responses, (1) more involvement of the central government, especially in assisting the municipalities on investments and providing additional funding from the central budget and (2) an increased financial autonomy or tax exemptions on municipal services.

The responses vary ostensibly according to the socio-economic development of provinces. Municipalities in more socio-economically developed provinces favor an increased financial autonomy whereas municipalities in less developed provinces are expecting more presence of the central government in local governance.[18]

Non-state Actors in Local Governance

The final section of this chapter focuses on the local components of governance and elaborates to what extent non-state actors are influential in local governance. The means of participation, the extent of participation and the factors affecting the involvement of citizens, private sector organizations and civil society organization in local governance will be looked at in detail in subsequent parts.

Citizen Participation

The direct involvement of citizens in local governance is relatively limited in Turkey. Largely, their roles and functions are rather advisory rather than actual decision-making or policy implementation.

In overall, there are three means for citizens to participate in local governance mechanism: *mahalles*, urban councils, and special committees of the municipal council.

Neighborhoods are governed in Turkey with a traditional institution called *mahalle*, which is headed by the locally elected *muhtar*. Muhtars are elected by the fellow residents of a neighborhood to organize the basic bureaucratic functions such as registering the residents, providing IDs and birth certificates. It is important to mark the difference of the functions between the muhtar in mahalles and muhtar in the village administration. In the latter, muhtars are the top civil servants in the village administration with responsibilities in organization and implementation of certain public services, whereas muhtars in the neighborhoods have only responsibilities on issuing official paper works.

The new provision in municipal law enhanced the function of the muhtar in local governance by allowing them to participate in the special committees of the municipal council to express opinions on locally

---

[18] More of this to come in Chapter 4, on my interpretation of findings from quantitative analysis.

related issues. It is expected from the muhtar to operate as a channel between the neighborhoods and municipal decision-making mechanism (Marcou 2006). Furthermore, the muhtar is also a member of urban councils. In a way, muhtars provide a semi-direct means of citizen's involvement in local politics.

The second institution for citizen participation is relatively a recent formation called 'urban councils'. Urban councils are established in 2006 inspired by the Local Agenda 21 program of the UNDP. Urban councils are ideal examples described by governance literature as they serve as a platform to exchange ideas among the urban stakeholders. The members include the representative of the central authority in localities (governor or district governor), the representative of the mayor, representatives of public institutions, muhtars, representatives of political parties, representatives from the city universities, representatives of trade and labor unions, and other civil society organizations. Their core functions are improving the democratic participation in urban governance, supporting sustainable development by preparing plans and strategies, supporting civil society institutions in the locality, supporting the active participation of different social groups in the local decision-making mechanism such as youth, elders, and women. Although the legislation mentions a wide array of governance functions for the urban councils, their actual participation is limited to providing opinions to be discussed in the municipal council.

The third means of citizen participation is through the expert committees in the municipal assemblies. The expert committees are composed of 3 to 5 councilors according to the ratio of political parties' representation in the municipal assembly. They are formed to prepare expert reports usually on specific tasks such as budget or land development planning. In accordance with the agenda item, muhtars, agents of central government and representatives from provincial administrations, academicians, civil society organizations, and local trade unions are allowed to participate in committee meetings and share their opinions without a voting right. Albeit not being a strong mean of citizen participation, these meetings mostly serve the purpose of information gathering for the councilors.

The question is to what extent local actors and citizens are influential on local decision-making. The graph on the importance of the communication with actors (see Fig. 3.6) suggests that despite the importance of central government on communication, communication with NGOs, muhtars, and urban councils are also seemingly important for mayors. In order to better grasp the weight of actors in the municipal

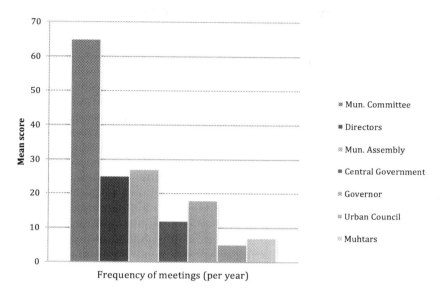

Fig. 3.6 Access to public managers

decision-making, the mayors and deputy mayors are asked to provide the number of regular meetings they hold with internal and external actors. Figure 3.6 presents the mean number of the meetings held by mayors with each actor per year. Accordingly, regular meetings with the representatives of citizens (i.e., urban council and muhtars) have the least weight in municipal communication with an average value of 3 to 4 times per year. These findings also imply that the access of local actors to managers is substantially more limited than the central government. Hence, the central government is not only more important in local governance in comparison to local actors but also have a better access.

Yet again, it is also possible that the mayors find less value in the participation of local actors in municipal decision-making. Therefore, the mayors are asked to assess the attitude of the member of urban councils during the meetings. Findings suggest that mayors overwhelmingly positive about the contribution of the urban councils and describe them as cooperative bodies suitable for collaboration and more engaged actions (see Fig. 4.1). It is remarkable, that despite the urban councils are perceived as cooperative and constructive; the mayors have less interest in engaging with them in local governance.

Although not being a local government, regional development agencies (RDAs) contribute also to local governance by fostering the cooperation between public, private, and civil society organizations on regional development. The organizational structure of RDAs consists of a development council, an executive board, and a general secretariat. The development council is the advisory body and it is composed of representatives of public and private sector and civil society organizations. Another function of the development councils is strengthening the bonds among the stakeholders and ensuring their participation in economic development. The development council advises to the executive board, which is the decision-making body and headed by the governor of one of the constituting provinces in the NUTS-1 area. Unlike the urban councils and the special committees in the municipal assembly, members of private and civil society institutions are allowed to join the executive board. Thus, RDAs can be described as the only compelling example of a fully-fledged inclusive local governance institution. However, the central government is still decisive in the selection of the participating non-state actors. Therefore, it is disputed to what extent the local actors participating in the executive board represent the local interests.

Private Sector Organizations

The theories on governance and public service delivery define an ever-growing role to private sector organizations both in co-production and also co-delivery of public services. In fact, the regulations on public–private partnerships (PPPs) are initiated relatively earlier in Turkey comparing to other countries. The earliest example of public–private sector cooperation in public services was in 1984 with the 3096-coded law regulating the rule of electricity production for non-public entities. However, the first operational model of a PPP was presented in 1994 with the law on Build–Operate–Transfer model (BOT). This law expanded the private sector involvement in areas of transportation, energy and water supply, and treatment (Tekin 2010). According to the BOT model, private sector organizations undertake the investment of the technology and high-capital intensive public projects in return preserve the rights of management for a specific period. Over the years, different BOT models were extensively implemented in the realization of large-scale investment projects, mainly concentrated on energy (e.g., electric production and distribution companies) and transportation sectors (e.g., motorways, bridges, airports, and ports). Especially, nearly a quarter of the electricity production in the energy sector is supplied by the PPPs (Tekin 2010).

In 2002, the legislation on public procurement has been revamped to harmonize the regulations with international and the EU standards. The revised law introduced new standards and instruments in procurement such as framework agreements, electronic procurement, and electronic auctions. Yet, a comparative study on the comparative international public procurement practices by the Global Legal Group (2011) suggests that certain limitations persist in areas concerning 'types of contracts, use of restricted procedure, application of negotiated procedures and direct procurement, methods for estimating the value of contracts and aggregating contracts, technical specifications and standards, publication of procurement notices, procedure and criteria for qualification of participants, procedure and criteria for contract award (selection of the best tender), existence of national preferences, and restriction of foreign-company participation'. Additionally, the report underscores certain difficulties with the bankability of international transactions under the current legal framework. There are ambiguities in contract negotiations and without a 'build' element in the project, the only option for transferring an existing infrastructure facility to the private sector is through the rigid concession method. Here, the strict interpretation of the Council of State's on transaction conditions delimitates the viability of some projects (GLG 2011).

In 2010, the Privatization Administration under Prime Ministry has published a working paper on the anticipated legislative changes on public procurement aiming to improve tendering standards and an improved legal framework for second-generation PPP projects. Accordingly, a legal definition, unifying standards, and the rule of the establishment of the PPP, extension of the PPP applications, the establishment of a new central PPP unit, rules on the resolution of disputes, risk-sharing, and project-cycle management are expected to be settled in a new law on PPP.

Nonetheless, at the moment there is neither a PPP specific law nor one single supervising governmental authority on PPPs (see SIGMA 2017). There are separate pieces of legislation which regulate five different models of public–private cooperation in Turkey; Build–Operate–Transfer (BOT), Build-Operate (BT), Transfer of Operational Rights (TOR), Long Term Rent (LTR), and Built–Rent–Transfer (BRT). Different responsible bodies assume specific roles in establishing PPPs. Ministry of

Development does macroeconomic planning, the Treasury secures the state guarantees, the Ministry of Finance looks into the budgetary issues and the Public Procurement Agency supervises the tenders. PPPs can be formed by the Privatization Administration through TOR, BOT, and other concessions; by the line ministries through BOT, BO, BRT, and TOR; by the municipalities through BOT, BO, and other concessions (Tekin 2010).

The laws on local administrations authorize municipal councils and provincial councils to establish corporate entities, to grant concessions, to use BOTs and to privatize public service provisions. The Privatization Law allows the granting of operation rights in infrastructure facilities to private entities up to 49 years. The areas allowed for private sector cooperation include the provision of drinking water, wastewater management, public transportation, and solid waste management. Concessions can be granted in these areas with the consent of the Council of State and approval of the Ministry of Interior.

Nevertheless, the PPPs are not widespread at the local level (Péteri and Sevinc 2011). The report prepared by the Local Administration Reform Program in Turkey explains the reasons for limited private-public cooperation as follows;

- Differences in management culture between the public and private sectors
- The investment and operation risks are not properly identified and shared.
- Lack of administrative expertise at the local level to manage complex projects.
- An absence of a comprehensive legal framework and a supervising governmental authority to guide the public entities throughout the public procurement process, and lack of institutional support from the central government.
- Lack of transparent decision-making, proper external audit, and design of exit strategies.

Civil Society Organizations

The arrival of civil society organizations as an actor in Turkish local governance system is a considerably recent phenomenon. Historically, civil society organizations in Turkey were constrained by trust foundations (*waqf*), trade unions, and business associations. However, this formation has radically changed following the 1995 United Nations Human Settlements (Habitat II) conferences in Istanbul. With the launch of the Local Agenda 21[19] program in 1997, the foundations of civil society involvement in local governance have been laid.

The first cases of collaboration between civil society organizations and governmental actors occurred following the massive earthquakes in 1999. Two successive high-intensity earthquakes occurred near Istanbul have caused the life of over eighteen thousand people and left more than three hundred thousand people homeless. The inadequacy of municipalities to conduct search and rescue operations with own sources paved way for the collaboration with various civil society organizations. 1999 was also the year when the EU candidacy of Turkey was officially announced. The EU candidacy brought a new dynamism to the activities of civil society organizations, as well as their involvement in local governance. Especially, the EU grants allocated for civil society institutions boosted the number of new CSOs. To this day, the EU remains the biggest donor organization in Turkey supporting the CSOs through various programs and funds.

About the regulative aspects, the Law on Associations has been renewed in 2005, which eased the rules on the establishment and financial activities for civil society organizations. Since then, the association numbers in Turkey are regularly growing.[20] The Directorate of Associations' statistics show that the majority of the associations are concentrated in the most populous and developed cities.[21] The data indicate

---

[19] The UNDP Turkey's Web site explains the purpose of the Local Agenda 21 as followed: 'In response to the global mandate as contained in Chapter 28 of Agenda 21, the Local Agenda 21 Program was launched in 1997 in Turkey under the auspices of UNDP Turkey and Capacity 21, and coordinated by IULA-EMME. The program, encompassing 59 partner cities as of October 2004, reflects a decentralized and enabling approach, based upon networking and collaboration among equal partners. Based on community participation, local stakeholder involvement, the establishment of local partnerships and decentralization of the local decision-making process, the LA21 Program of Turkey has provided a unique opportunity for the enhancement of local democracy and for practical implementation of the concepts of "good governance" and "sustainable development" in Turkey'.

[20] According to 2015 data, there are 105.201 active associations in Turkey (Ministry of Interior, Department of Association).

[21] The four biggest cities have the highest percentage of active associations per province: Istanbul 20.02%, Ankara 9.59%, İzmir 5.47%, and Bursa 3.98%.

a close correlation between the development level of the city and the number of associations existing in it.

A research conducted by Hirai (2007) provides some useful insights into the general features of CSOs in Turkey. According to the findings, a majority of civil society organizations in Turkey are social support groups (26.9%) and mutual organizations (16.5%). Especially, community support organizations are the most popular type of associations, which are followed by civil society organizations active in education (11.7%) and vocation (10.3%).

The Hirai's study shows that in terms of local governance activities, 'serving to the public' (43.5%) and 'informing society for public interest' (20.1%) are perceived by the CSOs as part of their responsibilities. CSOs are predominantly interested in 'regional and local development policies' (30.8%) and 'education and sports policies' (28.4%). Other notable policy areas are 'environmental protection' (13.4%), 'local governance' (11.2%), and 'health and welfare' (14.7%). The relation with the public authorities is mostly defined in terms of scrutiny instead of participation in decision-making. Only 8.2% of respondents state participating in the decision-making processes. The study also looks into the CSOs' relationship with political parties. CSOs are predominantly (around 80–90%) disclaiming any sort of relation with political parties. Yet, there are some associations, which openly favor one single political party. Among them, AKP has the biggest support with 11.4%, followed by CHP with 9%.

An important channel for CSOs to participate in local governance is the urban council. As previously mentioned, through urban councils various CSOs can participate in the meetings of provincial assemblies. Without any voting rights, CSOs can participate in the assembly meetings where they can express their opinions and discuss suggestions of local administrations in the formal council meetings. However, informal communication remains dominant in the relationships between public organizations and CSOs (Çaha 2010).

A research by YADA foundation (Keyman et al. 2010) clusters the most common problems faced by voluntary organizations in Turkey under eight categories:

1. *Infrastructural problems*: A major problem faced by voluntary organizations is the insufficient financial sources. Other problems under this category include the insufficient human resources, managerial incapacities and lack of institutionalization.

2. *Problems with voluntary people and members*: The lack of responsibility among members, insufficient professional staff and lack of communication.
3. *Relations with the public bodies*: The lack of formal relations with public bodies, the impact of partisanship and patronage on the relationship with public bodies, the lack of trust by public bodies in voluntary organizations.
4. *Organizational problems*: The lack of trust, personal conflicts and weak social relations among the members.
5. *Interorganizational relations between voluntary organizations*: The lack of communication and coordination among voluntary organizations and lack of institutional platforms to enable interactions among voluntary organizations.
6. *Relations with target groups and society*: Lack of public relations activities, the absence of communication channels with society, the prejudices of target groups against voluntary organizations, lack of reach to local TV channels and other communication means, and an absence of feedback mechanism from target groups.
7. *Relations with media*: mainstream media's favoritism among voluntary organizations; media's indifference against the activities carried by voluntary organizations.
8. *Conceptualization of 'civil society' among voluntary organizations*: The lack of awareness among voluntary organizations on their roles and duties within the concept of civil society, unwillingness to get involved into lobbying and interest representation, and a narrow perception on civil society organizations limiting them only with voluntary organizations.

To sum up, the CSOs' involvement in local governance is largely limited to opinion-sharing rather than co-production. There are some good examples of CSO's participation in local governance activities, which usually takes place through the urban councils. However, their involvement in policy implementation is limited and there are only individual cases for this matter.

SOME FINAL REMARKS ABOUT LOCAL GOVERNMENT REFORMS

Turkey has experienced an extensive public management reform in the 2000s and restructured its public administration system according to the New Public Management principles. An identifying characteristic of the reform process was decentralizing the central authority toward local government. The decentralization of the central authority was not initiated only to empower the local government but to increase the efficiency and effectiveness of public service delivery. To assess the impact of local government reforms, the chapter focused on the changes in local government's position vis-à-vis the central government in public governance. The findings point out that despite the increasing administrative and financial autonomy of the local government, the central government still upholds its influential position in local governance. A decade later after the initial decentralization reforms, the overall assessment of local government does not indicate a significant improvement in the local government's role in public governance in comparison to the pre-reform period.

The later phase of the reform process underscores simplifying the administrative structure and overlapping competencies, especially in metropolitan municipality areas. Removal of the first-tier municipalities and SPAs and proliferation of the metropolitan municipalities as semi-regional administrative bodies shows a movement toward simplification and streamlining in public governance. The reform on metropolitan municipalities was not only motivated to overcome the overlapping competencies and removing redundant organizations but also new metropolitan municipalities with wider economies of scale are anticipated to use the local sources more effectively on the delivery of the public services. The question is, can we identify this reform as a reversing trend on the decentralization trajectory of Turkey? Although this law was clearly an act of recentralization at the local level, the reform was not about returning the power to the central government. The metropolitan municipalities have higher fiscal autonomy in comparison with other types of local administrations, and the expanding administrative discretion of local government in provincial borders can even be interpreted as empowering the local government against central government. The caveat is, that the size of the metropolitan municipality does not necessarily match with the size of the urban zone, which is the source of generating income. Considering the own-source revenues largely rely on property taxation, the municipalities without a condensed population at the urban center are more likely to fail to generate higher income in property taxation. Especially, metropolitan municipalities in provinces with smaller urban centers and wider territories (e.g., Konya); in provinces with less populated urban center and more populated rural/town areas (e.g., Muğla, Kahramanmaraş), and poorer provinces with higher population (e.g., Van) are at higher risk to be adversely affected by the law. In time, these municipalities may require the involvement of the central government in public service delivery or can be heavily indebted to the central government for investments, which would undermine the role of local government in public governance.

What can we learn from Turkey's experience with public management reforms? The pattern in the reform process shows a clear resemblance with the NPM reform trajectories in France, Belgium, and Italy (Pollitt and Bouckaert 2004). The common characteristic of this so-called managerial modernizers is prioritizing the managerial practices over participatory practices. Turkey has experienced severe economic fallout following the political and economic crises in 1999 and 2001,[22] and the newly formed AKP government set a clear neoliberal reform agenda to downsize the public sector through privatizations and to increase its efficiency through NPM reforms. In a similar fashion to managerial modernizers, the local government is empowered through financial and administrative decentralization. Yet, the political aspects of decentralization have been largely disregarded. Especially, the distrust in the Kurdish political movement that is deeply embedded in the state and the wider societal level has limited the extent of political decentralization toward local government. About the non-state actors, their involvement in governance is largely delimited with the observer, opinion-giver or service-provider status rather than as a participant in policy making or a partner in public services. It appears that the administrative state reflexes in the local government remain strong despite the flexibility provided by the new regulatory framework. Undoubtedly, the high-intensity in politicization and securitization at the state level after 2016 complicates, even more, the initiative taking at the local level and pursuing more independent policies. Nevertheless, even before the political aspects kicked in, the diffusion of the NPM practices in local governance appears limited.

While this chapter assessed the overall regulative framework and other relational influences on the local governance, the following chapter will look into how public management reforms have influenced the governance capacities at the organizational level. Not only the internal capabilities of the local governance but also the exogenous factors affecting the organizational efficacy will be explored.

---

[22] The Turkish economy has shrunk 6.1% in 1999, and in 2000, Turkish Lira was devaluated about 40%.

REFERENCES

Bağlı, M. S. (2009). Kalkınma Ajansları. In V. K. Bilgiç (Ed.), *Değişik Yönleriyle Yerelleşme*. Ankara: Seçkin Yayıncılık.

Buğra, A., & Candaş, A. (2011). Change and Continuity under an Eclectic Social Security Regime: The Case of Turkey. *Middle Eastern Studies, 47*(3), 515–528.

Çaha, Ö. (2010). Women and Local Democracy in Turkey. *Journal of Economic and Social Research, 12*(1), 161–189.

Celbis, M. G., de Crombrugghe, D., & Muysken, J. (2014). *Public Investment and Regional Politics: The Case of Turkey. Maastricht Economic and Social Research Institute on Innovation and Technology.* Maastricht: Maastricht Graduate School of Governance.

Çınar, K. (2016). Local Determinants of an Emerging Electoral Hegemony: The Case of Justice and Development Party (AKP) in Turkey. *Democratization, 23*(7), 1216–1235.

Erdoğdu, S. (2003). *Kamu Personel Rejiminde Uyarlanma. Kamu Yönetimi Reformu İncelemeleri, Mülkiye'den Perspektifler, Tartışma Metinleri.* Ankara: SBF.

Eryılmaz, B. (2008). *Kamu Yönetimi.* Ankara: Okutman Yayıncılık.

GLG. (2011). *The International Comparative Legal Guide to: Public Procurement 2011. A Practical Cross-BORDER Insight into Public Procurement* (Chapter 30-Turkey). London: Global Legal Group Ltd.

Gözler, K. (2003). *İdare Hukuku.* Bursa: Ekin Kitabevi.

Güler, B. A. (1992). *Yerel Yönetimler.* Ankara: TODAIE.

Güler, B. A. (2003). Kamu Yönetimi Temel Kanunu Üzerine. *Hukuk ve Adalet -Eleştirel Hukuk Dergisi, 1*(2), 26–61.

Heper, M. (1991). Local Governments in Turkey with Special Reference to Metropolitan Municipalities. In J. Hesse (Ed.), *Local Government and Urban Affairs in International Perspective: Analysis of Twenty Western Industrialized Countries* (pp. 579–602). Baden-Baden: Nomos.

Hesse, J., & Sharpe, L. (1991). Local Government in International Perspective: Some Comparative Observations. In J. Hesse (Ed.), *Local Government and Urban Affairs in International Perspective: Analysis of Twenty Western Industrialized Countries* (pp. 603–621). Baden-Baden: Nomos.

Hirai, Y. (2007). Japon Perspektifinden Türkiye'de Sivil Toplumun Yapısı: Sivil Toplum Araştırmaları Çerçevesinde Türk Sivil Toplum Kuruluşlarının Ana Hatları ve Faaliyetleri. *Uluslararası, Hukuk ve Politika, 3*(9), 101–129.

Kaplan, G. (2005). 5216 Sayılı Büyükşehir Belediyesi Kanunu ile 5393 Sayılı Belediye Kanununa Göre Belediye Meclisi Kararları Üzerindeki Denetim. *Sosyal Bilimler Araştırma Dergisi, 3*(6), 233–256.

Keleş, R. (2011). *Yerinden Yönetim ve Siyaset* (6th ed.). Istanbul: Cem Yayınevi.

Keyman, E. F., Yeğen, M., Çalışkan, M. A., & Tol, U. U. (2010). *Türkiye'de Gönüllü Kuruluşlarda Sivil Toplum Kültürü*. İstanbul: Yaşama Dair Vakfı.

Kjellström, S. B. (1990). *Privatization in Turkey*. Washington, DC: The World Bank.

Marcou, G. (2006). *Local Administration Reform in Turkey: A Legal Appraisal Based on European Principles and Standards*. Paris: Université Paris 1 Panthéon-Sorbonne.

Ökmen, M. (2008). Türkiye'de Merkezi Yönetim-Yerel Yönetim İlişkileri ve Yerel Yönetimlerin Yeniden Yapılandırılması. In R. Bozlağan & Y. Demirkaya (Eds.), *Türkiye'de Yerel Yönetimler* (pp. 45–81). İstanbul: Nobel.

Ökmen, M., Baştan, S., & Yılmaz, A. (2004). Kamu Yönetiminde Temel Yaklaşımlar ve Bir Yönetişim Faktörü Olarak Yerel Yönetimler. In A. Yılmaz & M. Ökmen (Eds.), *Kuramdan Uygulamaya Kamu Yönetimi*. Ankara: Gazi Kitapevi.

Ortaylı, İ. (1985). *Tanzimat'tan Cumhuriyet'e Yerel Yönetim Geleneği*. İstanbul: Hil Yayını.

Ortaylı, İ. (1999, May 12). *Aslında Hepimiz Tanzimat'çıyız*. Istanbul: Milliyet Gazetesi.

Özcan, G. (2000). Local Economic Development, Decentralization and Consensus Building in Turkey. *Progress in Planning, 54*(4), 199–278.

Péteri, G., & Sevinc, F. (2011). *Municipal Revenues and Expenditures in Turkey and in Selected EU Countries. A Comparative Assessment with Recommendations*. Ankara: Local Administration Reform in Turkey (LAR) Phase II.

Peters, B. G. (2008). The Napoleonic Tradition. *International Journal of Public Sector Management, 21*(2), 118–132.

Pollitt, C., & Bouckaert, G. (2004). *Public Management Reform: A Comparative Analysis* (2nd ed.). New York: Oxford University Press.

SIGMA. (2017). *The Principles of Public Administration. Monitoring Report Turkey*. OECD.

Tan, E. (2014). Towards a Managerial State: Turkey's Decentralization Reforms Under the AKP Government. In C. Conteh & A. S. Huque (Eds.), *Public Sector Reforms in Developing Countries: Paradoxes and Practices*. New York: Routledge.

Tan, E. (2018). Quo Vadis? The Local Government in Turkey After Public Management Reforms. *International Review of Administrative Sciences*. https://doi.org/10.1177/0020852317752268. Article first published online May 2, 2018.

Tekeli, İ. (1992). *Belediyecilik Yazıları (1976–1991)*. IULA-EMME.

Tekin, A. G. (2010). *PPP in Turkey*. Ankara: Republic of Turkey Prime Ministry Privatization Administration.

TODAIE. (2007). *Belediye Yönetimi*. Ankara: TODAIE.

CHAPTER 4

Local Governance Capacities in Turkey

Systemic changes are never easy, and successful public management reforms profoundly rely on public sector organizations to adjusting their new roles and responsibilities under institutional and contextual conditions. Recent public management reforms in Turkey vested the local government with additional public service responsibilities and managerial tasks in public governance notwithstanding with less of an emphasis on the participative aspect of public governance. Nonetheless, the macro-level outlook of Turkish local government in the aftermaths of the public management reforms displays a limited change on the role of local government in public governance and a questionable outcome about the effectiveness of decentralization reforms in improving public service efficiency. Yet, this is only part of the story. The shift from administrative model to a managerial model in Turkey presumes a new toolkit of organizational and managerial capabilities for the success in governance. New responsibilities in public services and in managerial tasks as well as the advent of municipal enterprises deem necessary a different undertaking in local governance to maintain—let alone to improve—the quality of public service provision. Here, it is important to ask to what extent endogenous and exogenous conditions conform to new expectations in public governance, and how do subjectivities presumably affect the outcomes in public governance. Addressing these questions is not only important to fine-tune the research design on the relationship between decentralization and governance capacity, but also for the reliable interpretations of the findings from quantitative analyses.

© The Author(s) 2019

E. Tan, *Decentralization and Governance Capacity*, Public Sector
Organizations, https://doi.org/10.1007/978-3-030-02047-7_4

128   E. TAN

In compliance with the analytical framework on governance capacity, the chapter is structured around the input elements for governance capacity, namely financial, material, planning, communication, managerial, and human resources capabilities. The data used in this chapter is compiled from official accounts of Turkish government agencies, national and international reports, and surveys conducted with mayors and deputy mayors of provincial municipalities during the course of my field research in 2013.

FINANCIAL CAPABILITIES

Financial capabilities denote the adequacy of local government in covering public expenditures with available revenue sources without deteriorating debt outlook. The findings in the Turkish case draw a complex picture on this matter. Primarily, financial capabilities vary extensively among local government depending on the type, population, region, and economic development in the province.

Starting with the revenue sources, the intergovernmental transfer shares and shares from central government's tax revenues constitute the largest amount for all types of local government. According to 2016 data,[1] for all types of municipalities, the share of revenues from central government budget is around 60% of total municipal revenue.[2] For SPAs, the share of central government's budget is around 71%.[3] The difference is while municipalities receive their shares from central budget through the formula specified in the 5779-coded law by direct transfer to their accounts in the Bank of Provinces; the majority of transfers (about 42%) to SPAs are conditional, via provincial administrations (i.e., governorates and deputy governorates) and only for specific purposes. Therefore, revenues of the latter are under a more direct fiscal control of central government. Another distinction exists between municipalities and metropolitan municipalities in terms of allocation criteria. While the former predominantly depends on the population criteria, the latter is funded additionally by the place of origin. Other allocation criteria (e.g., development index) are relatively more important for SPAs comparing to

---

[1] Data source is Ministry of Finance www.muhasebat.gov.tr.

[2] The budget item is 'kişi ve gelirlerden alınan paylar'.

[3] The sum of budget items 'kişi ve gelirlerden alınan paylar' and 'merkezi yönetim bütçesine dahil idarelerden alınan bağış ve yardımlar'.

the municipalities. Ultimately, the weight of intergovernmental transfer shares in local government revenues suggests that the allocation criteria in tax sharing (i.e., population, geographic size, number of villages, rural population, and development index) have a varying but salient role in the financial capabilities of local government.

The second most important revenue source for municipalities is own-source revenues. Own-source revenues[4] originate mainly from municipal taxations,[5] fees and fines,[6] enterprise and property revenues, and capital revenues from movable and immovable properties. For the majority of municipalities, property taxation constitutes on average 60% of municipal taxation. Property taxation is calculated through land value, land tax, and building tax. The value of the land is assessed by a commission of experts composed of the agents of central authority and municipality. In every four years, the commission appraises the land value per square meter for the property taxation. The final land value is calculated after the addition of an annual revaluation rate set by the government. The land and building taxations are set according to the Law on Property Taxation whereby tax rates in metropolitan municipalities are set as double of other municipalities.[7] The same law also gives the discretion to the central government to modify the taxation rates from half up to three times the final rate. Consequently, municipalities have limited flexibility on setting the taxation rates in property taxes, and the actual difference between municipalities on revenues from property taxation is designated by real estate market conditions and tax-collection capacity of the municipality.

Similar to tax revenue, incomes from fees[8] and capital revenues vary according to economic development, and between metropolitan

[4] According to 2016 data, the share of own-source revenues is as follows: municipal taxation (15.1%), enterprise and property revenues (10.4%), and capital revenues (7.2%).

[5] Municipal taxes are property taxes (land, building) advertising tax, entertainment tax, communications tax, fire insurance tax, electricity and liquid petroleum gas consumption tax, and environment cleaning tax.

[6] Occupation fees, fee for working permissions on holidays, freshwater sources fee, commissioners fee, building user fee, land development fee, business opening permit fee, examination license and report fee, and health document fee.

[7] In municipalities, land tax for building plots is one per thousand, and for other plots of lands three per thousand. The building tax is for dwellings one per thousand and for other buildings two per thousand.

[8] Construction fee (25%), occupation fee (18%), wholesale market fee (12%), and building user permit fee (9%) are directly affected by market conditions.

municipalities and other municipalities. For example, metropolitan municipalities and metropolitan district municipalities are able to generate substantial income from the sales of building sites, whereas rents from immovable properties are more important for smaller municipalities (Péteri and Sevinc 2011).

Now, the question is to what extent municipal revenues match to the cost of assigned public services. Here again, we see significant discrepancies among municipalities according to their size and regional basis. The per capita own-source revenues between larger and smaller cities and between developed regions such as Istanbul, East Marmara, Aegean, West Anatolia, and other less developed regions diverge largely. In the least developed cities, even the cost of collecting revenues could be a financial burden simply because of the limited revenue-raising base and high local service costs. For instance, in the most underdeveloped five provinces (Ardahan, Muş, Ağrı, Şırnak, and Kilis), costs of financial administrative services (i.e., the collection costs, financial management, accounting costs) are above own-source revenues (Péteri and Sevinc 2011). Moreover, the 2016 data show administrative services (30%) constitute the biggest budget item in total municipal expenditure, which is followed by revenue-raising economic activities (22%), and housing and welfare activities (21.5%).[9] These numbers underscore municipalities predominantly use their financial sources for administrative expenses, and for economic activities to supply the own-source revenues.

Another dimension of financial capabilities concerns with debt structure and its influence on local government finances. The outlook of debt structure is important to assess whether municipalities use loans and credits to invest in public services and to expand their revenue base or to cover current expenditures. Needless to say, the latter indicates a deteriorating financial outlook for the municipality. Municipalities, which have to take loans for current expenses and interest payments of debts, would have limited flexibility in public service provisions and investments. Additionally, any decision to fund investment through borrowing has to be accompanied by debt management capability not to weaken the financial position and quality in public service provisions. Especially, the ratio of short-term payments to long-term payments indicates the capability of debt management. A lower rate indicates a higher flexibility in budget

---

[9] See the Appendices.

expenditure. According to 2016 data retrieved from Undersecretary of Treasury, 83% of the total debt owed to the Treasury belongs to the local government and municipal enterprises, among which 25% of debts are assigned as overdue, and half of the debts registered in municipalities have short-term obligations. This ratio points out deterioration in short-term debts, which were around 30% in the period between 2005 and 2010 (Péteri and Sevinc 2011). Nonetheless, restructuring of debts and periodic debt acquittance are common in the management of local government's public debt. For instance, in January 2018, a new law on public debts came into force to restructure short-term debt obligations up to 5 years with minimum interest rates.

In order to better understand the motivations of mayors in provincial municipalities on incurring debts, mayors of provincial municipalities are given five options (administrative costs, current expenses of public services, investment on infrastructure, investment on the superstructure, financial investment) in the survey to choose from. Among 25 respondents, investment on infrastructure and investment on superstructures received the top two choices with both 31%. A total of 28% of respondents assigned administrative costs and current expenses of public services as primary reasons on incurring debts. Remarkably, the debt for operational expenses (i.e., the sum of administrative costs and current expenditures) corresponds to the national rate of overdue debt among local government.

As a final note, the 2013 assessment report of VI. Financial Management in Local Administrations Forum organized by the Treasury and Union of Turkish Municipalities raises the following issues concerning with the financial capabilities in local government:

- The formula of intergovernmental transfer shares to metropolitan municipalities and district metropolitan municipalities should include additional criteria (such as development index) to offset low municipal revenues.
- A need for further fiscal decentralization to enhance own-source revenues through expansion of municipal taxes and fees.
- The regulations affecting municipal financial management should not be in the form of bag bills and should be designed through deliberations with local government.

Material Capabilities

While financial means and the flexibility in expenditure create one side of the story with the mobilization capacity of local government, the other side is about the material possessions to conduct its operations. Hence material capabilities are concerned with what local government owns to run its operations and whether it has the effective and efficient means to procure goods and services from external sources.

A basic aspect with material capabilities is about whether all departments are equipped with adequate means to carry out their responsibilities. The physical conditions of working places, the computerization of services, and assets of machinery, software, and hardware on public services are some of the indicators with material capabilities. Yet, the efficiency and economy criteria do not necessarily call for the ownership of goods but also having the capability of purchasing or co-sharing the properties in case of necessity. Without a doubt, the flexibility in purchasing is closely linked with financial capabilities. Yet, the effectiveness in purchasing increases with less red tape and effective methods in public procurement. Besides, municipalities do not necessarily have to purchase goods and services but through effective partnerships, with other local authorities, they can meet their needs without the limitations of financial capabilities.

Let's start with whether the Turkish local government has the adequate means to run its operations. Adequate means can vary from basic physical conditions of the working environment to advanced machinery and digital assets. There is not a regulative framework in Turkey specifying minimum conditions about material capabilities for efficient service delivery. Also, the data provided by municipalities about their material possessions are not consistent in each case as well. Therefore, it is difficult to make a comprehensive assessment, but there are some independent studies to help us to form an opinion about the material conditions in Turkish local government. For instance, the 2011 KENTGES report of Ministry of Environment and Urbanization found out severe inconsistencies on the number of registered material possessions among participated 2954 municipalities and concludes with that municipalities lack the capacity and means to provide satisfactory input on inventory and statistical data on their material possessions.

Akin to financial capabilities, KENTGES report emphasizes material capabilities differ with size and type of municipalities. Accordingly, it is common that rural and district municipalities lack the certain basic equipment to create urban strategies as expected from all municipalities. Indeed, the difference appears so high that the findings indicate that while 80% of metropolitan municipalities possess the adequate technical capabilities, the level is at provincial municipalities around 30%, and at rural and district municipalities only 5%. Yet, the study incorporates indicators about technical personnel into calculation thus these numbers only approximate material capabilities.

Notwithstanding with variances among local government, an overall digital transformation in government services is noticeable during the 2000s. Needless to say, this period also coincides with global trend in digital technologies and theories in digital governance, but a fourfold increase on ICT investments at government services from 2002 to 2011[10] infers prioritization of digital transformation as a government policy. Most notably, large-scale projects such as e-Transformation Turkey[11] and FATIH[12] have become salient on this effort. In December

---

[10] Data is retrieved from State Planning Office repositories.

[11] The e-transformation of Turkey was initiated in February 2003. The State Planning Organisation (SPO) was assigned to coordinate the project. A new institutional structure was formed by introducing e-Transformation Turkey Executive Board, e-Transformation Leaders, and an Advisory Board (Telli 2011).

[12] The following information is taken from a news piece in Today's Zaman (July 2, 2012): 'Undertaken by the Ministry of Education and supported by the Ministry of Transport and Communications, the Movement to Increase Opportunities and Technology (FATIH) Project is expected, once finalised, to be in use in 570,000 classrooms in 42,000 schools all around Turkey. According to government plans, teachers will be able to instantly access any document around the world they may need for their class, projecting it on the interactive smart board. The project will also facilitate long-distance learning programs while encouraging a gradual transition to e-textbooks and other electronic-learning materials for each class. In the second component of the project, there will be 110 in-service training centers connected to each other through a network that covers Turkey's 81 provinces for educator training purposes, where all the participants will able to interact with each other live through teleconferencing. The last component is the establishment of a secure and appropriate network infrastructure for all the schools across the country'. FATIH project was inaugurated in 2010, and initially, the project was expected to cost 4.9 billion TL in ICT investments in the education sector. However, the project's success has been seriously undermined after overly exceeding the initial costs (about 1 billion TL is earmarked for the project every year), and limited achievements with initial targets. In 2017, the Ministry of Education has announced according to the project targets '66% of the digital infrastructure at schools, 71% of interactive smart-boards, and 19% of tablet distribution' is completed.

134   E. TAN

2008, a unified, single entry gateway for e-government services '*e-Devlet*' is launched, and as of 2018, e-Devlet includes 3027 e-services of 423 different agencies, and a number of registered users about 36.5 million.[13]

Can we say these efforts have been fruitful on the digitalization of government services at local governance? A 2011 report by the Ministry of Interior shows that 97% of the population resides within the service area of a local administration with a Web site. Furthermore, the 2016 e-Government Benchmark Report of the EU marks e-government performance of Turkey as 'progressive' about the same with the EU average, and especially in user centricity (i.e., to what extent a service is provided online and its user-friendliness) Turkey significantly outperforms the EU average. Considering the average lower scores of education level and Internet users[14] indicators, the report highlights an adequate infrastructural basis in Turkey to undertake e-government services.

There are nonetheless certain shortcomings in e-government services concerning local governments. The report of the Ministry of Interior (2011) highlights the following weaknesses in e-government services at the local level:

- There is a lack of citizen trust in security systems to protect user data registered in e-government services.
- The legislative framework and regulations are inadequate to ensure the security of personal data on online services.
- Web sites of local government usually provide information rather than interactive services.
- Some available e-government tools are only limited to services provided by central administrations and they do not extend into local services.
- Not all municipalities keep a centralized IT system required for e-government services.

The second aspect of material capacity is about the efficacy in public procurements. Local government has three options in procurement: the State Supply Office (*Devlet Malzeme Ofisi*), municipal enterprises, and

---

[13] The information is taken from the European Commission report 'E-government in Turkey May 2018'.

[14] The performance scores for 'Education Level' and 'Internet Users' for the EU (31) average are, respectively, 0.29 and 0.79, whereas it is 0.15 and 0.51 for Turkey.

market. State Supply Office, is a state enterprise under the auspices of the Ministry of Finance, and its primary function is to supply public authorities with office materials at competitive prices. State Supply Office is supplied from several vendors and it supplies a large variety of merchandise to the public sector. Its profit is channeled as an income to the Treasury. The primary customers of State Supply Office are central government and its agencies, but it is also a popular choice for local government on public procurement.

All public procurements in local government are subject to the Law on Public Procurement. According to the law, there are three methods in public procurement: open tenders (open to all aspirants), negotiated tenders (participation is limited to three aspirants), and direct procurement. Direct procurements are usually for continuous and low-value purchasing, and it does not require a tendering procedure. For high-value purchases, open tenders are obligatory. The law on public procurement has been amended several times since 2002, to improve its compliance with the EU and WTO public procurement rules on transparency and procedural conditions. Nonetheless, in practice, the purchaser has a high discretion in setting the tendering conditions, and usually tendering procedures for middle and low-value purchases are decided according to the preference of purchasers. Especially, one rationale behind purchasing through municipal enterprises is mentioned as keeping municipal resources indirectly within the organization (Bozlağan 2000: 447; Atik 2009: 441). A study on the relationship between municipal enterprises and municipalities found out 7% of tenders, which is in value the equivalent of 25% of all municipal tenders, won by municipal enterprises (İlhan 2013).[15] Although these numbers do not necessarily point out a special relationship between municipal enterprises and municipalities, the ratio varies extensively among municipalities. For instance, in the cases of Eskişehir and Samsun, the value of public tenders granted to municipal enterprises is, respectively, 58 and 86% of total value.[16] It seems like while municipal enterprises have a bigger role in metropolitan municipalities, in provincial municipalities their significance in public procurement is limited. My survey findings among provincial municipalities show that State Supply Office (41%), and market (36%) are most frequently used

---

[15] The study is conducted in years 2008 and 2009 and comprises data from 86% of all tenders.

[16] Ibid.

and with the highest preference on covering material needs, and only 12% of respondents select municipal enterprises as their preferred source.

The remaining 11% selected other municipalities as the primary source for supplying their material needs. Indeed, another option for municipalities is forming informal or formal intermunicipal partnerships to support their material needs. Nonetheless, the effectiveness of formal intermunicipal partnerships seems limited in Turkey and they are limited to certain areas such as water management, waste management, and environmental protection. As it seems that the clauses regulating municipal partnerships under Law on Union of Local Administrations cause different interpretations about the extent of the law on employing intermunicipal partnerships to cover material needs. Furthermore, sustaining intermunicipal partnership requires certain managerial capacities including human resources and organizational efficacy, and the management costs of sustaining partnership stand out as a hindrance on the proliferation of intermunicipal partnerships (Jackson and Üskent 2010).

Similarly, my survey results show corresponding findings on intermunicipal partnership. The ambiguity of the current law on regulating municipal partnerships is articulated as the primary reason for avoiding intermunicipal partnerships. Other common reasons are 'no adequate personnel capacity to contribute to intermunicipal partnerships' and 'no adequate budget for intermunicipal partnership'. One respondent explained the impact of financial constraints on failing intermunicipal partnerships as 'Partnering municipalities expect support from each other due to financial constraints, and therefore joint projects fail to materialize'. Yet, municipalities are not abstained from forming partnerships, as half of the respondents expressed themselves open for partnerships, and 62% are engaging with unofficial partnerships. That shows there is room for improvement in municipal collaboration, and with regulative and capacity-related adjustments, municipal partnerships can be a viable alternative for public procurements.

COMMUNICATION CAPABILITIES

Communication capabilities reflect what extent the local government is capable to collect the information, which is most representative of local needs and priorities, process the information for the production of effective public policies, and share it effectively with citizens and other stakeholders outside of the organization. In a way, this description gives us three areas to study the communication capabilities in local government. First, inside the organization—the means and structure of communication between management and staff, among different departments, and between civil servants and political representatives. Second, outside the organization—the means and structure of communication between public managers and citizens, and between public managers and other stakeholders including the central authority. Third, effective and efficient communication systems inexorably depend on the ICT penetration in municipal governance. Therefore, as a crosscutting area, capabilities with ICT systems in processing, storing, and channeling the information will be part of the inquiry.

There are two lines of communication inside municipalities to assess intra-organizational communication capabilities: (1) the communication between councilors (or local political representatives) and head of administration (mayor or deputy mayors) and (2) the communication between managers (mayors, deputy mayors, and head of departments) and civil servants. While the former is an important component for democratic governance, the latter is substantial for effective implementation. Nevertheless, these two dimensions are not easily separable, and a holistic approach is important to assess the effectiveness in organizational capacities.

The evaluation reports of LAR II[17] present the most comprehensive findings on intra-organizational communication. According to 'Training Needs Assessment Report', only a small percentage of municipalities hold line-management structures where the heads of units meet regularly under the supervision of deputy mayor with rest of the municipal staff. For the rest, communication with civil servants is an ad hoc basis. Furthermore, the report underlines 'the physical nature of offices' and 'bureaucratic bottlenecks' hamper in some municipalities the effective organizational communication. Yet, more frequently, limitations with intra-organizational communication are substantiated by the lack of awareness and cooperative attitude at top-managerial level. Remarkably, the report points out that many municipalities are equipped with capable ICT infrastructure to maintain effective information management,

---

[17] Local Administration Reform in Turkey (LAR) is an IPA project funded by the EU accession grants, to support the implementation of local government reforms by the Ministry of Interior. The first phase (LAR I) took place in 2005–2007 and the second phase (LAR II) took place in 2009–2011.

but their effectiveness is limited as a result of unwillingness at managerial level to share information or of their disregard to store information. The absence of mutually agreed task descriptions and responsibilities and managerial deficits in cultivating effective interdepartmental meetings are other articulated reasons with shortcomings in administrative communication.

The communication between elected local representatives and municipal administration is also suggested as ineffective according to LAR II findings. In many municipalities, municipal councilors rarely or not at all meet with civil servants. Moreover, councilors are neither aware of how to effectively monitor municipal services nor capable of doing it, and it is suggested that there is a lack of guidelines or training possibilities to oversee municipal administration. Councilors, predominantly being local businessmen and artisans, are often adhered to party politics at municipal decisions, and party affiliation often prevails over the representation of local interests (Oktay 2016). Indeed, this sense of unity between local and central politics is widespread in the southern group of European countries (Page 1991). The findings suggest likewise that councilors rarely meet with their constituents if they do meet at all. By the same token, the residents appear to have little information on what a councilor does. Therefore, the effectiveness of councilors as local representatives and as a mechanism of deliberative governance is restricted.

In my research, I have also directed several questions to mayors related to the communication capacity of councilors. In one question, mayors are asked the number of petitions and written requests they receive from councilors per month. Only one mayor responded to ever receive a written request from councilors. Additionally, deputy mayors are asked whether there are guidelines or training options available for councilors to enhance their communication with municipal administration and citizens. Around 25% of respondents stated to provide guidelines or training for councilors to enhance their communication. Although the purpose of these questions was to form an insight into the role and capabilities of councilors in municipal decision-making process, and the number of respondents is too limited to suggest an overarching claim about councilors' role on municipal decision-making, the findings are coherent with the expectations of restricted role that councilors hold in municipal decision-making.

As the representativeness of local interests through elected officials is relatively ineffective, alternative means, such as muhtars and urban councils, gained upper hand in the representation of citizen's interests in local governance. Urban councils with their wider base in the representation of diverse and organized interest present a viable alternative to the municipal council about local representation. Nevertheless, the access of urban councils to municipal decision-making processes appears to be restricted. The findings from LAR II suggest there are some ad hoc committees initiated by urban councils to monitor decision-making processes at municipal council, but there are no formal means to facilitate the exchanges between them. It also appears that some exchanges with urban councils create mix responses on the municipal side, as their stance is taken as confrontational rather than constructive. Yet, in my research, mayors happened to be to a large extent positive toward urban councils, which are perceived as useful and cooperative bodies suitable for collaboration and more engaged action (see Fig. 4.1). However, this positive attitude toward urban council is not supported by other findings as mayors have fewer tendencies to engage with them in public governance.

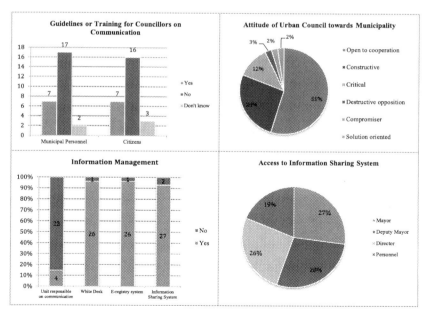

Fig. 4.1 Information structure

140   E. TAN

On the other hand, the muhtars' role as a medium in local representation is also contingent on the mayor's initiative. Under favoring conditions, muhtars can find easier access to municipal decision-making. Yet, these cases are sporadic and do not suggest as a viable mode of participation in local governance.

The limited access granted to urban council and muhtars to municipal decision-making has been backed by my findings as well. A significant finding from surveys was the number of regular meetings with central government and governors per year exceed the number of regular meetings with local representatives (i.e., the urban council and the muhtars) in average by 18 meetings per year. If we rank the frequency of regular meetings, intra-organizational meetings come at first in municipal communication then it is followed by agents of central government and later by representatives of local interests. This shows that the access of the central government in municipal decision-making is far ahead of the access of local stakeholders. This finding together with responses of mayors on the importance of communication with the central government over local representatives (see Fig. 3.5) clearly suggests that central government holds prevalence over local components in public governance.

The absence of effective local representation in public governance seemingly encouraged citizens to search for more direct means of access to the municipal administration. LAR II findings suggest that most municipalities hold one form of a direct communication mechanism between mayor (or deputy mayor) and citizens. In many municipalities, there are public desks for questions and complaints of citizens, as well as local TV channels and newspapers supported by municipalities as alternative means of communication. However, LAR II findings also suggest that citizens are largely unaware of these means, thus raising doubts about their effectiveness. The working cases of direct communication extensively rely on the predisposition of mayors.

Reasonably, the most convenient way of direct participation in governance is through the means of e-government. We have seen that the e-government infrastructure in local government is relatively advanced in the Turkish case. However, the effectiveness of e-government and e-participation is also dependent on the penetration of Internet usage and the ICT infrastructure at the local level. Here, Turkey appears to be closing the gap with EU countries. According to Eurostat Information Society Indicators, the percentage of households with Internet access in Turkey is 81% and percentage of individuals using Internet once a week is 61%.[18] A similar upward trend is also apparent on e-government indicators, including 'percentage of individuals using the Internet for interacting with public authorities', 'percentage of individuals using the internet for obtaining information from public authorities in Turkey', 'percentage of individuals using the Internet for downloading official forms from public authorities in Turkey', and 'percentage of individuals using the internet for sending filled forms to public authorities in Turkey'.[19] However, according to transparency indicators, Turkey is relatively underperforming.[20] Another report by the Ministry of Interior,[21] on the other hand, shows that at least one means of e-participation (e.g., online surveys, voting systems, interactive discussions) is present in municipal Web sites corresponding to 87% population coverage.

Yet, there is a caveat with e-governance and e-participation, their effectiveness is heavily contingent on socio-economic and demographic factors. For example, age differences, literacy, and education level are strongly correlated with effective Internet usage. Turkey has a high level of young population under 24 (close to 50% of total population), and the level of Internet usage among young population is distinctively higher than country average.[22] This serves an advantage as it indicates the sustainability of upward trends in e-government indicators. However, high regional socio-economic differences create a disadvantage. Regions with higher socio-economic level perform better in e-government

[18] The data is retrieved from Eurostat Web site on May 29, 2018. The EU average of each measure is, respectively, 87 and 81%.

[19] For Turkey, the percentages are, respectively, 42, 38, 22, and 30%. The EU average is for the same, 49, 41, 30, and 30.

[20] According to EC's e-Government Benchmark 2016 report, Turkey is falling under the category of 'fair' at 'Transparent Government' with an overall score of 56. The measure indicates to what extent the government is transparent regarding (i) their own responsibilities and performance, (ii) the process of service delivery, and (iii) personal data involved.

[21] General Directorate of Local Administrations (2011). *E-devlet (yerel) uygulamaları anketi raporlaması*. Ministry of Interior.

[22] The Internet usage for the age group 16–24 is 87.5%, which is significantly more than the country average of 66.8% (Turkish Statistical Institute 2017). Also among OECD countries, the difference in Internet usage between 16–24 and 55–74 age groups is highest in Turkey (OECD 2017: 170).

142   E. TAN

rankings.[23] In overall, country statistics infer penetration of e-government services in Turkey is improving and catching up with the EU, but lack of transparency at local governance, and differences among regions can impede its effectiveness as an alternative to representative and direct forms of citizen participation in local governance.

Another dimension with communication capabilities is about having an information management system to use the collected data effectively in municipal decision-making. Information management is in fact beyond communication capabilities only and it has crosscutting features with material and managerial capabilities. In the surveys, municipalities are asked, whether they have (1) a unit responsible for interdepartmental communication, (2) a desk[24] for citizens to appeal their complaints and requests, (3) an electronic registry system to store the complaints received from citizens, (4) an information sharing system and who has access to it. Figure 4.1 shows that almost all participants responded affirmatively to having a desk for complaints and requests, as well having an e-registry system to store them. This shows that municipalities usually hold the means of retrieving information from citizens. However, in terms of internal management of information, the findings are less assuring. Only 15% of municipalities mention having a unit responsible on interdepartmental communication. Although the level of access into information sharing system is fairly balanced, an effective management is important to turn the collected data to sound policy practices. Once again, this finding suggests that communication capabilities in Turkish local government is fairly capable in terms of ICT infrastructure but less assuring on effective use of the collected information.

The last dimension that we will look under communication capabilities will be about information sharing with other public sector organizations. Insofar as ICT capabilities, Turkey made considerable advances in connecting the digitalized government services through *the e-Devlet* gateway. However, about connecting local government services into a unified database and information sharing system, Turkey has been lagging behind. In fact, the efforts to create a unified system connecting local and central information sharing are going on for a long time since

---

[23] Two socio-economically most lagging behind NUTS regions in Turkey; Southeastern Anatolia, and East Black Sea Regions perform the lowest scores on the percentage of households with a broadband connection (69 and 67%), while Istanbul region scores 89%.

[24] This desk is usually referred to as 'white desk'.

the initiation of 'YerelBilgi'[25] project. The project was launched in 2001, with the collaboration of the Ministry of Interior and TODAIE,[26] to create a unified databank pooled by information from local authorities including affiliated enterprises of municipalities. The activation of the project has been prolonged by a number of problems such as software incompatibilities, difficulties in data registry, and using the system. As of 2018, the system is still not functional and does not allow data sharing despite being integrated into the *e-Devlet* gateway. Consequently, communication among local government and the central government has been constrained to personal links and takes place often through means of party affiliations.

Lately, the Union of Turkish Municipalities as a platform for information sharing and deliberation among local government is gaining importance. The law on the union of local governments sanctioned the establishment of two nationwide unions, one for municipalities and the other for SPAs, where all respective local governments are natural members. The core functions of unions are to defend and protect the interests of their members at the central level and to develop awareness through training and seminars on new regulations and practices at the local level. Besides these, there is also a limited number of regional unions,[27] focusing on information sharing and collaboration at a regional scale.

Planning Capabilities

Effective decision-making in public governance hinges on effective planning capabilities as much as communication capabilities. Especially, the recent reforms in Turkey brought to local government new planning responsibilities with strategic planning and performance budgeting.

The legal framework for new planning responsibilities is set by the Public Financial Management and Control (PMC) Law. The Art. 9 in PMC Law obliges the local government to perform certain practices as part of strategic planning such as setting the mission, vision, and the

---

[25] 'YerelBilgi' literally means local information.

[26] Public Administration Institute for Turkey and the Middle East (TODAIE) is a public body inaugurated in 1952 to conduct research on public administration and to provide training to civil servants. YerelBilgi Project is taken over by the Ministry of Interior in 2004.

[27] The most prominent one is the Union of Marmara Municipalities.

144   E. TAN

strategic goals; defining measurable outcomes and performance targets with predefined indicators; including supervision and evaluation stages. Moreover, strategic planning should incorporate the participation of stakeholders in setting targets. To ease the transformation process with planning responsibilities, several guidelines are prepared by the relevant state agencies. For example, the Handbook of Strategic Planning for Public Institution (2006), prepared by the SPO,[28] explains various analysis methods for each stage of strategic planning. Additionally, strategic planning should be integrated into budget preparation through performance indicators set for objectives. Here, another guidebook prepared by the Ministry of Finance (2004) explains the basics of performance-based budgeting. The guidebook promotes performance-based budgeting as the link between strategic planning and budget preparation. The system anticipates each public sector organization to set annual performance targets for objectives and to assign matching activities and budgets. Success criteria for each activity should be indicated in the performance charts. Additionally, the guidebook expects an activity-based appraisal in performance budgeting.

Yet it seems like the effectiveness of strategic planning in municipal decision-making is rather mixed, as both national and international observers report substantial discrepancies in planning processes. For instance, the 'Training Needs Assessment Report' of LAR II highlights that managers and councilors in the municipalities do not think strategic planning is linked to the operational effectiveness of the administrations. The pilots demonstrated strategic plans are usually prepared as academic practices with very little participation from inside and outside of the organization. Furthermore, the report underlines that there is a very little sense of ownership by lower-level managers over the plans inferring the plans do not serve as key management tools.

I have also directed some questions in surveys about strategic planning. For example, mayors are asked to select the actors, who participated in strategic planning and their means of participation (see Fig. 4.2). Accordingly, the strategic plans are predominantly compiled via participation of the managers (deputy mayors and directors), rather than via participation from outside of management and organization.

---

[28] The State Planning Organisation was restructured as the Ministry of Development in 2011.

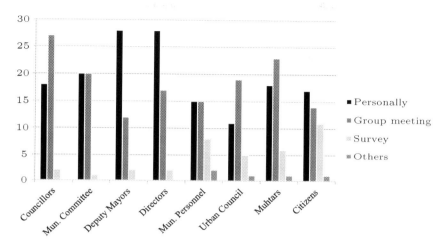

Fig. 4.2 Structure of participation in strategic planning

As a deliberation method, personal communication is preferred inside the administration, while group meetings are usually preferred for the rest such as councilors, urban council, and muhtars. Concurrent with findings on communication capabilities, managers prefer personal contacts with citizens as well, which infers a limited representativeness of citizen input in strategic plans. A further question was whether municipalities received any external consultancy during the preparation of strategic plans. 5 out of 29 respondents stated that they receive external help for the preparation of strategic plans.

Similar to strategic planning, the effectiveness of performance budgeting seems to be limited to the Turkish case. Çatak and Çilingir's (2010) give a comprehensive insight into practices and problems in that regard. The report underlines the following problems with performance budgeting in Turkey:

- *Inadequate and incomplete legislation* caused by (i) deficiencies and ambiguity in strategic planning, performance programming, budgeting and accountability reporting regulation; (ii) preparation of investment and operational budgets as separate documents; (iii) preparation of performance programs and budgets as separate documents; (iv) short coverage period of performance programs;

(v) short budget approval period by Parliament; (vi) unaligned complementary legislation.

- *Incomplete and unclear performance budgeting methodology* caused by (i) ambiguity in the performance budgeting approach; (ii) lack of a systematic approach for strategic planning; (iii) deficiencies and ambiguity in the performance programming methodology; (iv) ambiguity in linking strategic plans to higher-level policy documents, performance programs to strategic plans, budgets, accountability reports and detailed expenditure programs to performance programs; (v) lack of program classification; (vi) ineffective performance budgeting documents in determination of budget ceilings; (vii) appropriations of administrations and ambiguity in rules and procedures of budget negotiations.
- *Weak coordination and guidance* caused by (i) two regulatory administrations (i.e., Ministry of Interior and Ministry of Finance) in the performance budgeting system; (ii) inadequacy of the assessment of the strategic plans and performance programs; (iii) insufficient guidance for strategic planning and performance programming processes; (iv) disconnected performance budgeting legislation and disconnected budget negotiations.
- *Improper and ineffective implementation* caused by (i) delays in the budget calendar; (ii) lack of activity-based costing, feasibility analysis, risk assessment and cost accounting.
- *Disabling administrative and external factors* such as (i) organizational problems of the Strategy Development Departments; (ii) insufficient political ownership and supervision; (iii) lack of infrastructure to obtain, track and evaluate performance data; (iv) inadequacy of the e-budget system.

Some of these shortcomings have been addressed in time with certain regulatory adjustments. For instance, in 2016, a bylaw[29] issued by the Ministry of Interior, introduced new rules in budgeting and accounting records to standardize performance budgeting and to monitor performance appraisals in local government. Yet, at the moment, it is still too early to assess the impact of these regulations.

In overall, the planning capabilities of local government are seemingly limited to promote effective decision-making in public governance.

---

[29] The bylaw 'Mahalli Idareler Bütçe ve Muhasebe Yönetmeliği' is issued in May 2016.

4 LOCAL GOVERNANCE CAPACITIES IN TURKEY 147

The reasons are both systematic and organizational. Despite all limitations, advancements in planning practices as set by law can potentially contribute to improvement in local governance capacity.

MANAGERIAL CAPABILITIES

Managerial capabilities refer to personal qualities of senior managers and head of units encompassing their functional and technical skills in management. Yet, managerial capabilities are not only limited to personal qualities of managers but also includes management systems inside the organization. However, management systems have various applications, and some relevant aspects have already been elaborated as part of communication and planning capabilities. Therefore, to avoid repetition, in this part, I will focus primarily on the personal qualities of managers and practices empowering managerial capabilities.

Certain qualities of a good manager are overarching whether it is the public, private, or voluntary sector. Especially, leadership qualities, qualified educational background, and experience attribute to a good manager. Unfortunately, there is limited aggregated data showing personal qualities of mayors in Turkey. The database of Supreme Electoral Council of Turkey holds some data about gender and age composition of mayors in Turkey. For instance, according to the data of 2009 local elections, the age disposition of mayors gives a bell curve shape where 63% of mayors fall within the age range of 40 to 55. A similar disposition is also present among councilors. On the other hand, the gender data show a heavily disproportionate representation of gender, that 99.1% of mayors and 95.6% of councilors are men. A similar finding on my study was that women only occupy 11% of managerial positions in provincial municipalities.

A 2011 study conducted by Yörük et al. gives further insight on leadership and personal qualities of mayors. Among 530[30] mayors, 66% have at least a bachelor degree, and about 60% of mayors have a middle/upper middle income.[31] The study provides interesting findings of the leadership styles assumed by mayors and the factors affecting their choices of democratic or autocratic leadership styles. Accordingly, 65% of mayors assume a democratic leadership style. Experience in politics and age appear to be correlated with preference for democratic management

---

[30] It is about 17% of all mayors.

[31] In 2011, an average monthly middle income was between 2000 and 4000 TLs.

148   E. TAN

style. Furthermore, democratic management style is more frequently present in municipalities larger in size, especially in comparison with town municipalities.

In case managers lack experience or occupational expertise with their position, training can reinforce managerial capabilities. Municipalities can provide internal training or send their managers to external training. For example, unions of municipalities regularly provide training and information sessions for municipal personnel.[32] Some international organizations, such as the UNDP and EU, provide also occasional training to enhance managerial capabilities. However, there is not an accredited training program available in municipal management, and participation in training remains limited among mayors.

In the surveys, mayors are asked whether their deputy mayors and directors have received occupational training in last 12 months. 86% of participants responded positively, with an average of 3 pieces of training in 12 months. A few respondents have noted the training and seminars provided by the Union of Turkish Municipalities were, in fact, useful in complementing their internal training.

Managerial practices to foster staff motivation and performance are also linked with managerial capabilities. For that, effective awarding is substantial to invigorate staff motivation and to promote good practices. Effective awarding can be either through financial means, such as salary bonus or gifts or through promotion. Yet, as a result of overstaffing in municipalities and politicization at managerial level, it seems that promotion is not a viable option for managers, and many managers serve in the same position for years (LAR II 2010). In some cases, posting to municipal enterprises are used as a form of promotion for senior managers. LAR II findings suggest that limitations with staffing and posting have led managers to a sense of fatigue. The report points out that managers are not regarded as 'result-oriented' or 'problem-solvers' by councilors but rather seen as 'doing the minimum to keep their position'. Furthermore, managers are reported to be rarely taken initiatives themselves and usually do whatever the mayor asked them to do.

Figure 4.3 illustrates the management of performance and staff motivation in municipalities according to survey responses. Several questions

---

[32] In 2017, Union of Turkish Municipalities provided 676 pieces of training with 46,234 participants from municipalities (i.e., mayors, councilors, municipal personnel) (TBB 2017: 75).

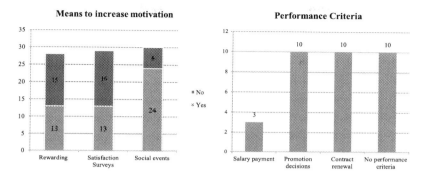

Fig. 4.3 Staff motivation and performance

are directed about awarding system, satisfaction surveys, and social activities. The responses indicate 46% of municipalities adopt a form of awarding system for high performance. For about 70% of municipalities, awarding takes a financial form such as bonuses or premiums. Other popular means of awarding include letters of appreciation, gifts, or placards. 45% of municipalities undertake satisfaction surveys among personnel; in average one time per year and 80% of municipalities organize social activities for their personnel on average 4 times a year. Furthermore, integration of performance measurement in municipal decisions regarding promotion and awarding is substantial to endorse high municipal performance. On that regard, 52% of participating municipalities expressed to relying on performance criteria on their municipal decisions. Among them, 21% use performance criteria on salary payments, while 71% use performance criteria for promotion decisions and contract renewals.

One last topic concerning managerial capabilities is the level of cooperation and coordination among managers. Once again, party affiliations appear to have a substantial role on the effectiveness of cooperation at the managerial level. Mayors are frequently obliged to cooperate with heads of unit, which are selected among other party candidates, and political calculations are influential in assigning roles and responsibilities inside the administration. Another interference in coordination is municipalities usually lack a commonly agreed term of reference which either cause duplication or negligence of work (LAR II 2010). In my study, 76% of municipalities expressed in adopting a term of reference to avoid duplication of work.

Human Resources Capabilities

Implementation capacity relies on the capabilities of human resources as much as managerial capabilities. Human resource (HR) capabilities are, first of all, associated with the quantitative and qualitative adequacy of personnel to achieve organizational objectives. Indicators about personnel, skills, training, and motivation are some key aspects of evaluating HR capabilities. Moreover, HR capabilities are linked with the quality of human resources management (HRM), which is essential for efficient use of human resources. Thus, the efficiency of the HRM system is equally important in the evaluation of HR capabilities.

The 2018[33] data indicate there is a total of 2,414,018 public employees employed at local agencies of central government whereas 212,400 public employees are employed at local government. The working and employment conditions of public personnel are regulated in the Civil Servants Law.[34] Accordingly, there are four categories of employment in civil service: public servant, contracted personnel, permanent worker, and temporary worker. Since the beginning of the public management reform process in Turkey, there have been regular public debates and announcements[35] on reforming the Civil Service Law to comply better with modern managerial practices and to unify different public employment regimes, but as of early 2018, the former law is still in practice.

The graphs on public employment in the previous chapter showed that there are two salient trends in public employment at the local level. First, municipal enterprises have become a significant alternative to inside municipality employment, and second, contract-based employment is preferred over permanent employment despite politically motivated occasional interventions from central government through regulations. We can infer from these trends municipalities prefer flexible employment conditions, which can be an opportunity for more effective usage of performance criteria in employment, yet on the other hand, a convenient

---

[33] Data are retrieved from Public Personnel Directorate's repositories (Devlet Personel Başkanlığı).

[34] The 657-coded Civil Service Law is enacted in 1965 and has been subjected to minor amendments since then.

[35] Most recently, a new draft bill for civil service regime is expected after June 2018 general elections.

means to use politically motivated employment policies which can cause inefficient employment at local government. The findings of the 2011 SIGMA assessment report infer the latter by underlining the following needs for improvements in the civil service system: '*narrowing the scope of the civil service, including a more precise delimitation of the boundaries between politics and administration; improving the merit-based system for recruitment and management; establishing a unitary, simpler, transparent and fair salary system; reinforcing rights and duties of civil servants; using mobility and training as important human resources management tools; cutting favoritism and patronage; eliminating the abuse of temporary appointments as a way of circumventing normal recruitment and promotion procedures; abolishing the immunity of civil servants and the permission system for being prosecuted; emphasizing impartiality as a fundamental civil service value; regulating the right to strike; removing restrictions on the freedom to unionize; increase social dialogue*'.

It is well known that lack of professionalism and political polarization among civil servants favor cronyism and partisan practices in public employment at local government. Yet, causes of inefficiency in public employment spread further than mere lack of professionalism, as regulative and institutional conditions also impinge on the effective use of human resources. Public employment in municipalities is not balanced among departments nor equally distributed across the country. Two macro-level factors are seemingly influential on that. Regulative constraints impede internal mobility among departments (SIGMA 2011), leaving municipalities with uneven personnel capabilities across departments. Moreover, the absence of HRM mechanisms both at central and local level encumbers the effective use of human resources at the organizational and institutional level. Despite some recent developments, there is not an operational central civil service registry system to standardize the HRM information system in municipalities (SIGMA 2017); HR function is performed by individual authorities with limited cohesion among them (SIGMA 2017); and there is less use of strategic HRM compared to the OECD average (OECD 2012).

The absence of effective HRM mechanisms and regulative restraints on personnel employment, as well as the transfer of public personnel from dissolved local authorities, has led to overstaffing in many municipalities. Especially, smaller municipalities with least resources suffer the most on excessive personnel expenditures that are snowballed through irrational employment policies in time. Moreover, changes in census

152 E. TAN

system in 2007[36] have adversely affected municipalities in less developed areas, whose residents often work and live in bigger cities while officially being registered in their hometowns. Bearing in mind the weight of population criteria in transfer shares from the central budget, the financial burden of overstaffing has become even more encroaching on municipalities with declining populations.

There have been, however, certain efforts to deal with the overstaffing problem in public institutions. A noteworthy development in 2007 was the adaptation of 'norm cadre' system in municipalities and affiliated agencies. The system sets the standards and ceiling numbers for every position and category of personnel for employment. Every year, the Ministry of Interior publishes the norm cadre numbers for each municipality according to population and economic activity criteria, thus declaring the optimum number of personnel required for operations. Furthermore, in 2011, the approval of 6111-coded law allowed the removal of redundant permanent workers in municipalities into field agencies of the Ministry of Education and the General Directorate of Security.[37] Moreover, the introduction of performance criteria in municipal management can be regarded as another precaution against overstaffing. However, performance-related pay is not used in public employment and the extent of performance-based decisions in HR is limited with contract renewal and career advancement (OECD 2012).

Notwithstanding with staff overstaffing, lack of qualified or technical personnel is a common phenomenon in municipalities. One part of the problem is an unequal distribution of labor force among geographical regions. Another part of the problem is the limitations of available training programs to improve the quality of existing personnel. For the latter, the Training Needs Assessment Report of LAR II underscores the following key findings on training in human resources:

---

[36] The new census system is designed on the basis of residence addresses of the citizens instead of a one-day enumeration on a 'de facto' basis. The main purpose of the system is to prevent the population overcount which was usually the case in the former system.

[37] See Art. 166 of the Law.

- There is a lack of coordination among various training providers, and there are no commonly agreed training courses or packages. Furthermore, there are neither recognized standards nor an accreditation system for trainers.
- Training is implemented by a 'supply-led' approach rather than 'demand-led', where managers decide on training topics for their staff. Therefore, training programs seldom cover the real training needs of personnel.
- Only a few of local administrations have the capacity within their HR department to assess and monitor their training needs.

The survey findings among provincial municipalities, however, suggest that necessary means of training are largely available inside provincial municipalities. In the surveys, respondents are asked (1) is there a unit responsible inside the municipality to assess training needs?; (2) is there a municipal training program for the personnel?; (3) is there a particular budget allocated specifically for municipal training? Among 27 responding municipalities, 78% has a responsible unit inside the organization to assess training needs; 70% has a municipal training program for the personnel, and 62% allocates a particular amount of budget (in average 75,000 TL per year) for training.

Conclusion

So where are we now with the governance capacity of the Turkish local government? Governance capacity, insofar as the input capabilities of financial, material, and human resources, varies across size, geographical regions, and type of local government. In overall, bigger municipalities have larger revenue basis for financial and material capabilities in comparison with smaller municipalities; municipalities in socio-economically more advanced areas have a larger pool of resources in terms of human resources and more advanced e-government infrastructure and user profile; and metropolitan municipalities have more expenditure autonomy over their own-source revenues in comparison with other types of municipalities. This implicates that a reliable analysis of the relationship between decentralization and governance capacity should rely on the comparison between same tiers of municipalities as well as control the influence of the size of the municipality on this relationship. Furthermore, at least for the Turkish case, socio-economic differences—or *local*

154   E. TAN

capacity as conceptualized—among provinces are expected to play a role in the relationship between governance capacity and decentralization. Correspondingly, mayors' responses to the open-ended question[38] about government capacity adequacy suggest the mayor's perception vary along with municipal revenue basis. Mayors of poorer provinces commonly bring up constraints with financial resources as most urgent issues, whereas responses from wealthier provinces hardly mention financial capabilities as a pressing concern. Mayors reporting capacity constraints in financial resources likewise mention constraints in material capabilities (e.g., a need in reparation and maintenance of equipment and machinery, or insufficient physical conditions). All in all, three types of requests or concerns are expressed about central government's role on financial capabilities: (1) more involvement of central government in cofinancing of investments with large financial burden, (2) more financial autonomy to levying taxes, removal of indirect taxes to municipal services, and more fiscal decentralization, (3) concerns about the misbalance between municipal responsibilities and existing financial resources. Especially in terms of the misbalance, there are two outstanding positions. First, municipalities from poorer provinces underline local sources are insufficient to generate income in scarcely populated and poorer areas for adequate public services. Secondly, municipalities, which are granted the metropolitan municipality status following the 2014 elections, point out the additional financial burden to be brought by indebted district municipalities once these municipalities become part of their jurisdiction. It is not hard to imagine, municipalities from richer provinces lean more toward fiscal decentralization, unlike municipalities from poorer provinces, which look for more central government's involvement in financing projects. Furthermore, regulative framework affecting intermunicipal partnerships and public-private partnerships seemingly have an impact on municipal choices of not seeking alternative sources to supply their material needs, which could be another reason why municipalities with financial constraints look for more central government involvement. Yet again, this could be only a matter of convenience, as municipalities in

---

[38] See the Appendices.

poorer regions mostly belong to AKP and political allegiances are strong between central and local governments.

Indeed, the political affiliations in management and in municipal assembly appear to have an impact on choices in management and implementation. Managers usually prefer an insular decision-making with less involvement from elected representatives or other stakeholders in planning processes. Even though the means of e-government, despite overall fairly adequate institutional and organizational capabilities, the influence of citizens and local stakeholders is limited in strategic decisions. Bureaucratic inertia, partisanship, and having little incentive to encourage citizen participation seem to be the culprit for insular decision-making process rather than the incapability of councilors or citizen's disinterest in governance. A similar outcome is observable on mayor's responses with capacity needs. Only a minority of municipalities raises concerns over planning and communication capabilities or effectively engaging with the citizen. One mayor was more receptive in relation to the shortcomings in engaging with local stakeholders and effectively using the information collected from citizens. The mayor stated that the necessary structure for effective use of information is missing inside the municipality by underlining the deficiencies 'to request the input from citizens, to make sense out of it and to transform it into meaningful services'. The rest, who shared anything about planning and communication capabilities, expresses to have adequate capabilities in planning and implementing projects also in successfully engaging with citizens. My impression is, noting the relatively less emphasis on citizen participation in public management reform acts, municipalities lack the awareness of how to integrate citizens and local stakeholders in decision-making, as well as citizen participation, is not taking as a necessity but rather as a nuisance in public governance. Therefore, it is not surprising why agents of central government appear to have more weight in municipal decisions in comparison with urban councils or muhtars.

The lack of qualified personnel is, on the other hand, a pressing concern for municipalities. A clear majority of survey respondents underline that they either lack educated and technical personnel, or they have a mediocre capacity in human resources. The absence of incentives to attract qualified personnel as a result of legislative limitations, such as maximum wage allowed to the contracted personnel cannot surpass 25% of the highest ranked civil servant's salary, and performance payments

156   E. TAN

are restricted to certain criteria,[39] and the absence of qualified personnel in smaller or poorer municipalities are expressed as primary reasons. Here, training provides a little solution to improve HR capabilities, as most municipalities already undertake training programs but nevertheless lack qualified personnel. Remarkably, political polarization among personnel has been mentioned several times as the cause of why municipalities cannot benefit from some in-house qualified personnel in managerial positions. Additionally, differences in educational background and poor communication caused by heavy workload are stated as other factors for poor collaboration among directors. One mayor stated that there is a 'learned helplessness' among directors that municipalities are dysfunctional places and this creates inertia and distrust in management.

One final remark from surveys is that none of the respondents reported an arbitrary involvement of central government in municipal affairs, but several respondents mentioned political differences in personnel and management have been influential in poor performance of policy implementation. Thus, I surmise different party affiliations inside the municipality, as well as political differences between mayors and central government to have an exogenous role on the dynamics between decentralization and governance capacity. All these and more will be tested in the next chapter on the quantitative analyses of the data retrieved from provincial municipalities.

REFERENCES

Atik, E. T. (2009). Belediye İktisadi Teşebbüsleri ve İktisadi Açıdan Değerlendirilmeleri. *Ulusal Kalkınma ve Yerel Yönetimler Sempozyumu Bildirileri*. Ankara: TODAİE Yayını.

Bozlağan, R. (2000). Belediyelerin İktisadi Teşebbüsleri ve Özelleştirme Tartışmaları. *Yerel Yönetimler Sempozyumu Bildirileri*. Ankara: TODAİE Yayını.

Çatak, S., & Çilingir, C. (2010). Performance Budgeting in Turkey. *OECD Journal on Budgeting, 10*(3), 1–39. https://doi.org/10.1787/budget-10-5km 4d7941142.

[39] Article 49 of the Law on Municipalities states personnel expenses cannot exceed 30% of municipal revenues. For the municipalities with less than 10,000 residents, the regulation is that personnel expenses cannot exceed 40% of municipal revenues. Moreover, the same article states that the performance payments are only applicable to permanent civil servants, they cannot be allocated more than twice a year and limited with the 10% of municipal personnel.

General Directorate of Local Administrations. (2011). *E-devlet (yerel) uygulamaları anketi raporlaması*. Ankara: T.C. İçişleri Bakanlığı.

İlhan, İ. (2013). Türkiye'de Belediyeler ve Şirketleri Arasındaki Ihale Ilişkileri Üzerine Bir Araştırma. *Sayıştay Dergisi 88*. Ankara.

Jackson, J., & Üskent, S. (2010). *Municipal Partnerships Support Network*. Ankara: LAR Phase II.

LAR II. (2010). *Training Needs Assessment Report*. Ankara: Local Administration Reform in Turkey Phase II.

Ministry of Environment and Urbanization. (2011). *KENTGES Belediyeler Anketi*. Ankara: T.C. Çevre ve Şehirçilik Bakanlığı.

Ministry of Finance. (2004). *Performans Odaklı Bütçeleme (Pilot Kurumlar İçin Taslak)*. Ankara: T.C. Maliye Bakanlığı Bütçe ve Mali Kontrol Genel Müdürlüğü.

Ministry of Interior. (2011). *E-devlet Yerel Uygulamaları Anketi Raporlaması*. Ankara: T.C. İçişleri Bakanlığı Mahalli İdareler Genel Müdürlüğü.

OECD. (2012). *Human Resources Management Country Profiles*. Turkey: OECD.

OECD. (2017). *Digital Economy Outlook 2017*. http://dx.doi.org/10.1787/97 89264276284-en.

Oktay, T. (2016). Municipal Councils in Turkey After the Local Administration Reform. In Y. Demirkaya (Ed.), *New Public Management in Turkey: Local Government Reform* (pp. 98–128). New York, NY: Routledge.

Page, E. (1991). *Localism and Centralism in Europe*. Oxford: Oxford University Press.

Péteri, G., & Sevinc, F. (2011). *Municipal Revenues and Expenditures in Turkey and in Selected EU Countries: A Comparative Assessment with Recommendations*. Ankara: LAR Phase II.

SIGMA. (2011). *Assessment Turkey 2011*. OECD.

SIGMA. (2017). *Monitoring Report: The Principles of Public Administration Turkey*. OECD Publications.

SPO. (2006). *Kamu İdareleri için Stratejik Planlama Kılavuzu*. 1.Sürüm. Devlet Planlama Teşkilatı.

TBB. (2017). *Faaliyet Raporu 2017*. Türkiye Belediyeler Birliği.

Telli, Ç. (2011). *Broadband in Turkey: Compared to What?* Washington, DC: World Bank infoDev.

Turkish Statistical Institute. (2017). *Youth in Statistics*. Press Release 16 May 2018. http://www.turkstat.gov.tr/PreHaberBultenleri.do?id=27598.

Yörük, D., Durmuş, D., & Topçu, B. (2011). Leadership Styles of Mayors in Turkey and Factors Effecting Their Leadership Styles. *Ege Academic Review, 11*(1), 103–109.

CHAPTER 5

What Is the Relationship Between Governance Capacity and Decentralization?

Here, we are with the core question of the book, and this chapter is about shedding some light on the answer with empirical findings from the Turkish case. So far, in Chapter 2, we have seen the theoretical and conceptual dimensions, which constitute the relationship between decentralization and governance capacity. In Chapters 3 and 4, I have discussed the country case of Turkey and its idiosyncratic subtleties to contextualize the relationship between governance capacity and decentralization. In this chapter, I will present the findings and models explaining the relationship between decentralization and governance capacity in Turkish local government. The chapter starts with presenting the methodological choices and operationalization of key variables used in the analysis. Later on, I will test the hypotheses followed by a rigorous analysis of the empirical data and interpret the role of key variables in substantiating the relationship between decentralization and governance capacity.

RESEARCH DESIGN AND DATA

As Creswell (2003) suggests, in case the problem is identifying factors that influence an outcome, the utility of an intervention, or understanding the best predictors in outcomes, then a quantitative approach is the best choice for the researcher. However, the quantitative research design has its own limitations. The structured data collection instruments for quantitative research usually fall short in capturing intangible or abstract

© The Author(s) 2019
E. Tan, *Decentralization and Governance Capacity*, Public Sector
Organizations, https://doi.org/10.1007/978-3-030-02047-7_5

159

notions. Especially, measuring capacity encompasses several intangible elements, which are difficult to reflect in quantifiable data. Besides, the rigidity of quantitative data collection can easily fail to capture other influential factors. As a remedy, during the interpretation of findings, I will embrace qualitative responses from open-ended questions, which have been frequently referred to in previous chapters. The qualitative responses will not only supplement the interpretation of statistical findings but also help us to complement the big picture on how governance capacity and decentralization mutually affect each other.

One major challenge with quantitative research design is to secure an adequate sample size. The basic principle of 'more is better' in statistical analysis is not easily attainable in social sciences, especially if the unit of analysis is not individuals. Statistical inferences based on the population of public bodies or states are inevitably restricted by the possible data size. Similarly, this research is bounded by the available number of municipalities. As discussed previously, there are in total 1391 municipalities in Turkey, which differ significantly in terms of capacities. Bigger municipalities (i.e., municipalities at the provincial level or bigger district level) have higher capabilities in almost every aspect of governance capacities, and additionally, the legal rights and autonomy of metropolitan municipalities differ from other types of municipalities. Consequently, this delimits even further available data size to draw reliable inferences.

Therefore, the first challenge of this research was to select an optimal level of comparison to safeguard a workable data size and yet to draw reliable inferences between capacity levels and the degree of decentralization. Eventually, I decided upon provincial municipalities as the unit of analysis. The field research in Turkey was conducted in 2013, and at that time, there were in total 16 metropolitan municipalities and 65 provincial municipalities. Just as a small reminder, in 2014, Turkey enacted a new law that promoted 14 provincial municipalities to the status of metropolitan municipalities. At the time of the field research, this law was not in force but the municipalities were already informed about upcoming changes in their status.[1] From a data size point of view, this means a

---

[1] Careful readers may have realized in the previous chapter that some opinions shared in the surveys already reflect on these upcoming legislative changes (see the Conclusion section of Chapter 4).

bigger pool of data sample to buttress statistical findings. Nevertheless, even with the most optimum outcome in data sample size (in other words if n is 65), this data set could invoke understandable concerns on the robustness of statistical findings. Acknowledging this challenge, I have ended up with a more meticulous choice in controlling the reliability of findings and devoted an ample space for discussion, which could be more than usual. I apologize for this from more 'up to the point' readers, and they are free to skip these parts.

The primary data are collected via surveys with mayors and deputy mayors of provincial municipalities, and the secondary data rely on government records. Two separate surveys were distributed in each municipality, one for the mayor and the other one for the deputy mayor. Mayor's survey involves mainly opinion-based questions, while deputy mayor's survey contains a large extent of technical and factual questions. The organizational structure of provincial municipalities varies in each case. Yet, in each municipality, the mayor is the highest authority in management and deputy mayors are in charge of different departments. Typically, there exist several deputy mayors in a municipality, yet only one survey is dispatched to deputy mayors. The decision on who should fill the survey has been left unaccounted, as some questions require the gathering of data from different departments. The rest of the data are from official documents and information published by the municipalities or by the relevant state institutions. All data comprise the information from the accounts of 2012. More information on data sources and coding of indicators can be found in the list of indicators in Appendices.

In the surveys, 25 questions are directed to mayors and 37 questions are directed to deputy mayors. The questions are clustered according to financial, material, communication, planning, managerial and human resource capabilities, and questions about the discretion of central government in local government. The majority of the questions are based on a 5-point Likert-type scale where higher numbers indicate better performance or the questions ask for factual data on administrative and financial aspects of local government. There are some semi-open and open questions that are used to get further insight into the numerical responses or the process of inquiry. Additionally, one broad open question is directed to mayors for the personal evaluation on the capacity of their municipalities. The responses to this question and other received remarks are already been covered in previous chapters. The English translations of surveys can be found in Appendices.

All surveys are affected by certain biases on sampling, response, and measurement stages. For that, I have benefited from the Total Survey Error (TSE) method to control possible biases and errors in findings. TSE does not suggest a single uniform design, but it identifies certain categories of possible errors that could occur during survey-based research. Basically, TSE refers to sampling and non-sampling error affecting the reliability of survey results. Non-sampling errors can be broken down into three further categories such as coverage error, nonresponse error, and measurement error.[2]

Sampling error occurs when the sample of cases does not fully represent the whole population. The cause of sampling error could be either the bias on selecting the cases or the selected cases do not reflect the variance on population. In this research, the target population covers all provincial municipalities and thus sampling error is not a relevant issue.

Coverage error can manifest itself when sampling frame does not include a part of the target population (i.e., under coverage) or when ineligible units are part of the sampling frame (Groves et al. 2004: 54). In this research, the population of interest is the mayors and deputy mayors and/or the head of departments. Throughout the research, the follow-up calls were conducted with the mayor's assistants or with the heads of staff. Coverage errors can be broken down further into coverage bias and coverage variance. Coverage bias occurs when elements in the population are systemically excluded from the sampling frame (Gideon 2012: 42). A possible coverage bias is if other people than the addressees fill out the surveys, especially on opinion-based questions. To mitigate this risk, a foreword is added about the study and who should fill out the surveys. Three weeks after posting the surveys, follow-up calls were made to ensure the surveys arrived at the addressee. In case the addressees did not receive the surveys, the surveys were sent via e-mail to the head of staff or assistants of the mayors.

Nonresponse error occurs when respondents choose not to respond to some of the questions (item nonresponse) or for the whole questionnaire (unit nonresponse). A systematic nonresponse of a category of participants could lead to bias, as the survey statistics then may not be representative of the population parameters. The nonresponse bias can be calculated as the differences between respondents and

---

[2] 'Total Survey Error = Sampling Error + Coverage Error + Nonresponse Error + Measurement Error' (Gideon 2012: 40).

non-respondent means multiplied by the nonresponse rate. There are several statistical techniques to mitigate the impact of nonresponse. In the case of unit nonresponse, weighting techniques can be adjusted to compensate for the nonresponse bias. For item nonresponse, single or multiple imputation techniques are used to prepare the data for statistical analysis. Nevertheless, techniques such as weighting or imputation can increase the uncertainty in our results by replacing the bias with variance.[3]

Measurement error occurs when there is a difference between the estimated value and the real value of the target variable. According to Gideon, there are various factors which could cause measurement error on survey results such as 'poor question wording, unclear question instructions, erroneous skip patterns, lengthy questions, inadequate response options, the topic of the questionnaire, timing, sponsorship, confusing visual designs, data collection methods, interviewer characteristics, faulty interviewer training, interviewer actions (whether indicated by the training or unforeseen behaviors), interviewer expectations, respondent reactions (whether to the topic or to the interviewer appearance), social pressure in the interviewer-respondent interaction, and respondents' memory erosion among many others'.

Psychological factors due to the interaction between the interviewee and interviewer are not a cause of worry in this research as the surveys are posted to the addressees. However, the downside is any measurement error resulting from potential misunderstanding, cannot be corrected on the spot by a surveyor. As a precaution, the experts in the Union of Municipalities of Turkey have assessed the surveys before the field research. Furthermore, most of the questions are formulated in closed or semi-closed questions in Likert-scale form, in order to minimize variances on the responses. For that, the respondents are asked to pick a number from 1 to 5 where '1' is stated as the lowest degree and '5' is the highest degree for the statement without necessarily stating the verbal equivalent of each numerical value.

In order to avoid any social pressure on the deputy mayors or other lower-ranking managers, the questions on the second survey are mostly framed as factual questions instead of opinion-based. The opinion-based questions are kept mostly in the questionnaire of mayors. The few opinion-based questions directed to deputy mayors are addressed to

[3] Ibid.

mayors in their questionnaire as well (e.g., Q-13 and Q-14/3, respectively, in surveys) to mitigate the risk on measurement bias. With regard to any bias due to sponsorship, the Union of Municipalities of Turkey is a largely independent body whose main objective is to voice the problems or needs of the municipalities to the central government. Therefore, the support of the Union of Municipalities is not expected to indicate any bias in responses. Social desirability could be a matter of concern as mayors are asked to self-evaluate on the capabilities in different areas. However, the questions can hardly be regarded as politically sensitive, and the collected data on opinion-based questions were taken either into factor analysis or used as supplementary information to control the findings of the statistical analysis. Therefore, any impact of social desirability is expected to be minimal.

Before moving further, a few words are needed for the choices with Likert-type questions. Even though the range of scales can vary from 3 to 11 values, most psychometric studies adopt 5 or 7 point Likert scale for measurement. In principle, the response error should diminish with a higher number of available values, as the measurement bias would be lower. Measurement bias occurs if the respondent cannot find the most representative value for its assessment and is compelled to select the closest value. However, with a higher number of similar Likert-type questions in a survey, the scale of questions matters less. The difference between 5 and 7 points of value is relatively more important in larger sample sizes, which was negligible for this research. Also, to reduce the respondent's fatigue, the 5-point Likert scale is preferred in the survey design.

It has been much debated in the methodology literature how to measure Likert-type questions, a dichotomy caused by the ordinal nature of Likert items but frequently treating them as interval scales in measurement. In a nutshell, the pro-ordinal scale arguments emphasize the numbers are anchored with verbal labels (such as 'strongly disagree' or 'neutral') that do not necessarily imply equal distances between integers. Consequently, any descriptive statistics or factor analysis would be statistically not interpretable. Yet, Likert scale is different from Likert-item or Likert-type item despite the frequently interchangeable usage of the terms (Clason and Dormody 1994; Boone and Boone 2012; Uebersax 2006). A Likert scale is composed of Likert-type or Likert-items and unlike Likert-item data Likert-scale data can be analyzed at an interval measurement scale (Boone and Boone 2012). For example, while in a regular multiple-choice test answers are categorized under 5 options (a, b, c, d, e), the test scores are treated at interval level (e.g., 90 out 100). The indicators in the research measured by Likert-type questions incorporate at least two items into Likert-scale data by taking their mean score. There are only two indicators (MOB4 and IMP1) using single-item measures, and these are treated in the analysis as ordinal.

A common way of controlling the internal structure of Likert-scale items is by measuring Cronbach's alpha score. Yet, there are some caveats on interpreting the results of Cronbach's alpha score. First of all, the alpha score does not only depend on the magnitude of the correlations among the components, but also on the number of components in the scale. Scales with larger numbers can misleadingly give higher scores, while average correlation might remain the same. Second, two scales, each measuring a different aspect, when combined together can give higher alpha scores without necessarily measuring the same attribute. Third, a significantly high number on alpha coefficient score may indicate redundant items, which probably measure the same attribute rather than a common attribute. Nevertheless, the Cronbach's alpha coefficient will provide an idea of the internal structure of the variables, which in the later stage will be taken into further analysis. Further aspects of the validity and reliability of data collection will be addressed in the data screening section of this chapter.

RESEARCH VARIABLES

The research hypotheses from Chapter 2 call for the operationalization of three key variables, namely local government capacity, local capacity, and decentralization. Local government capacity is divided further into mobilization capacity, decision-making capacity, and implementation capacity. There is one theoretical and one methodological reason behind this choice. The theoretical reason is the division of local government capacity into functional categories provides further insight into how different capacities are related to the outcomes of decentralization. The methodological reason is, as we will see soon, local government capacity variables hinge on a substantial number of indicators, and considering the limitations with data sample size, this impedes to run a sensible factor analysis to reflect local government capacity as a single factor.

In addition to the core variables, four control variables, namely population, political diversity, party affiliation, and the influence of central government, are selected within the framework of Turkish local government. The choices in the operationalization of each variable are elaborated below.

Decentralization

Typically, in comparative empirical studies, decentralization is operationalized as the extent of subnational government's influence/discretion/share over administrative, political and fiscal dimensions. The theoretical underpinnings of the relationship between decentralization and governance presume that local government is financially and politically dependent on local constituents and has the discretion to implement its policy decisions. In this study, I excluded administrative dimensions of decentralization as provincial municipalities have the same administrative rights and autonomy in governance. Additionally, provincial municipalities are elected organizations, and in principle, they are accountable to their constituents. Yet, depending on exogenous conditions (such as the centralization of political parties), the policy prioritization between citizen's interests and central government's interest might vary among municipalities. Here, I expect provincial municipalities that are financially more dependent on local sources to be more financially accountable on local constituents. Therefore, fiscal autonomy is selected as the locus of analysis.

OECD Fiscal Decentralization Database provides a wide array of possible indicators[4] for the comparative study of fiscal decentralization. Nevertheless, most of these indicators are more suitable for country case comparison. In Turkey, the local government's autonomy on municipal taxation and expenditures is set by law and limited, and thus any related indicator (for instance, tax autonomy, expenditure, fiscal rule indicators) is not significantly relevant for the comparison. Besides, the indicators about the financial flexibility of local government in expenditure (such as debt and budget balance) are included in the analysis as part of the financial capabilities under mobilization capacity. In terms of revenues, local governments in Turkey have two key sources: own-sources and intergovernmental transfer shares. These sources constitute together about 90% of all municipal revenues. The intergovernmental transfer shares are allocated from general budget according to a formula without any discretion from central government. Therefore, the share of intergovernmental

---

[4]These are 'tax autonomy', 'intergovernmental transfer', 'expenditure', 'revenue', 'tax revenue', 'intergovernmental transfer expenditure', 'intergovernmental transfer revenue', 'user fees', 'tax revenue as a share of total revenue', 'intergovernmental transfer revenue as a share of total revenue', 'balance', 'debt', 'fiscal rule indicators', and 'the recurrent tax on immovable property'.

transfer revenues does not necessarily influence the financial autonomy of provincial municipalities. Consequently, the share of own-source revenues to overall revenues is the most representative indicator of financial autonomy, and it is used in the measurement of decentralization variable.

Local Capacity

The relational approach to public governance necessitates that local government should have access to sufficient relational resources at the local level. In that meaning, local capacity is most comprehensively inferred from the socio-economic development of the province. Socio-economic development is an umbrella concept; it refers to the endogenous capacity of locality both economically and socially. In that sense, the 'Socio-Economic Development Ranking Survey of Provinces and Regions (SEGE-2011)' conducted by the Ministry of Development in Turkey provide the most comprehensive and contemporary data on socio-economic development levels of provinces. In the study, 61 indicators from eight subcategories (demographics, education, health, employment, competition and innovation capacity, fiscal capacity, accessibility, and quality of life) are used to create an index to score the socio-economic development levels of provinces.[5] I employed the index score of provinces for the measurement of the local capacity variable.

Mobilization Capacity

Mobilization capacity indicates the capacity of the local government in mobilizing essential financial and material resources for services and functions. Mobilization capacity brings together financial and material capabilities and encompasses three subcategories: (1) the ability in bringing in financial resources for purchasing, (2) the capability in channeling the financial resources for purchasing goods and services, and (3) the adequacy in financial and material means for municipal functions.

For the first subcategory, two indicators are selected: (1) 'property taxation' reflects the ability of municipality on collecting property taxes, which contribute the biggest share in municipal tax revenues; (2) 'utilization of immovable property', which indicates the ability to

---

[5] See the Appendices for the details of SEGE index and scores.

generate income from municipality's immovable properties. These indicators together reflect the municipality's capability in generating income by focusing on the two most important items in own-source revenues (i.e., tax revenues, and enterprise and property revenues). Both indicators are expected to be in the same direction as the mobilization capacity.

The second subcategory is about a municipality's ability in utilizing the revenues for purchasing goods and services required for public services. Two aspects are important in this regard: (1) the financial flexibility in purchasing goods and services and (2) the effectiveness of the public procurement system. The financial flexibility decreases when current administrative expenditure (e.g., personnel cost, social security cost) holds a big share in overall expenditures and/or when short-term debt level is too high. Thus, three indicators are selected for the second subcategory: (1) debt structure, (2) public procurement, and (3) purchasing power. 'Debt structure' is measured by the ratio of short-term debts (with a due date less than a year) to long-term debts. 'Public procurement' is a 5-point Likert-scale variable composed of 4 items: (a) the sufficiency of public procurement in supplying the needs of the municipality, (b) the speed of public procurement, (c) specialized personnel in public procurement, and (d) e-procurement infrastructure. 'Purchasing power' is measured by the ratio of the expenditures on goods and services to the overall municipal expenditures. 'Debt structure' is expected to be in reverse direction with mobilization capacity, as higher ratios would indicate the municipality has lesser flexibility in purchasing due to debt obligations. Other two indicators are expected to be in the same direction with mobilization capacity.

The third subcategory focuses on financial and material adequacy in the provision of public services. Three indicators are selected: (1) material adequacy in public services, (2) adequacy of financial resources, and (3) physical and technical adequacy in administration. 'Material adequacy in public services' is measured by the mean score of mayors' satisfaction scores about the material adequacy in fourteen different municipal services. 'Adequacy of financial resources' is measured on an ordinal scale by the satisfaction of mayors' with available financial resources. 'Physical and technical adequacy' is measured by the mean score of 5 Likert items on the adequacy of (1) computer and computer hardware, (2) technical equipment and machinery, (3) Internet connection and computer software, (4) physical condition of civil servant's offices, and (5) physical condition of manager's offices.

5 WHAT IS THE RELATIONSHIP BETWEEN GOVERNANCE CAPACITY ... 169

In sum, mobilization capacity refers to an aggregate indicator of eight indicators (property taxation, utilization of immovable, debt structure, adequacy of financial resources, purchasing power, physical and technical adequacy, material adequacy in public services, and public procurement).

Decision-Making Capacity

Decision-making capacity indicates the capacity of the local government in determining how to allocate and where to allocate resources. The former signifies the planning capabilities in strategizing how to allocate local government's resources to service areas. The decision on where to allocate resources also demands adequate and effective means in information gathering and processing. Thus, decision-making capacity incorporates indicators of planning and communication capabilities.

In terms of planning capabilities, municipalities should strategize between their means and needs, apply this strategy to a feasible budget plan, and carry out their operation in concurrence with these plans. Eventually, three indicators are selected: 'the success in strategic planning', 'performance budgeting', and 'the importance of strategic and performance plans on actual decision-making'. Accordingly, 'success in strategic planning' is the mean of mayors and deputy mayor's evaluation scores on previous year's strategic plans. Here, deputy mayors are asked to evaluate the success of stages in strategy planning, while mayors are asked to assess the overall success in strategic planning. 'Performance budgeting' reflects the assessment with performance budgeting system including: (1) timing in budget planning; (2) integration of budget plans with performance plans; (3) implementation of performance criteria on budget negotiations; (4) coherence with strategic planning; (5) integration of activity-based costing, feasibility analysis, risk assessment and cost accounting in budget plans; (6) adequacy of equipment to monitor and assess performance; and (7) adequacy of e-budget system. The 'importance of strategic plan and performance plans on actual decision-making' encompasses to what extent the plans are important for mayors on municipal operations and politically sensitive decisions.

About the communication capabilities, seven indicators are selected, namely 'intra-organizational communication', 'the importance of local representatives on decision-making', 'data sheets', 'citizen polls', 'e-government system', 'e-participation system', and 'website visitors'.

'Intra-organizational communication' incorporates seven areas: (1) communication among departments, (2) communication between deputy managers and directors, (3) share of information inside the municipality, (4) adequacy of IT systems, (5) storing of information, (6) division of work and collaboration among departments, and (7) communication between civil servants and councilors. 'Importance of local representatives on decision-making' reflects the mayor's assessment of urban council and muhtars' influence on the formation of the municipal program. 'Datasheets' and 'Citizen polls' indicate the number of times spreadsheets and polls are used in 2012 for the purpose of information gathering. 'e-government system' shows the sophistication of e-government services and measured by the mean score of dummy variables on different government services accessible via municipality's Web site. 'e-participation system' is the mean score of dummy variables on e-participation means available in the municipality's Web site. 'Visitors to the website' is measured according to the Alexa Traffic Ranking indicating the frequency of visitors on the Web site, in which lower ranks mean a higher number of visitors. Therefore, except 'visitors to the website', all variables are expected to be in the same direction with decision-making capacity.

Implementation Capacity

Implementation capacity encompasses the capacity of local government in management and human resources. The managerial dimension incorporates individual skills and qualities of managers, but also management practices to increase organizational performance. For the managerial dimension, 6 indicators are selected: 'education level of the mayor', 'years in office', 'initiative taking in management', 'collaboration in management', 'management practices', and 'seniority in directors'. 'Education level of the mayor' is a categorical variable indicating the education level of the mayor. 'Years in office' indicates the experience as a mayor showing the number of years in the office. 'Initiative taking in management' is the mean score of mayor's evaluation on the level of initiative taking by deputy mayors and directors. 'Collaboration in management' is the mean score of responses about the degree of collaboration between deputy mayors and directors, and deputy mayors and mayor. 'Management practices' denotes practices to improve the effectiveness of management staff, and it is measured by the mean score of 3 Likert items: (1) practices to increase motivation among staff, (2) training on leadership and management, and (3) practices to increase initiative taking in directors and other personnel. Finally, 'seniority in directors' indicates the experience of directors measured by the range of years in the occupation.

The human resource dimension of implementation capacity incorporates eight different indicators: 'seniority in personnel', 'norm cadre', 'technical personnel', 'specialized personnel', 'personnel in municipal companies', 'human resources management system', 'employment policies' and 'formation'. 'Seniority in personnel' captures the years of occupation among personnel similar to 'seniority in directors' indicator. 'Norm cadre' indicates the adequacy and efficiency of municipal employment by taking the ratio of norm cadre to the total number of employees. Accordingly, values higher than 1 suggest overstaffing, while values less than 1 underscores understaffing. The optimal values should be close to 1. Technical personnel is important for the delivery of specialized services inside the municipality, and 'Technical personnel' indicator is measured by the ratio of the number of technical personnel to the total number of municipal personnel. Similar to 'norm cadre' indicator, more is not always better for this indicator since values closer to 1 would indicate overstaffing in terms of technical personnel. Therefore, both variables could create nonlinear relationships that could require logarithmic transformation before further analysis. 'Specialized personnel' shows the rate of personnel who has either a specialized higher education degree or an equivalent vocational training degree. 'Personnel in municipal companies' is the ratio of personnel employed in municipal companies to all personnel. This indicator encompasses the impact of employment outside of municipal administration. 'HR management system' shows the effectiveness of human resource management system capture by a Likert-scale variable of seven items: (1) functionality of HR management system, (2) sufficiency of HR management system, (3) coherence of the HR management plans with the municipality's needs, (4) competence of HR department, (5) implementation of HR strategies, (6) monitoring and assessing the training need, and (7) training meet the municipality's needs. 'Employment policies' is another Likert-scale item with four items: (1) sufficiency in personnel number, (2) sufficiency in qualified personnel number, (3) efficiency of employment policies, and (4) match of new recruits with the job criteria. And finally, 'formation' shows the hour of occupational training received per personnel in 2012.

172   E. TAN

All indicators are expected to be in the same direction with implementation capacity. However, for 'norm cadre' and 'technical personnel' indicators, the degree of relationship might be reduced due to potential nonlinear relationships with other variables.

Control Variables

Population has 80% weight in the calculation of intergovernmental transfer share, which is the most important budget item for most municipalities. Since decentralization variable is calculated by the ratio of own-source revenues to all revenues, the population may have an impact on decentralization via its impact on the dividend. Yet, provinces with larger population may also lead to higher income in own-source revenues. At the same time, these provinces would have an access to a larger pool of human and financial resources, which may influence the local government's capacity. In overall, the population is an essential variable to control for any external impact on the relationship between decentralization and capacity.

Political diversity is a proxy variable[6] indicating whether the municipality is governed by the governing party in central government (i.e., AKP) or by opposition parties. Municipalities governed by opposition parties could be less willing to cooperate with the central government, or central government might pursue uncooperative policies toward municipalities. This can have an impact on the relationship between governance capacity and decentralization.

Party affiliation indicates the political power of the governing party in municipal management. Different party affiliations inside the municipalities can cause unwillingness for cooperation among managers or inefficiencies in implementation. The measurement relies on the percentage of votes that the governing party received in the 2009 local elections.

Influence of central government reflects the perception of the mayor on the extent of the central government's influence on local governance. Local government's discretion in governance does not always suggest the 'real decentralization'. Instead, the central government can impose

---

[6] The value is '1' if the mayor is from AKP, and '0' if the mayor belongs to an opposition party.

influence via indirect means on the political, administrative, and fiscal discretion of local government.

Two assumptions can be built on the impact of the central government's influence on the relationship between decentralization and governance capacity. The first assumption is that central government can influence the decision-making process of local government, which can adversely influence the decision-making capacity by undermining the citizen-based communication or intra-organizational communication. Additionally, the influence of central government can undermine the importance of strategic planning on municipal decisions. The second assumption is if the local government lacks certain capacities, local government can look for central government's involvement in local governance. Then, the influence of central government can increase in the case of lower governance capacity.

The influence variable is measured by the mean of the cumulative scores on 8 areas: own-source revenues, aids, loans and credits, municipal partnerships and collaborations with civil society organizations and private companies, decision-making on municipal services, administrative activities, implementation of municipal services, and investment decisions.

OVERVIEW OF THE FIELD RESEARCH

Over a duration of 8 months in 2013, out of 130 surveys distributed in 65 provincial municipalities, 24 municipalities sent both surveys back, 9 municipalities sent only one survey back, either from the mayor or the deputy. In total, 33 municipalities provided data indicating a response rate of 51% of the population.

It is important to say a few words on my personal experience and challenges I have encountered during the field research. Even though engaging with high-ranking public officials for research purposes has always been a challenging task for researchers, a research on this scale was a particular challenge given the geographical extent of the target area and the complexity of hierarchical structures in Turkish public administration. First of all, the unfeasibility of personally conducting surveys in 65 provinces necessitated the reliance on intermediary agents in municipalities for distribution, application, and collection of the surveys. These agents have varied from personal secretaries or executive assistants to deputy mayors depending on the internal structure. Without an initial personal contact and relying only on phone conversations and e-mail exchanges, the fieldwork required extensive time to follow up and a diligent preparation for pinpointing key people inside organizations.

I am not disregarding the possibility that some surveys might not have been filled out by the mayor personally but instead by an executive assistant or a similar respondent. It is virtually impossible to ensure the genuineness of the opinion-based answers of the addressee. But, as a precaution, clear written and oral instructions were provided to respondents on how to complete the surveys.

Secondly, the stiff hierarchy in some municipalities has often necessitated several contacts with different respondents to climb up the hierarchy. In some municipalities, this procedure was particularly easy considering the absence of an initial personal acquaintance; yet in some, it was almost impossible. One observation is that some municipalities are keen and have more awareness in participating in these sort of studies, yet in some others, executives are unwilling to cooperate and more suspicious toward surveys. In fact, I anticipated a certain extent of distrust in filling surveys. As a precaution, before the field study, I made personal contacts with principals from three main political parties, namely AKP, CHP, and MHP, who have been either in charge of the affairs with local governments or close to the person in charge of the affairs with local governments, and asked their endorsement for the cooperation of mayors affiliated with their parties.[7] Moreover, I have contacted the Union of Turkish Municipalities, whose general secretary provided a support letter that was attached to the surveys. The only party that I was not able to make a personal contact was BDP, despite my extended efforts to contact with the person in charge of the affairs with local governments. One party affiliate explained to me that BDP is not structured like other political parties which have a vertical relationship between the party center and local representatives, and instead, there are influential names inside the party who can endorse the collaboration of local governments. Nevertheless, I was not able to break through the BDP hierarchy for endorsement, which may be the reason for a relatively poor response rate I received from BDP municipalities.

---

[7] I would like to thank personally to Furkan Tanrıverdi, Umut Oran, and İbrahim Durak for establishing the contacts inside the political parties.

There have been also certain technical difficulties during the distribution of surveys. The surveys were dispatched via post to municipalities addressing the mayors. Disappointingly, out of 130 surveys, only about half of them reached their destinations, the rest either due to the failure of postal services or internal delivery mechanisms did not make it to mayor's office. Therefore, the second round of surveys was sent via e-mail to intermediary agents. It was relatively easy to conduct the research via e-mails, yet there have been cases where municipalities were not able to provide a functioning e-mail address, and even in one case, the municipality did not have an e-mail address or a fax number despite their genuine interest to participate in the study.

The length of surveys and especially the questions that necessitate compiling factual data from different departments have augmented the challenge in filling the surveys. Nevertheless, the quality of responses has been highly satisfactory. Remarkably, except a few cases, all factual data were provided thoroughly and in almost half of the surveys, the respondents were willing to provide further feedback and additional comments about related issues. Considering the genuine answers and high attention in filling in the surveys, I surmise governance capacity and decentralization are vital concerns for Turkish municipalities.

Furthermore, survey responses are not restricted to a certain geographical area or socio-economic level but rather well dispersed. To control whether an underlying response bias was present on non-participating provinces, the socio-economic level[8] of non-participating provinces was compared with participating provinces. The t-test of the comparison did not indicate a statistically significant relationship between the response rate and socio-economic differences.

Additionally, the representativeness of political parties among responded municipalities has been close to the disposition of political parties according to 2009 local election results. As noted before, only BDP has been somewhat underrepresented in the data list (Table 5.1).[9]

---

[8] Socio-economic development is measured according to SEGE-2011 index scores.

[9] After 2009 local elections, the political distribution of provincial municipalities has been as follows: AKP (Justice and Development Party): 38 provinces; CHP (Republican People's Party): 11 provinces; MHP (Nationalist Movement Party): 8 provinces; BDP (Peace and Democracy Party): 7 provinces; others: 1 (Sivas) province.

176   E. TAN

Table 5.1   Survey responses from municipalities

Name	Population	Governing Party (in 2013)	Surveys received
Adıyaman	217.463	AKP	Both
Afyonkarahisar	186.991	AKP	Both
Aksaray	186.599	AKP	Both
Amasya	91.874	AKP	Both
Ardahan	19.075	AKP	Both
Artvin	25.771	CHP	Both
Bilecik	51.260	AKP	Both
Bitlis	46.111	AKP	Only from the deputy
Bolu	131.264	AKP	Both
Burdur	72.377	AKP	Both
Çanakkale	111.137	CHP	Both
Çorum	231.146	AKP	Only from the mayor
Denizli	525.497	AKP	Only from the deputy
Giresun	100.712	CHP	Only from the mayor
Gümüşhane	32.444	MHP	Only from the mayor
Kahramanmaraş	443.575	AKP	Both
Karabük	110.537	MHP	Both
Karaman	141.630	AKP	Both
Kars	78.100	AKP	Both
Kastamonu	96.217	AKP	Both
Kütahya	224.898	AKP	Only from the mayor
Manisa	309.050	MHP	Both
Mardin	86.948	AKP	Both
Muğla	64.706	CHP	Both
Muş	81.764	AKP	Both
Niğde	118.186	AKP	Both
Rize	104.508	AKP	Only from the deputy
Sivas	312.587	BBP (later independent)	Both
Tokat	132.437	AKP	Only from the mayor
Trabzon	243.735	AKP	Both
Uşak	187.886	MHP	Both
Van	370.190	BDP	Only from the mayor
Yozgat	78.328	AKP	Both

AKP Justice and Development Party; *CHP* Republican People's Party; *MHP* Nationalist Action Party; *BDP* Independent Democracy Party; *BBP* Great Unity Party

Data Preparation and Screening

The raw data[10] contained several missing values to work on before further analysis. A quick glance at the data set revealed that most missing values are caused by the absence of one survey (either from the mayor or the deputy mayor), thus a pattern in missing values is evident. For the rest, the missing values are random and less than 10% for most variables. There have been only two variables (MOB2 and MOB6) with a considerably high number of missing values.[11] MOB2 is about utilization of immovable property, shows the ratio of annual generated income from immovable properties. In fact, municipalities do not necessarily keep these data for their budget plans. Therefore, the extra work needed to collect or to find the data for the question might be the reason for the lack of responses. MOB6, on the other hand, reflects the physical and technical adequacy in the municipality. The variable is the mean score of 5 Likert-items capturing the adequacy in (1) computer and computer hardware, (2) technical equipment and machinery, (3) internet connection and computer software, (4) physical situation of civil servant's offices, and (5) physical situation of manager's offices. There could be several reasons for the lack of responses, but since it is an opinion-based question addressed to deputy mayors and/or head of departments, the respondents might have been reluctant to provide a genuine answer about the physical conditions of the municipality. Furthermore, one municipality has sent the survey back with missing the page that included the information for the variable.

There are several ways to deal with missing data. An easy and safer way is the listwise or pairwise exclusion of missing cases. However, considering the limitations on the sample size, listwise exclusion of cases with one survey would mean a 30% decrease in sample size, which is an extreme loss of information. The missing data values are generated using multiple imputation methods and to avoid any misinterpretation of the created variables, the composition of each variable is checked from a theoretical standpoint. Accordingly, the variables, which are taking an ordinal value between 1 and 5, are rounded off to the nearest acceptable

---

[10] See the Data list in Appendices.

[11] MOB2 has 21% of missing values, and MOB6 has 17%.

number. Nevertheless, there have been only a few variables to round off and their distance to the acceptable numbers is significantly limited.

The internal validity of Likert-scale variables is controlled with Cronbach's alpha scores,[12] and the unidimensionality is further controlled with factor analysis. The only variable with an alpha score relatively lower than the acceptable limit and with a spurious solution in factor analysis is IMP4. This variable is the composite score of the same question directed to mayors and deputy mayors about the level of collaboration in management. Therefore, it is certain that the index variable is covering the same construct.

The common source bias is controlled with Harman's one-factor test, and the normality and linearity assumptions are controlled with histograms and Skewness-Kurtosis tests. Later, the factorability of variables and the suitability of sample size are checked with Bartlett's test of sphericity and Kaiser-Meyer-Olkin (KMO) measure, respectively. All tests have suggested the data are reliable for further analysis.

Data Analysis

Following the ex-ante tests, the intercorrelations of each local government's capacity variable are controlled with polychoric correlations matrixes. Polychoric correlation analysis provides more reliable results if the data set contains ordinal and categorical variables. The absolute value of correlation coefficients less than 0.2 is treated as 'no relationship' or 'a negligible relationship', and an absolute value above 0.4 treated as 'strong relationships'. Among the three correlation matrixes, the only indicator with a value of less than 0.2 has been the 'debt structure' under mobilization capacity. 'Debt structure' indicates the ratio of short-term debts (a due date less than a year) to overall debts. Higher values indicate that the municipality has less flexibility in allocating funds for purchasing goods and services. However, almost 30% of respondents selected '0', indicating that they don't have any short-term debt obligations, thus the variance in responses is quite limited. The rest of the variables show largely strong binary correlations, which is a good indication of the suitability for the factor analysis.

---

[12] The alpha scores give the estimate of reliability, where a score between 0.7 and 0.9 is treated as acceptable and any score lower than 0.5 is interpreted as unacceptable.

The exploratory factor analysis with *varimax* rotation resulted in factors, which are theoretically representative of each local government's capacity variable. A general rule of thumb on factor selection is to retain the components with an eigenvalue higher than 1, as lesser values account for less variance than the original variable. Another method is the scree plot analysis. It is also important to evaluate the cumulative number that accounts for the percentage of the total variance measured by the factors. Accordingly, mobilization capacity and decision-making capacity variables have resulted in only one factor that satisfied all the selection criteria. However, implementation capacity has resulted in three different factors fulfilling the selection criteria. Since mobilization capacity contains most variables in comparison with other two capacity variables, it is expectable the data can capture different standalone variables. In fact, a closer look at the data has shown that Factor 1 is mostly related with the systems and practices in implementation and least influenced by qualitative and quantitative features of mayor and staff. Factor 2 is mostly influenced by management capacity components demonstrating rather the management capacity. Factor 3 is, on the other hand, influenced by the quantitative aspects of human resources that can be interpreted as the sufficiency of staff. Eventually, Factor 1 is selected as the most representative factor for the implementation capacity variables. The pairwise correlation of each constructed variable confirmed that the local government's capacity variables are significantly correlated with each other ($p < 0.05$).

Table 5.2 presents the descriptive statistics of mobilization capacity (MOB), decision-making capacity (DM), implementation capacity (IMP), decentralization (DEC), local capacity (LC), central

Table 5.2 Descriptive statistics

Variable	Obs.	Mean	Std. dev.	Min	Max
MOB	33	−8.78E-09	0.918457	−2.594843	1.358933
DM	33	−4.06E-09	0.9456926	−2.19453	1.535497
IMP	33	−5.42E-09	0.9435443	−2.325766	2.099706
DEC	33	0.2506061	0.1067889	0.053	0.527
LC	33	−0.2148455	0.6977461	−1.7329	1.0493
Inf	33	2.849865	0.7824249	1.25	4.5
Pop	33	158,030.4	121,153.4	19,075	525,497
PolDiv	33	0.6969697	0.4666937	0	1
Party	33	0.4573636	0.0763339	0.31	0.65

180   E. TAN

government's influence (Inf), size of the province (Pop), the political diversity between governing party at local and central government (PolDiv), and the strength of governing political party in municipal management (Party). The data are normally distributed, and standard deviations show a good variance of the sample in local government capacity variables.

The scatterplot graph between *Pop* and *DM* hinted a logarithmic relationship indicating that with a population increase, there is a decreasing slope in the decision-making capacity. In fact, an increased population could lead to increased flow of information from the locality, and thus inclusion in the decision-making process would be more challenging. In order to examine if the logarithmic transformation of *Pop* would indicate a better fit with *DM* variable, a new variable '*lnPop*' is generated. A re-run of the correlation analysis with *lnPop* has provided better results, even though *DM* remained the only key variable with a higher correlation. Furthermore, both *DEC* and *Party* range between 0 and 1. A logarithmic transformation of both variables fits better for the visual and statistical interpretation of the relationships. The new variables '*logDec*' and '*logParty*' are created by $\log(x)=\log(x/1-x)$.

Table 5.3 shows the final correlation matrix after logarithmic transformations, where high and significant correlations are highlighted in bold. First of all, the matrix shows that all key variables of local governance capacity, local capacity and decentralization are highly correlated. As far as the control variables are concerned, *PolDiv* has a high negative correlation with *IMP* and *LC*, but a high positive correlation with *Inf* and

Table 5.3 Correlation matrix

	MOB	*DM*	*IMP*	*logDec*	*LC*	*Inf*	*lnPop*	*PolDiv*	*log-Party*
MOB	1								
DM	**0.742**	1							
IMP	**0.422**	**0.388**	1						
logDec	**0.688**	**0.716**	**0.384**	1					
LC	**0.597**	**0.734**	**0.326**	**0.896**	1				
Inf	0.077	−0.025	0.079	0.157	−0.047	1			
lnPop	0.292	**0.441**	0.165	0.224	0.214	0.015	1		
PolDiv	−0.175	−0.199	**−0.505**	−0.139	**−0.322**	**0.438**	0.033	1	
logParty	0.244	0.177	0.066	−0.102	−0.220	0.227	**0.419**	**0.304**	1

logParty. This relationship suggests that AKP municipalities have usually lower implementation capacities, are present in the provinces with lower socio-economic development, and perceive the central government's influence in local government high. This statement is also consistent with the input from previous chapters that the distance between local and central government is strikingly narrow in the case of AKP, and the central government is an important actor in local governance. Moreover, the relationship between *PolDiv* and *Party* suggests that AKP municipalities are elected mostly with strong electoral support, which implies a stronger control of party politics in municipal management. I think the most interesting implication of this set of relationships is that this homogenous concentration of party politics in local government shows a distinctively negative correlation with implementation capacity, which suggests the municipality does not find much incentive to invest in the management systems and practices to improve the effectiveness in implementation. Tentatively, we can even infer from this relationship a presence of clientelistic relationship that the municipal management is more driven by the influence of political actors. In fact, this interpretation is consistent with Goldfrank's findings in Latin American cities; '*In cities with a strongly institutionalized party, decentralization will likely result in elite capture and exclusionary politics*'.

On the other hand, the correlation between *lnPop* and *PolDiv* suggests that the governing parties in more populous provinces usually have stronger electoral support. It is noteworthy to mention, that the population variable shows a significant correlation neither with decentralization variables nor local government capacity variables except the decision-making capacity. However, without regression analysis, it is premature to omit any possible influence of population or other control variables may exercise over the relationship between decentralization and capacity variables. This will be looked into in the following part.

REGRESSION MODELS

The correlation analysis of key variables supported the argument that there are linear correlations between local governance capacity, local capacity, and decentralization. The next step is to understand how these relationships are wired and which model can best explain the variance in the decentralization variable. It is also important to control any conditional effect of government capacity variables affecting their influence on decentralization variable. For instance, the effect of implementation capacity on decentralization can increase (or decrease) for different values of decision-making capacity or mobilization capacity. Therefore, the government capacity variables are regressed separately, together and with the interaction terms against decentralization variable by using ordinary least square (OLS) methods. Later, local capacity and control variables (i.e., population, political diversity, party affiliation, the influence of central government) are included in the regression models, and any extraneous relationship is controlled. Since the sample size is relatively limited, the significance level of the p-value is selected starting from $p < 0.1$.

Before OLS regressions, the underlying assumptions of linearity and normality are controlled visually (scatterplot and QQ-plots) and via statistical tests (Kolmogorov-Smirnov). The relationships among variables do not signify any nonlinearity. Only mobilization capacity has shown characteristics of a negatively skewed data due to three significant outliers. The outliers are kept in the analysis as there is no particular reason to remove them and the Kolmogorov-Smirnov test did not show that the normal distribution assumption is violated.

Table 5.4 presents the regression results of the relationships. The first three models indicate that each local government capacity variable is individually a significant predictor of the variation of $logDec$. However, if all variables are included in multiple regression analysis, mobilization capacity and decision-making capacity remain the only two significant predictors. When local capacity is added into the equation, the changes in R^2 and Root MSE show a significant increase in the predictive value of the model. Nevertheless, the most striking change in the later model is that the coefficient of decision-making variable drops significantly, and its p-value becomes insignificant. This shows that local capacity has a confounding effect on decision-making variable. Unlike an intermediate variable, a confounder does not imply a causal relationship between the independent and third variable, but it removes the distortion which can obscure the relationship between independent and dependent variables. One explanation for this phenomenon could be that e-governance capacity indicators have an important influence on measuring decision-making capacity and higher e-governance capacity largely relies on the socio-economic factors (e.g., infrastructure, literacy level, and the number of computers in the household). Bearing in mind, that other alternative

Table 5.4 OLS regressions

Ind. Var. logDec	Model 1		Model 2		Model 3		Model 4		Model 5		Model 6		Model 7		Model 8		Beta coef.
	Coef.	Std. err.	Coef.	Std. err.	Coef.	Std. err.	Coef.	Std. err.	Coef.	Std. err.	Coef.	Std. err.	Coef.	Std. err.	Coef.	Std. err.	
MOB	0.5****	0.1					0.238*	0.14	0.299*	0.16	0.274**	0.1	0.312***	0.1	0.283***	0.088	0.388
DM			0.507****	0.09			0.315**	0.13	0.4**	0.14	0.027	0.1	0.009	0.1	0.024	0.091	0.034
IMP					0.272***	0.19	0.052	0.1	0.102	0.1	0.061	0.06	0.068	0.06	0.049	0.054	0.069
MOBxDM									−0.193	0.13	−0.078	0.08	0.021	0.09	0.001	0.078	0.001
MOBxIMP									0.25	0.19	−0.02	0.13	0.054	0.13	0.003	0.114	0.004
DMxIMP									−0.178	0.17	0.113	0.12	0.005	0.12	0.05	0.106	0.055
MOBxDMxIMP									−0.264	0.16	−0.2*	0.1	−0.147	0.1	−0.165	0.089	−0.289
LC											0.756****	0.12	0.753****	0.13	0.779****	0.106	0.812
Inf													0.167**	0.07	0.174***	0.062	0.204
lnPOP													0.05	0.08			
PolDiv													0.126	0.12			
logParty													−0.139	0.23			
R^2	0.47		0.51		0.15		0.57		0.66		0.871		0.912		0.904		
Adj. R^2	0.46		0.5		0.12		0.53		0.56		0.828		0.858		0.867		
Root MSE	0.49		0.48		0.63		0.46		0.44		0.278		0.252		0.244		
F-value	27.8****		32.56****		5.35***		12.87****		6.92****		20.25****		17.17****		24.17****		

Note $N = 33$, $*p < 0.1$, $**p < 0.05$, $***p < 0.01$, $****p < 0.001$

participation channels, such as through proxies or representatives, are mostly ineffective in municipal decision-making, e-governance channels may have even a larger weight in that regard.

Another notable change is that the 3-way interaction term ($MOBxDMxIMP$) becomes a significant predictor and the significance of mobilization capacity as such increases in the later model. Unlike theoretical expectations, the negative coefficient of interaction term indicates a reverse relationship with decentralization variable. The plot between two variables, however, shows a positive trend and two influential negative outliers explain the negative relationship. Therefore, I have reservations about reporting any significant relationship between the 3-way interaction of governance capacity variables and decentralization.

Among control variables, only influence of central government has a statistically significant p-value. As external factors are not necessarily an integral part of the hypotheses, the control variables except Inf are removed in the final model. Expectedly, the removal of the control variables did not make any significant change in the R^2.

The question at this stage is whether there is a measurement error that can explain the strikingly high R^2 value. There are three common causes of high R^2 value that can hint a measurement error. First, there can be too many regressors in the model creating inflation with a little prediction value. The adjusted R^2 is a useful way to control the inflation caused by a large number of variables. In our case, the adjusted R^2 value is almost as high as the R^2 value; thus, this option can be ruled out. Secondly, collinearity and multicollinearity are the usual suspects of high R^2 values, where two or more covariates have high correlations with each other. The problem with multicollinearity is that it does not reduce the predictive power of the model but it affects the calculations regarding the predictors. The correlation matrix of variables shows that there are already high correlations among local government capacity variables (especially between MOB and DM) and LC variable, and there is a chance this could have a certain impact on the value of R^2 value. The extent of collinearity is controlled with Variance Inflation Factor (VIF) of independent variables, but the findings did not point out a problem with multicollinearity. Thirdly, the high R^2 value could be caused by a convenient regressor, which might be related to the dependent variable, thus measuring the same underlying construct. The most important change in the models occurs when LC

5 WHAT IS THE RELATIONSHIP BETWEEN GOVERNANCE CAPACITY ... 185

is included in the equation. 61 different indicators measure the aggregate variable of local capacity, among which two indicators can have an indirect inference with the revenues of municipalities. These are 'budget revenues per person' and 'provincial tax revenues' share in Turkey'. 'Budget revenues per person' measures the per capita value of people living in the province in terms of their contribution to the general budget. 'Provincial tax revenues' share in Turkey' measures the national share of per capita value in revenue and corporate taxes that are potentially collectible in the province. Both indicators can be related with decentralization variable through their influence on municipal revenues. However, it is difficult to argue that higher values would indicate higher values of decentralization, as this influence should be more present in the transfer of shares from the general budget. Moreover, two indicators among 61 indicators would have limited impact on the index value, and thus, it is highly unlikely to explain the high correlation by arguing these two indicators and decentralization variables are measuring the same underlying construct. Therefore, the more plausible explanation of high R^2 value is local capacity variable has high explanatory power with its sixty-one constituting elements, instead of a concealed measurement error.

Following the post-estimation and reliability tests on linearity, multivariate normality, multicollinearity, and homoscedasticity, the Model 8 is selected as the most rigorous and representative model. According to Model 8, a one-unit change in local capacity is associated with an estimated 0.779 unit change in the logarithmic transformation of decentralization by keeping constant other variables. This means that a unit increase in the socio-economic development value would result in a 78% change in the ratio of own-source revenues to all municipal revenues. This is a significant indicator showing the extent to which the socio-economic development influences the financial autonomy of Turkish provincial municipalities. On the other hand, the standardized beta coefficients show that one standard deviation increase in the local capacity variable would result in 0.812 standard deviations change in the dependent variable, which is followed by the influence of mobilization capacity with the standardized beta coefficient 0.388 and of *Inf* with 0.204. This shows that the impact of the change in local capacity on the decentralization variable is almost twice of mobilization capacity and four times higher than the influence of central government variable.

Interpretation of Findings

So what are the highlights that we learn from the Turkish case on the relationship between decentralization and governance capacity? Here are the primary findings and their interpretation:

1. In relation to the research hypotheses set in Chapter 2, we can reject the null hypothesis that local capacity does not have an effect on decentralization. We can also reject the null hypothesis that mobilization capacity does not have an effect on decentralization. Yet, we cannot reject the null hypothesis for decision-making and implementation capacity. In addition, the observed significant relationship between the 3-way interaction of local government capacity variables and decentralization has failed to pass the reliability tests.

2. The standardized beta coefficient scores indicate that the impact of local capacity on the change of the standard deviation is more than two times higher than mobilization capacity. This shows that the local capacity is the most important variable to explain the variance in the financial autonomy of provincial municipalities. Another implication of this result is that a change in the socio-economic conditions would have a distinctively higher impact on the success of decentralization—by referring to its financial autonomy—than any local government capacity change. Therefore, theoretically, we should expect socio-economically more developed provinces to have better outcomes in decentralized governance even with limited local government capacities. By the same token, local governments in socio-economically lagging areas would have limited success in decentralized governance even with higher local government capacities.

3. A change in the local capacity variable is associated both with the change in local government's capacity and decentralization variables. We observe this influence on the change in the p-value of decision-making capacity when local capacity is included in the model. This change shows that local capacity is a confounding variable since it covaries both with local government's capacity and decentralization variables. The confounding effect of local capacity removes the influence of decision-making capacity on decentralization; without local capacity, decision-making capacity befalls as

the most influential local government capacity on decentralization. Confounding influence does not necessarily imply causality but a strong indication of causal relationship. Further studies with structural equation modeling or causal path analysis could provide further insights into causal relationships among local capacity, local government capacity, and decentralization.

4. Among local governance capacity variables, mobilization capacity variable is the only significant predictor of decentralization. Considering that the mobilization capacity is partly captured by the ability to collect taxes and generating revenues through owned immovable, it can directly affect the financial autonomy. However, this effect is much smaller than the influence of socio-economic development on financial autonomy.

5. The only statistically significant predictor among control variables is the perceived influence of central government in local governance. *Inf* does not have any significant correlation with any of the key variables[13] but it explains the variance of decentralization, which is not captured by local capacity.[14] Interestingly, this influence is in a positive direction. This may seem paradoxical but one plausible explanation is that the municipalities in socio-economically more advanced provinces perceive the presence of central government in public governance as more than necessary or asked for. The influence of *Inf* is revealed when the local capacity variable is included in the equation, and it remains a significant predictor only if local capacity is in the equation. Therefore, any alternative theory suggesting that central government is more willing to intervene in economically developed provinces would be invalid, because it would require observation of a significant correlation between *LC* and *Inf* variables.

6. Besides *Inf*, no other control variable has a significant influence on decentralization. This finding is important because it disputes

---

[13] See the correlation matrix in Table 5.3.

[14] This phenomenon happens because *LC* is so highly correlated with *logDec*, the inclusion of *Inf* exposes a relatively small amount of variation that has been previously masked. In order to control whether this argument holds true, a new variable is generated for the residuals between *LC* and *logDec*, and I found out that this variable is significantly correlated with *Inf* and *logDec*.

the role of the municipality's size on the outcomes of decentralization and leaves the socio-economic development as a more important indicator of financial autonomy than the population of the province. Similarly, political differences inside the municipality or with the central government do not suggest a significant influence on the financial autonomy. This does not mean that an arbitrary act by the central government would not adversely affect the financial autonomy of the municipality. Rather, the presumed effect will be limited if local capacity conditions are sufficient enough.

7. The final model has a distinctly high R^2 value, which is uncommon in social sciences. Neither the statistical tests nor the logical analysis of the relationships pointed out a measurement error to justify high R^2 value. The most plausible explanation is that local capacity variable has a high explanatory power due to sixty-one constituting elements. Additionally, the model relies on relatively limited data sample size, and with a larger data set, the high R^2 value can decrease to a certain extent. Nevertheless, the model has a very high explanatory power on the variance of decentralization (Fig. 5.1).

About the hypothesized relationships between governance capacity and decentralization, the findings in the Turkish case suggest

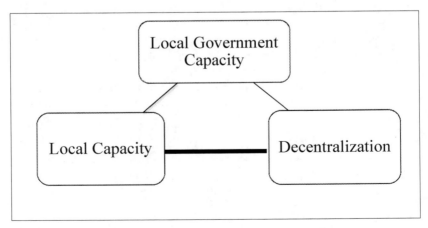

Fig. 5.1 The relationship between decentralization and governance capacity

that local capacity influences decentralization through local government capacities, most saliently in the case of decision-making capacity, but local government capacities also influence decentralization independently through mobilization capacity. Yet, the latter is subservient to the direct influence of local capacity exercises over decentralization.

This relationship is best represented by H2, which assumes both local capacity and local government capacities influence decentralization.[15] Although the direction of relations cannot be derived from the regression analysis, it is logical to interpret that local capacity causes a change both in financial autonomy and local government's capacities. A counter-intuitive argument could suggest a reverse causality between decentralization and socio-economic development. This argument would entail an indirect causality suggesting that an increase in financial autonomy brings better governance of public services and thus affects the indicators measuring the socio-economic development. However, the indicators measuring socio-economic development are not directly affected by municipal services. Indicators in relation to health, education, life quality, and transportation in the province are mostly under the responsibility of central government. Therefore, this alternative explanation of the direction of the relationship between decentralization and local capacity would be theoretically less convincing. Nevertheless, this explanation is valid insofar as the relationship is unidirectional instead of bidirectional. It is still possible to construct a bidirectional relationship between decentralization and socio-economic development. I will return to this point in the following chapter.

CONCLUSION

This chapter tested the theoretical expectations between governance capacity and decentralization in the case of Turkish local government. Financial autonomy of local government is treated as the quintessence of successful decentralization in terms of public governance. The reason rests on the assumption of if local government's finances are more

---

[15] The thickness of lines is not representing the actual level of influence among the variables rather it suggests that the influence of local capacity on decentralization is higher than government capacity.

dependent on local resources; then, the local government should be more responsive to local needs and thus more accountable, transparent as well as effective in local governance. The question here was whether the local government's managerial and organizational capacities or local socio-economic conditions were more decisive—or decisive at all- on the extent of financial autonomy.

The primary empirical finding has been that financial autonomy is strongly associated with local socio-economic conditions and to a lesser extent with local government's capacities, more specifically with mobilization capacity. This finding suggests that, with decentralization, we should expect socio-economically more developed provinces to improve their public governance even with limited managerial and organizational capacities. By the same token, local governments in socio-economically lagging areas would have limited success even with higher managerial and organizational capacities. However, the confounding relationship observed between socio-economic development and decision-making capacity; as well as high correlations between local government capacities and socio-economic development suggest socio-economically more developed provinces have higher local government capacities. So, in reality, envisaging a substituting relationship between local capacity and local government capacity could have limited practical implications. Instead, it is more likely, socio-economic development dictates the outcome of public governance.

The question is now to what extent these findings are generalizable to other country cases? In decentralization studies, it is difficult to find robust indicators for cross-country comparisons, especially concerning with subnational government capacities, which are limited and extremely contingent on contextual conditions. In the same vein, in Turkish case, regulative and politico-cultural conditions may have accentuated the impact of socio-economic development on financial autonomy.

So it is important to look for other empirical cases, which can back up the observed relationship between socio-economic development and decentralization outcomes. Furthermore, is this a phenomenon limited with developing countries, which usually experience more stark regional differences in terms of socio-economic development, or is it a global phenomenon encompassing developed countries as well? On the other hand, what are the implications of these findings on development literature, where some studies presume a causal link between decentralization and development? These and more on how asymmetrical decentralization policies may improve public governance outcomes will be discussed in the next and final chapter of the book.

REFERENCES

Boone, H. N., & Boone, D. A. (2012). Analyzing Likert Data. *Journal of Extension, 50*(2). https://www.joe.org/joe/2012april/tt2.php.

Clason, D. L., & Dormody, T. J. (1994). Analyzing Data Measured by Individual Likert-Type Items. *Journal of Agricultural Education, 35*(4), 31–35.

Creswell, W. J. (2003). *Research Design: Qualitative, Quantitative, Mixed Methods Approaches.* London: Sage.

Gideon, L. (2012). *Handbook on Survey Methodology for the Social Sciences.* New York: Springer.

Goldfrank, B. (2007). The Politics of Deepening Local Democracy: Decentralization, Party Institutionalization, and Participation. *Comparative Politics, 39*(2), 147–168.

Groves, R. M., Fowler, F. J., Couper, M. P., Lepkowski, J. M., Singer, E., & Tourangeau, R. (2004). *Survey Methodology.* Hoboken, NJ: Wiley.

Uebersax, J. S. (2006). Likert Scales: Dispelling the Confusion. *Statistical Methods for Rater Agreement Website.* Available at: http://john-uebersax.com/stat/likert.htm. Accessed July 18, 2018.

CHAPTER 6

Conclusion: Toward an Asymmetrical Decentralization Design

Turkish case has shown us the strong influence of socio-economic development on the outcome of decentralization vis-à-vis local government's capacities. It is important to question whether this is a country-specific phenomenon or we can trace comparable findings in other cases.

But before taking the argument any further, let us first rewind and remember the theoretical underpinnings linking decentralization to better governance. As the argument goes, endowing local government with political and administrative authority on public service provision, making it more dependent on its own resources and letting local governments compete for attracting citizens (i.e., the sources of income), leads to higher allocative efficiency in public service provisions. Furthermore, local government once assumes the responsibility for public service delivery, utilizes its proximity to citizens to pinpoint public needs more effectively, and thereby promotes allocative efficiency in the delivery of public goods. These two sets of formal theories of decentralization, the competition-based and information-based theories, are further enriched with new public governance and new public service delivery theories, by attributing a higher role to citizens and societal actors in public services through co-creation and co-production, which enhances governance innovation and thus production efficiency in decentralized governance. Besides, making the local government more dependent on its own sources makes local government more responsive on local needs and demands, and thus creates a mutual interest between society and local government to further the conditions of democratic governance such

© The Author(s) 2019
E. Tan, *Decentralization and Governance Capacity*, Public Sector Organizations, https://doi.org/10.1007/978-3-030-02047-7_6

193

as accountability, transparency, and citizen participation, increasing the effectiveness of public governance.

And many scholars, indeed, found out positive findings suggesting that decentralization leads to improved governance, but these studies are often conflicted by failing cases in developing and transition countries, and several institutional, organizational and cultural contingencies are brought up to improve the predictability of decentralization reforms in governance outcomes. So, the question is, to what extent socio-economic development can explain the differences in decentralization outcomes and whether decentralization policies based on socio-economic differences can improve public governance.

Thus, this final chapter's goals are (1) to evidence that a certain level of socio-economic development is necessary in order to decentralization theories to hold; (2) to argue an asymmetrical decentralization design based on provincial socio-economic development can improve the predictability and success of decentralization policies; (3) and to share certain policy recommendations to support effective implementation of asymmetric decentralization arrangements and on capacity building practices in public sector organizations.

DECENTRALIZATION AND DEVELOPMENT—PRECARIOUS RELATIONSHIP?

Let's start with the relationship between decentralization and development. 'Decentralization leads to development' is a widely promoted idea among international donor organizations such as the UNDP, EU, and World Bank. For example, 'Decentralized Governance for Development' program of UNDP advocates that decentralized governance is 'crucial to attaining human development and MDGs'. Not only donor organizations in developing and transitional countries but also OECD promote fiscal decentralization policies to enhance economic growth among its members.

Basically, the idea is that decentralized governance improves the institutional development and economic growth more effectively than redistributive mechanisms of central government. Remarkably, there are no formal theories, which directly link decentralization to development; instead, there are theories that suggest certain pathways whereby decentralization may lead to development (Martinez-Vazguez and McNab 1997; Buser 2011). Our knowledge on the relationship between decentralization and development relies predominantly on the empirical studies from the political economy literature, where the main body of scholarly work focuses on the relationship between decentralization (primarily fiscal decentralization) and economic growth. Nonetheless, as we have briefly seen in the Introduction chapter, the findings are inconsistent to confirm a relationship between these two concepts, and there are wide discrepancies between findings depending on the type of decentralization (e.g., revenue-based or expenditure-based fiscal decentralization), selection of country cases (e.g., OECD countries or a mixture of developing and developed countries), the extent of time-series data, or the level of analysis (subnational or cross-country comparison). Even studies from same country cases appear to have diametrically opposing findings. For instance, in two studies on China, a time-series analysis from 1970 to 1993 found a significant and positive correlation (see Lin and Liu 2000), whereas a time-series analysis from 1980 to 1992 (see Zhang and Zou 1998) found a significant and negative correlation. Moreover, the findings do not necessarily suggest a divergent pattern between developed and developing countries, albeit most inconsistencies (i.e., failure to find a significant relationship or finding a negative relationship) pertain to the studies incorporating developing countries.

Indeed, most critical studies against decentralization theories stemmed from the findings in developing and least developed countries; however, there are not many studies underline a causal pathway between the level of development and the outcome of decentralization. Rather, these critical studies mostly underscore administrative and regulative deficiencies encompassing state apparatus, the absence of democratic and participative institutions that mostly hinge on cultural or historical dynamics, and lacking organizational and managerial capacities at the subnational and national level as the culprit of decentralization failures. The problem is institutional heterogeneities, and differences in politico-cultural elements in cross-country studies hinder the effective control of these potential exogenous influences on the relationship between decentralization and development.

Remarkably, a number of empirical studies in single country cases treat the relationship between decentralization and development from a counter-causal perspective, arguing that decentralization leads to socio-economic development in subnational level (see Bartlett et al. 2013, 2018; Alibegovic 2013). The problem with these causal claims is that in the absence of formal theories to support empirical findings, these findings can easily turn into counterintuitive arguments. For instance, in her essay about the impact of decentralization on local regional development in Croatia, Alibegovic (2013) implements methodologically similar choices to my study in Turkey to analyzing the relationship between decentralization and local development. Alibegovic adopts regional GDP per capita[1] as the indicator of regional development and regressed it against several indicators for fiscal decentralization and observes a statistically significant relationship between regional development and subnational government's share of own tax revenues. She concludes that a higher level of fiscal autonomy is expected to exert higher local and regional development and recommends central governments to pursue fiscal decentralization for local and regional development. Although two studies draw different conclusions, the statistically significant relationship between regional/local development and decentralization hints the generalizability of results in other country cases. Yet, interpreting this statistical finding as the impact of decentralization on development is, to say the least, overly optimistic. Personally, a more logical assumption would be that higher regional economic development affects the own tax revenues, thus increasing the subnational government's financial autonomy.

Nonetheless, we can still theorize certain pathways, albeit not directly, from decentralization to development. A possible causal pathway between decentralization and development can be established via improvements in public governance (see Oates 1993). Decentralization theories hypothesize several links between decentralized governance and more efficient and effective public governance. Additionally, public governance is important for instance in the delivery of sustainable development goals (Bouckaert et al. 2016). It is also possible to create a bidirectional relationship, such as socio-economic development is important in order for decentralization to lead better public governance, and better public governance leads to socio-economic development. However, not to create a tautological argument, let us first take a look to what extent socio-economic development can explain the relationship between decentralization and effective public governance.

To start with, there are indeed some studies reporting the impact of socio-economic development in explaining different governance

---

[1] Although higher GDP per capita does not fully indicate socio-economic development, it is the most widespread measurement of access to wealth, and higher wealth is highly correlated with higher socio-economic parameters.

6 CONCLUSION: TOWARD AN ASYMMETRICAL DECENTRALIZATION DESIGN   197

outcomes following decentralization reforms. For example, Lessman (2012) suggests that the relationship between decentralization and regional inequality depends on the level of economic development.[2] Accordingly, decentralization tends to increase regional inequality in poorer countries whereas it decreases it in richer countries. Hence, he recommends different decentralization policies should apply to developing and developed countries. Similarly, Hodge et al.'s (2015) research about the relationship between decentralization and neonatal mortality rates in the case of Indonesia suggest that the situation in poorer regions has been worsened following decentralization reforms, whereas it has improved in richer regions. Concurrently, Thede (2009) reports divergent results in seven developing countries from Asia, Africa, and East Europe about health and education services. In these cases, decentralization has created more venues and access to health and education facilities, yet in the meantime, it led to a greater differentiation in access to higher quality services between richer and poorer municipalities. Finally, Barrett et al. (2007) also emphasize the conditionality of socio-economic development at local and regional level as a potential determinant on the outcome of decentralization practices, but there the socio-economic conditions are addressed as part of contextual realities of the country cases, and the question of how socio-economic conditions influence decentralization outcomes has been left intact.

Here, Bardhan (2002)'s work can unpack certain causal pathways to show how socio-economic regional differences can lead divergent results among richer and poorer regions and thus undermine convergence assumption of fiscal decentralization theorem. Bardhan brings forward six possible ways, whereby fiscal decentralization may lead to divergent results among regions in developing countries. First, the idea of mobile citizens voting with their feet fails to apply in developing countries as residents are often restrained from revealing their preferences with public goods, and many of the public goods are site- and community-specific which allows the exclusion of outsiders. Second, accounting and monitoring systems are usually weaker in developing countries, which compel the central government to adopt certain incentives and devices to check on public service bureaucracy in order to minimize transaction costs in

---

[2] Lessman (2012) mentions a possible cutoff value of US $2900 GDP of per capita and suggests countries lower than this threshold might experience negative redistribution outcomes with expenditure decentralization, while richer countries might benefit.

the allocation of funds due to corruption. Third, even in a few democratic developing countries, the institutions of local democracy and public accountability are weak. Thus, local elite captures and clientelistic arrangements are more often the concern in the case of developing countries, where higher transaction costs in public expenditures can be even more detrimental in regions with socio-economic deprivations. Fourth, the efficiency in public service delivery can be secondary to reaching out to poor and disadvantaged communities on assessing the governance performance in developing countries. Especially, the redistributive pressures can inflate local and state borrowing at the local government (as in the cases of South Africa, Brazil, and Argentina) undermining the macroeconomic stabilization. Furthermore, often in developing countries, the central government is in a more advantageous and potent position to safeguard redistributive mechanisms to disadvantaged groups especially concerning education, health, and investment services. Fifth, income is often geographically concentrated in developing countries, and natural resources and infrastructural facilities are confined in specific areas. Therefore, the assumption of through revenue decentralization an interregional competition can be engendered has certain limitations in applications. Maybe consequently, decentralization in developing countries is primarily about providing central tax revenues to lower levels of government accompanied by increased public expenditure assignments, rather than empowering local government to collect taxes.[3] Sixth, technical and administrative capacities are not equally distributed among regions or among administrations. Although Bardhan acknowledges that this is not only a concern for developing countries, the conditions are more severe in developing countries. Most of the time talented people are stationed in the capital city either by appointment or by market forces, whereas local governments can hardly attract trained and more qualified personnel in administration.

However, we know that developing countries are not affected only by socio-economic deprivations but they also suffer from institutional weaknesses. For instance, the widely acclaimed work of Acemoğlu and Robertson 'Why Nations Fail?' places the strength of institutions at the core of their thesis to predicate different development outcomes in developing and transition countries. Therefore, in order to argue that socio-economic development, indeed, determines the efficiency of

---

[3] Actually, this is very representative for Turkey.

decentralized governance, it is important to look at the cases of developed countries. For instance, the study of Warner (2003) on US rural government suggests that rural governments lacking certain managerial and local capacity conditions cannot support the interjurisdictional competition to attain efficiency in public service delivery. Although this study does not make a distinction between managerial and local capacity, it does hint that capacity differences among rural governments are more systemic than circumstantial. A recent study by Alonso and Andrews (2018) on English local government is, however, more illustrative on the impact of socio-economic development on the efficiency outcomes of decentralized governance. Alonso and Andrews state that fiscal decentralization can increase the productive efficiency of public service delivery, but this benefit is contingent upon deprivation levels, i.e., local socio-economic development level. The authors state; *'our evidence indicates that local governments can potentially become more efficient by raising more of their own tax revenue, the efficiency gains that those serving deprived populations can realize by doing this may be small compared to those achievable in affluent areas... it may be that budgetary autonomy should be encouraged in prosperous areas, but that a more nuanced evaluation of its costs and benefits is required in deprived areas'*. This finding is strongly in congruence with my findings in Turkish local government.

So, the efficiency argument of decentralized governance is susceptible to varying socio-economic conditions that are more adamant in developing countries but not exclusive to developing countries. However, effective public governance through decentralization does not only rest on efficient delivery of public goods and services but also on the democratic accountability of local government in a decentralized system. Therefore, it is legitimate to assume that adverse effect of resource deprivations in productive efficiencies can be mitigated (at least to a certain extent) by the creation of more democratically accountable local governments and supportive regulative frameworks. The problem is, as Bardhan implicitly points out, only a few developing countries have developed local democratic institutions; therefore it is difficult to control the influence of democratic accountability separate from the influence of development. Here, the findings of Treisman (2002) in an exhaustive study among 166 countries can be suggestive. In one of the few cross-country decentralization studies that include both democracy indicators and economic development indicators, Treisman reports that economic development is positively correlated with the indicators of decision-making, electoral, appointment, and personnel decentralization, as well as fiscal decentralization if the country size is controlled. Treisman interprets this finding as in more developed countries, subnational units are more likely to have significant decision-making autonomy, to have veto power over central decisions, to have a larger share of total public administrative employment and fiscal responsibilities, and to have officials who are locally elected rather than centrally appointed. Hence, Treisman is suggesting here, democracy or democratic governance is, in fact, a condition augmented by the level of socio-economic development. This argument is supported by a further finding of the study that the correlation between democracy and decentralization disappears when the impact of economic development is controlled, because of the high correlation between democracy[4] and development. The only type of decentralization indicator which remains correlated with democracy after controlling the impact of development is that 'proportion of subnational tiers with elected executives', which indicates whether the central power is devolved or deconcentrated. So not only local governments are more prone to assume increased autonomy in more developed countries, but also central government's decision on decentralization toward lower tiers of government is shifting in congruence with the development level of the country. In fact, this statement is supported by my findings at the Turkish local government. Local governments with better socio-economic hinterland perceive the influence of central government more than necessary, suggesting that they are more willing to presume power from central government, whereas socio-economically less developed provinces are looking for more central government's involvement and investing more on the relationships with central government.[5]

---

[4] In the Treisman's study, democracy is measured by the Freedom House's political liberties ratings.

[5] Here, I want to open a small parenthesis for the case of Porto Allegre. Porto Allegre's experience with participatory budgeting and effective inclusive policies toward marginalized groups has been an exemplary case of successful local initiatives and is been often cited in development literature and by international donor organizations to argue how decentralization policies can be successful in developing countries. When I first observed the strong role of socio-economic development in the Turkish case, I started to look for other countries whether socio-economic development can explain effective decentralized governance outcomes, and I also looked to Porto Allegre. I was positively surprised to learn that Porto Allegre has one of the highest socio-economic indicators in Brazil, despite not being one of most populous (see http://www.socioeconomicatlas.rs.gov.br and http://www.atlasbrasil.org.br).

6 CONCLUSION: TOWARD AN ASYMMETRICAL DECENTRALIZATION DESIGN 201

Does it mean that if a local government does not have an adequate socio-economic basis, the central government should replace the local government in service provision? Also what about the market alternatives? Market-led public good provision or privatization of public services could be less of a viable alternative in developing countries, but in more dynamic market conditions of developed countries, private markets can deliver certain public services directly thus allowing the local government more effectively to manage its resources in public governance.

There are nonetheless at least two potential fallacies in this line of argumentation. First of all, decentralization theories assume that local government should rely on the local resources in order to support productive efficiency and democratic governance. This is, in fact, a point raised by Rodriguez-Pose and Ezcurra (2011): '*An important, but often forgotten, initial premise is that fiscal decentralization implies a mobilization of resources. Subnational governments, by the simple fact of being granted greater autonomy and funds, are compelled into mobilizing the resources in their own territory, rather than wait for solutions or for the provision of public goods and services to come from a central, more remote, authority*'. Furthermore, the prominence of local government on public service provision is not solely for its proximity to citizens but also local governments are politically accountable on their local constituents unlike field agencies of central government. Therefore, from a principal-agent perspective, local governments are expected to be more responsive to citizen's needs under democratic conditions. For example, Faguet (2001) reports that in the case of Bolivia, devolution made the local governments more responsive to local needs in policy prioritization even in the poorest and smallest municipalities. Another interesting study in Bolivia by De la Fuente and Vazquez (2005) reports, the people interviewed from rural indigenous communities claim that decentralization has brought them greater wealth, despite their analysis did not support that decentralization had a demonstrable impact of poverty reduction in rural areas (also see Thede 2009). This finding suggests there might be a behavioral impact of decentralization on marginalized communities by creating a sense of communal empowerment; even it is not backed by (at least immediate) tangible outputs. Similarly, some recent studies found out decentralization is associated with higher trust in public institutions (Ligthart and Van Oudheusden 2015), and people tend to express higher satisfaction with the decentralized delivery of public services regardless of the actual improvement in public service quality (e.g., Hellman et al. 2003; Diaz-Serrano and Rodríguez-Pose 2015).

Secondly, the study of Warner[6] shows that the rural governments relying on private markets and privatization of public services have higher inequality on service provision in the face of uneven markets. In these cases, rich people can afford the good quality public services while poor people have to content themselves with poor quality public services. Yet from a critical point of view, we can question whether income inequality undermines necessarily the underlying principles of decentralization and better governance thesis? In many countries, private markets deliver various public goods including health and education services, which allow governments to reduce costs and increase the efficiency of public service provisions. In practice, the ways that income inequality can impair the underpinnings of decentralization theorem are manifold. First, countries with lower levels of income inequality tend to grow faster (Persson and Tabellini 1994; Birdsall et al. 1995; Deininger and Squire 1996). Second, countries with higher income inequalities usually have less social capital, i.e., elements that buttress trust, reciprocity, and cooperation in a society (Wilkinson 2000). Third, high levels of inequality and/or low levels of social capital in a country predict high rates of antisocial behaviors (Elgar et al. 2009; Hermann et al. 2008). In other words, with higher levels of income equality, higher efficiency and effectiveness in governance through co-creation and co-production with citizens is much harder to attain. Fourth, higher income inequality and thus lower social capital appears to increase the psychological stress among the poor thus making poor unhealthier and also leading higher crime rates and violence in society (Chon 2012; Elgar and Aitken 2010; Hsieh and Pugh 1993; Daly et al. 2001).[7] Consequently, even cost-saving in public expenditures through privatization of public service provisions can be untenable in the case of higher income inequalities. A more astounding finding is that the influence of income inequality appears to be independent of the absolute levels of poverty (Wilkinson 2000). So not the level of poverty but more the perception of citizens on inequality to access public good would undermine the effectiveness of private markets as an alternative in public governance. I will return to this point later on discussing

[6] Ibid.

[7] For a more extensive discussion on the relationship between income inequality, public health, violence, and crime, see Sapolsky (2017: 291–296).

6 CONCLUSION: TOWARD AN ASYMMETRICAL DECENTRALIZATION DESIGN   203

the design of effective decentralization policies, but at that moment, it is important to keep in mind that the absence of socio-economic parameters does not necessarily suggest replacing local government in public service provisions by central government or private markets. Rather, it suggests a smart design in the share of responsibilities between local and central government, and effective supportive mechanisms in public governance when it is needed.

ASYMMETRICAL DECENTRALIZATION FOR BETTER GOVERNANCE

In the previous section, I argued that socio-economic development could, in fact, explain the relationship between decentralization and better public governance both in subnational level but also in cross-country level. Its impact is not limited to the efficiency argument of decentralized governance but also expands to the democracy aspect of decentralization theories. So in this section, I will attempt to create a theoretical explanation why decentralization policies contingent on provincial socio-economic development can lead to higher returns of improvement in public governance. For that, I will refer to political economy and public administration theories, and discuss how an asymmetrical decentralization design can improve certain shortcomings of symmetrical decentralization designs. But first, I will take a look at the applications of asymmetric decentralization in public administration literature and discuss some possible ways of asymmetric arrangements in public governance.

Asymmetric Decentralization

Asymmetric decentralization among same level subnational government is not something new in public administration, but its applications to public governance have been limited. A majority of scholarly work on asymmetrical decentralization stems from federalism studies (see Tarlton 1965; Bauböck 2001; McGarry and O'Leary 2012). In federalism literature, the idea of asymmetric decentralization is usually treated as an instrument in accommodation of diversities and against secessionist movements of regions that differ ethnically, culturally, and/or historically from the rest of the country. In this definition of asymmetrical federalism/decentralization, asymmetry is usually the result of bottom-up demands and power relationship between central government and regional/local government (e.g., asymmetric federalism in Spain and in Russia).

Recently, a new area of studies has started to appear to distinguish asymmetric arrangements beyond the federalist understanding of asymmetric decentralization (see Holzhacker et al. 2016; Watts 2005; Wehner 2000). Accordingly, asymmetrical decentralization can refer to politically- or capacity-driven asymmetries; de facto and de jure (constitutional) asymmetries; between constituent units and peripheral constituent units[8]; and between transitional (as 'variable speeds') and permanent asymmetries (as 'variable geometry') (Watts 2010).

Insofar to my knowledge, the earliest account[9] on asymmetric decentralization to improve public governance appears in 'Rethinking decentralization in developing countries' (Litvack et al. 1998: 23). The core argument here is different instruments may have different effects in different circumstances, especially concerning with underlying economic, demographic, and social diversities in a multitude of governments and regions, and therefore different approaches may be needed to achieve similar (or acceptable) results. In order to accommodate these different approaches, the central government should adopt different policies for different units ('treating different units differently');

> An important element of such an approach is the principle of asymmetrical decentralization. For example, in many countries, it may be feasible decentralize political, economic, and administrative responsibilities to large urban areas. Similarly, at the regional level, fiscal and administrative capacity may make it easier to decentralize responsibilities only to some provinces or states. In other cases, it may be feasible to decentralize responsibilities directly from central government to the private sector rather than to local governments.

[8] For example, overseas territories or incorporated territories can be regarded as peripheral constituent units.

[9] Actually, in an earlier account, Shah (1994) proposes asymmetrical arrangements at local government based on certain capacity conditions as a way to improve public service efficiency. However, in the paper, asymmetric decentralization is treated as the allocation of different public services between upper and lower tier of local government, and the idea of asymmetric arrangement across the same tier of local government is only tentatively touched upon.

6 CONCLUSION: TOWARD AN ASYMMETRICAL DECENTRALIZATION DESIGN

Litvack et al. suggest asymmetric assignments of public services to manage administrative capacity problems in the post-apartheid South Africa, where many newly established regional and local authorities lacked the capacities to effectively deliver health and education services. They propose to assign the delivery of public services only to those cases, which show the capacity to manage these services. Acknowledging the political difficulty to convince elected representatives to receive less autonomy than their counterparts, they propose conditionality and regulative arrangements to ensure compliance with asymmetric arrangements:

> Depending on the country, solutions may be sought through such means as making the application of particular decentralization provision conditions on the satisfaction of a number of preconditions, on the voluntary assumption of certain financing or other obligations, or on the signing of a contract that permits individuation of both the timing and extent of decentralization. Such legislation assures the ultimate decentralization of political and economic powers and does not leave it to the discretion of the center, but rather, to the actions of elected representatives of subnational governments.

This paragraph sets out the discussion on how an asymmetrical decentralization design can be possible. From the paragraph, we can infer three principles on the design of asymmetrical decentralization (1) decentralization of powers and associated responsibilities in governance should rest on objective criteria that are acknowledged by all parties, (2) decentralization decisions regarding fiscal and administrative provisions should be free from the discretion of central government, and (3) the design should be flexible enough to allow subnational governments to assume further powers in time with the condition to deliver certain results. However, this idea of asymmetric decentralization design has not been much dwelled by scholars and policy practitioners and remained as a fringe area in public administration literature. I think the central impediment to further the idea was to decide upon the initial precondition to buttress the system. Here, the prevalence of socio-economic development, hereafter I will use it interchangeably with local capacity, in explaining governance outcomes presents a chance to further this idea's application in public administration. Ditto, the first condition of the asymmetric decentralization design can be fulfilled with an arrangement according to the local capacities of provinces. As an initial stage in reform design, local governments can be clustered under different development levels that match different fiscal and administrative autonomies and discretions in public service delivery. In this system, provinces with higher indices can be authorized with higher fiscal autonomy such as levying taxes and higher self-financing responsibilities in expenditure assignments, whereas regions with lower indices can have co-financing options and share of responsibilities in public services with central government's agencies.

The second principle, exempting decentralization decisions from the discretion of the central government, is essential to create trust and sustainability within the system. Overlooking this dimension can foster passing the buck or blame-avoidance in public governance. In other words, if the decision of furthering decentralization is left to central government's discretion, it will be difficult to keep the local government accountable on poor performances, as the blame can easily be shifted to central government's political intentions. The challenge here is, in the absence of central government's discretion, there is a need of linking the extension of administrative and financial rights with certain thresholds of local capacity. This creates several complications. For instance, is it better to have a gradual increase in fiscal autonomies (such as more flexibility on setting taxation rates or allocation of public expenditures) or to allow levying taxes in additional areas? Or the autonomy in service provision, should it be allocated according to the scale of services or area of services? There is not a shortcut answer to these questions, and country-specific conditions might dictate different strategies for more suitable arrangements. However, we can expect those socio-economically more developed provinces to be able to alleviate the repercussions of enhanced autonomies more efficiently and effectively with heightening citizen inclusion, transparency, and accountability in governance. That would not only improve productive and allocative efficiency but also encourage democratic innovations that suit better to sociocultural conditions.

The challenge with an extension of decentralized autonomy can be moderated with allowing the local government to assume more power from the central government. This brings us to the third principle. Flexible arrangements in asymmetric decentralization designs are important to effectively cope with changes in local capacity. Capacity is by nature subject to change endogenously and exogenously, and administrative arrangements should consider this temporal dimension. For example, local capacity can change in time with the mobility of people

6 CONCLUSION: TOWARD AN ASYMMETRICAL DECENTRALIZATION DESIGN

or changes in politico-economic conditions, and a static decentralization design can lead to inefficiencies in governance. Furthermore, strict arrangements may engender deterministic attitudes in local governance that might deter policy innovations and foster inertia and underperformance. Here, a possible policy instrument could be the adoption of a comparative benchmarking system that allows comparison of local governments at the same development level. Such a benchmarking system can foster horizontal interjurisdictional competition, yet it can also encourage dissemination of good practices and interorganizational learning as similar level local governments would be facing similar challenges. Moreover, citizens can judge the performances of their own local government by comparing with the performance of similar local governments that can create further political pressure on local governments to perform well.[10]

Flexibility is also important to effectively address diminishing returns in productive efficiencies that derive from methodological choices on the initial design of asymmetry. Any choice of yardstick to cluster development levels of local governments will be arbitrary, and this can create certain disadvantages for local governments that are close to the margins. However, for the effective use of flexible arrangements, it is necessary to introduce some means of conditionality to avoid abuse of power. Here, there could be two possible ways of policy action. One option is, as Litvack et al. suggest,[11] through a contractual agreement[12] between the central government and local government, that conditions further powers to certain improvements in service outputs in a specific time period. The local government's performance can be evaluated at the end of the period according to the predefined performance indicators and according

---

[10]There are some caveats with the effectiveness of benchmarking systems in improving public service performance (see Knutsson et al. 2012; Kuhlmann and Bogumil 2018) that may call for different benchmarking methods in different country cases. However, broad comparative benchmarks are reported to be more persuasive to citizens in comparison with reflexive benchmarks (see Charbonneau and Van Ryzin 2015).

[11]'The central government also must clarify the fiscal rules of the game and follow them. For example, it should first clearly assign expenditure responsibilities to each level of government. After these responsibilities have been assigned, tax instruments should be assigned to subnational governments to increase their access to own-revenues, and arrangements should be fixed for three to five years to improve predictability' (Litvack et al. 1998).

[12]A similar contract-based or staged approach is also suggested by Bird and Ebel (2006) to grant greater autonomy to administrations with higher capacities.

to the level of citizen satisfaction. The alternative to contractual arrangement could be through an adjustment period. In this period, the local government can have gradually more responsibility and autonomy from the central government, which may be followed by a period of performance monitoring.

So, setting clear sets of rules, in the initial phase of asymmetric decentralization and also on subsequent decentralization decisions, and allowing flexibility are important on the effective design of asymmetric decentralization policies. However, there is one particular challenge, which is unique for asymmetric decentralization, and it is not only confined to the design phase but also extends to implementation. The handicap of asymmetric decentralization is, unlike to symmetric arrangements, it does not comply with the 'equal rights and responsibilities for the same status of administration'. Instead, local governments with weak capacities receive less autonomy regardless of their administrative status. Asymmetric decentralization allows central government (or regional government in federal systems) to allocate more effectively public resources at the state level, but also the central government is expected to take an enhanced role in provinces where the local capacity is weaker. These make the asymmetric decentralized systems more vulnerable concerning with public accountability and local resistance. In fact, this downside of asymmetrical arrangement is also underlined by Smoke (2015) on his analysis of public sector decentralization in developing countries. In his words:

> Implementation is commonly approached in a standardized and mechanical way. A more "developmental" approach would involve systematic asymmetric treatment of local governments with varied capacities as they move towards assuming new roles at different paces. Capable local governments could be left more on their own to adopt devolved powers, while others might assume powers more slowly (according to clear criteria) in conjunction with targeted capacity building and support. Such an approach can be justified because allowing strong local autonomy without basic functional capacity and a degree of accountability to local citizens is a recipe for poor performance. There are two core challenges with this type of approach. The first is how to determine an appropriate initial balance between upward and downward accountabilities, which can evolve as local governments mature and are better able to manage functions more independently. A second is how to reduce opportunities for the approach to be undermined by the complex political economy dynamics outlined earlier. Some local governments could sidestep national processes if they are well connected or monitoring is weak.

6 CONCLUSION: TOWARD AN ASYMMETRICAL DECENTRALIZATION DESIGN 209

Certain aspects of accountability problems that Smoke draws attention, especially about managing the change, can be addressed to a certain extent with allowing flexible arrangements and clear sets of rules on advancing decentralization. However, setting up the role of central government in public governance and its means of involvement in lagging provinces are important for public accountability and deserve further deliberation. As earlier mentioned, theoretical premises of public governance suggest that local government has certain advantages over central government to foster public accountability, and therefore, it should preserve its principal role in public service delivery. For public accountability, local government should encourage citizen participation in decision-making and implementation processes of public services, and also be transparent on financial management processes. However, socio-economically lagging regions are afflicted by certain disadvantages with citizen participation. First, since local governments usually do not rely on local resources in public service delivery, they have less incentive to include citizen's effectively in public service design and implementation processes. Second, even though the local government prioritizes citizen's involvement in public governance, certain groups and power elites usually have easier access and higher leverage in decision-making processes which may create a bottleneck on the transmission of information from society to management (especially from marginalized communities). Third, even if the management decides to prioritize the involvement of marginalized communities in governance, that would require the allocation of limited resources for that purpose and thus put additional pressure on the budget. Fourth, in severe cases with socio-economic development, such as lower level of literacy rates, limited communication and transportation infrastructures, or limitations with economies of scales, the marginal cost of citizen participation can exceed its return on allocative and productive efficiency. Each of these scenarios may call for a different way of central government's involvement in public governance.

The first scenario, that local government depends highly on central government resources, calls for a mixed policy of effective use of intergovernmental transfer shares and adopting policies and instruments to encourage citizen's participation in governance. The intergovernmental transfer shares can be based on a formula of socio-economic development, where the least developed regions receive the highest share from intergovernmental transfers. Here, the central government can introduce conditional grants to foster citizen participation in governance.

For example, transfer shares can be allocated to local government in block payments, and by fulfilling certain performance criteria about citizen participation in governance, additional grants can be unlocked for the usage of local government. This way, the local government can have both further incentives to include citizens in public governance, but also efficiency in income redistribution can be fostered.

The second scenario applies for the cases when local elite captures or certain sociocultural elements encumber inclusion of certain groups in public governance. Policy instruments such as conditional grants or certain community empowerment projects by central government and/or donor organizations can be instrumental to overcome these limitations. For instance, Galasso and Ravallon (2001) report that in Porto Allegre, elite capture has been mitigated in time with insisting on participative budgeting. Participative budgeting's governance structure prioritizes inclusion of poor and disadvantaged groups, and in both cases, their involvement and influence in budgeting process have improved in time. So encouraging local governments to continue with inclusive policies can be another role of central government and/or its agents to play in public governance. Additionally, a combination of decentralization policies and 'yardstick competition' can also be influential in coping with elite capture and strengthening accountability (Seabright 1996; Besley and Case 1995). The idea behind 'yardstick competition' is the effort or competence of public officials is mostly not directly observable by citizens, and interjurisdictional comparison under decentralization may help voters to decide whether they should replace their government. The limitation of this idea is in the symmetrical design of decentralization policies; politicians can always plead that they did the best under given circumstances (Bardhan 2002). As earlier mentioned, a comparative benchmarking system under an asymmetrical decentralization design can further the effectiveness of yardstick competition, by extenuating claims of blame-avoidance by local governments.

The third scenario concerns with, despite attempts to enhance citizen participation, there could be less willingness or awareness of citizens about participation and accountability processes. For instance, in Turkish case, the municipal councilors as the representatives of citizens have limited awareness about their roles and thus limited effectiveness in public governance. Here again, the central government along with NGOs, civil society organizations, or international donor organizations can play a role to enhance citizens' awareness with capacity building programs

6 CONCLUSION: TOWARD AN ASYMMETRICAL DECENTRALIZATION DESIGN   211

targeting communities or representatives of communities. Furthermore, the central government can allow grants to civil society organizations and to other civil initiatives working on the area of citizen participation. In short, the central government's efforts can be concentrated more on a societal level.

The fourth scenario may necessitate central government or upper-tier regional/local governments to take a more extensive role in public service delivery, where more nuanced and case-specific solutions on financial and administrative arrangements can be possible. For example, the central government can allocate conditional grants, matching for services in specific areas, which are expected to create a spillover effect upon socio-economic development (e.g., education, health, and transportation). Another option could be co-sharing responsibilities on the delivery of certain public services with the upper tier of local governments or central government. The co-sharing responsibility for certain public services can also be arranged with more autonomous, neighboring local governments and thus creating higher allocative efficiency for both local governments.

Basically, asymmetric decentralization designs should be complemented by fine-tuned instruments that enhance political accountability and citizen inclusion in public governance, and in the meantime, central or federal governments should take a supportive role in alleviating socio-economic conditions. Clearly, enhancing the role of central government in local governance makes local government more vulnerable to state predation. Therefore, it is vital to ensure transparency in the processes of central government's involvement, and the discretion of central government on changing the fiscal rules of the game should be limited. Some developing countries endure nevertheless severe weaknesses of democratic and judicial institutions, and in those countries, the central government can exploit its role against opposition parties, especially if they govern regions strategically and economically more valuable provinces. Diaz-Cayeros et al. (2005) call this mechanism 'tragic brilliance' when an authoritarian or weak democratic regime perverts elections to serve as a mechanism of social control rather than citizen choice. A case in Mexico, however, suggests that more developed regions, thus more decentralized according to our asymmetric model, can resist better to the 'tragic brilliance' acts of central government. In the 1990s, many of the localities in Northern Mexico voted for the opposition party, in order to remove the central control on the delivery of local services, which were necessary for the newly emerging light export industry to the USA (Weingast 2014). The central government has punished these areas with reducing the revenue transfers and through other predatory acts, such as padding the labor budget by mailing money to supporters throughout Mexico and charging user fees for improved local services (Rodriguez 1995). However, these local governments were able to resist the central government by removing corruption and introducing user charges to public services, such as solid waste disposal, water, and road maintenance, and in a few years turning the 70% of state funding in budget to over 70% local funding (Rodriguez 1995; Weingast 2014). Remarkably, Northern Mexico has the highest GDP per capita ratings in Mexico.

On the other hand, political polarization between central and local government can trigger local resistance to comply with asymmetric arrangements. There could be several reaction points here. An asymmetrical design does not necessarily mean a demotion in autonomy, but political and cultural competitions among localities may provoke political objection to having less autonomy from counterparts. In regions with different ethnic and historical identities, this objection can be imbued with distrust to the central or federal government, thus may engender populist reactions and stronger resistance to comply with asymmetric arrangements. I think there are two contingency factors, which can mitigate the severity of local resistance. First of all, the asymmetric arrangement according to socio-economic development brings to certain impartiality on asymmetric designs in comparison with alternative models based on local government capacities. Indeed, many propositions in the literature (e.g., Litvack et al. 1998; Wehner 2000; Bird and Ebel 2006; Smoke 2015; Holzhacker et al. 2016) presume government capacities as the baseline for asymmetrical arrangements. Given that local governments are political organizations, it is inherently difficult to ensure the compliance of all local governments to have less autonomy from their counterparts only on the basis of organizational capacities as its measurement gives too much room for interpretation. Plus, the studies between government's capacity and decentralization do not provide a comprehensive picture about which organizational capacities are more important on governance outcomes. The second contingency factor against local resistance can be through flexible arrangements and benchmarking systems. The former allows the local government to assume further power, and the latter gives the possibility of citizens to independently monitor their government's performance by comparing with counterparts. I expect these two instruments to mitigate the possibility of blame games and political resistance, and thereby, the system can reach a better balance in time.

At this juncture, it is fair to ask whether there is real-life evidence that asymmetric decentralization improves governance outcomes and serves as a better alternative to uniform designs of decentralization. Although it is difficult to give a perfect example, there are country cases where asymmetric arrangements are preferred by the central government to improve governance outcomes. For example, in Indonesia, Holzhacker et al. (2016) identify an emerging trend of 'variable geometry multi-level system' referring to asymmetric formal and operational arrangements between central government and local government, as a response to the failure of earlier uniform practices of decentralization. On the other hand, earlier phases of market transition and decentralization in China resemble very closely how an effective asymmetrical decentralization might look like. In the 1970s, Chinese government under the leadership of Deng allowed higher autonomy to certain coastal areas with higher endogenous capacities to experiment with institutional reforms, whose successful practices later spread to other areas (Bardhan 2002). For example, Guangdong's success in economic transition compelled other regions that were resisting to change, to imitate successful practices as well.[13] Successful local governments have been granted further fiscal and administrative autonomy under a policy called 'one step ahead' (Weingast 2014), and additional financial incentives and budget flexibilities (Oksenberg and Tong 1991; Qian and Weingast 1997) to promote economic and land reforms. For example, from 1983 provincial governments were allowed to deal with joint venture applications for projects with an upper limit of US$ 3 million. The limit was raised to US$ 10 million in 1985 and then to US$ 30 million for certain coastal provinces in 1988 (Zhang 1994; Chien 2007). Furthermore, Weingast (2014) underlines special fiscal contracts with the central government

---

[13]Weingast (2014) gives, for instance, the case of Heilongjiang Province. Heilongjiang Province reacted to Guangdong's market reforms by increasing the standard subsidies of the socialist system. Yet Guangdong's reforms lowered the market prices of the same goods below the subsidized price. Because Heilongjiang accomplished the same result at great fiscal cost, fiscal incentives led its leaders to dismantle their expensive subsidies and imitate Guangdong (see also Montinola et al. 1995).

allowed most provinces to raise their own tax revenues,[14] which took the following form: The province shared 50% of all revenue raised up to a specified revenue level with the central government, and then the province to retain 100% of all revenue beyond that level. Additionally, central government has implemented a form of 'yardstick competition' to foster interjurisdictional competitiveness (Bardhan 2002) and managerial incentives by conditioning the career advancement of centrally appointed local leaders to the economic performance of localities (Burns 1987; Heilmann and Kirchberger 2000; Huang 1996, 2002; Ma and Wu 2005; Chien 2007[15]). Needless to say, Chinese government's certain centrally led policies, such as policy authority conditions and hard budget constraints (Montinola et al. 1995; Oi 1992; Shirk 1993), had been easier to implement in the absence of constraining democratic institutions; nevertheless, even in this context, Guangdong Province, an exemplary successful case of transition, has been able to resist politically by preventing the proposed anti-reform reaction by central government[16] (Shirk 1993: 194–195; Montinola et al. 1995).

China's remarkable success in economic growth and poverty reduction has been praised by the international community and taken as an exemplary case of a successful transition in developing countries, yet the role of decentralization policies in this transformation has drawn limited

---

[14]The average province faced a marginal tax retention rate of 89%; and 68% of all provinces faced a marginal retention rate of 100% (Jin et al. 2005).

[15]Chien (2007) describes the Chinese model of decentralization as 'asymmetrical decentralization' referring to central government holds an upper hand while granting autonomies to local governments to promote their own policies. Personally, I think Chinese decentralization resembles a controlled model of decentralization with certain elements of asymmetry. In my understanding of asymmetric decentralization, the central government should take a more benevolent role in local governance, such as enhancing its involvement in places needed and withdraw from places where there is adequate local capacity.

[16]In July 2018, I had the opportunity to listen in a roundtable discussion on the administrative reform plans of Chinese Society for Public Sector Reform. The reform plans put a high emphasis on centralization and enhanced party-led coordination among jurisdictions. The plan appears to be still at its early stage with regard to reforms at local government; however, centralization at the local level and bringing higher party centralization on the coordination of local governments appear to be the course of action. I inferred from their presentation that a possible reversal of decentralization policy might take place in coming future, limiting the autonomy of local and provincial governments by enhancing central government's control and/or coordination at local governance.

attention in public administration literature. Further studies on China's decentralization practices from a public administration perspective can significantly advance our knowledge of how to promote successful decentralization policies in developing countries.

Comparison of Symmetric and Asymmetric Decentralization Designs

In this concluding section about asymmetric decentralization, I will argue why asymmetrical decentralization can have theoretically better governance outcomes in comparison with symmetric decentralization. For clarification, I use the term asymmetric decentralization to refer asymmetric fiscal and administrative arrangements at same tier of elected governments that have equal legislative status in administration. This means that here, I will not refer to asymmetric decentralization models, such as in Spain, Russia, or the UK, that are largely derived from political calculations to keep ethnically, culturally, or historically different entities within national unity. I will also not refer to asymmetric fiscal and administrative arrangements between upper and lower tier of governments, for instance, between metropolitan and district municipalities, or between different functional local administrations, such as town municipalities and village administrations. The reason is in most country cases,[17] different administrative tiers of government have diverse responsibilities and autonomies in public governance. My following argumentation on asymmetrical decentralization will exclusively rest on the same tier of local governments with the same autonomies, rights, and responsibilities.

Decentralization of autonomy typically hinges upon the administrative divisions, wherein upper tiers of government have wider roles, responsibilities, and instruments in public governance for reasons such as economies of scale, externalities, and income redistribution and therefore retain broader autonomies than lower tiers of governments. In a way, public service responsibilities and available fiscal and administrative instruments vary in vertical scale of government, on the contrary to the horizontal scale of government, where the same tier of administrations is

---

[17] Remarkably, there are country cases, where different tiers of government have the same rights and responsibilities in public services. For instance, I was surprised to learn that in Slovakia, even villages with a population as less as 13 residents have the equal public service duty and rights to the central government.

expected to have equal rights and similar responsibilities in public service delivery. The ideological roots of the horizontal equality within the same tier of government probably stem from the legal principle of 'equality before the law', whereby local governments as the representatives of people have similar rights before the law. However, this divergence of decentralization policies toward hierarchical and vertical scales of government carries an inherent contradiction. The vertical variation of autonomies presumes that bigger municipalities (either bigger in territory or population) hold larger endogenous capacities to justify their extended roles and responsibilities in public service delivery, and since same tiers of government have relatively similar size, they have equal opportunities to use their endogenous capacities. The problem with this presumption is twofold. Administrative boundaries usually hinge upon historical path dependencies,[18] and they do not necessarily coincide with present economic and demographic realities. Globalization, along with increasing mobility of capital and people, has created economic hubs and areas of agglomeration not only in certain geographical territories but also within urban areas, and as the New Trade Theory (see Krugman 1991) suggests the economic regions with more production continue to be profitable and thus foster further growth asymmetries. Moreover, the impacts of macroeconomic forces are not confined with growth asymmetries, but they also reinforce socio-economic asymmetries by creating areas of deprived and marginalized communities with poor access to public services. Here, it is also important to reassess the influence of post-industrial evolution of cities (see Schragger 2010) on the endogenous capacities of local governments. Innovation-based industries and finance-based economies depend on the highly sophisticated workforce and generate limited employment opportunities, and the work is not restricted by stationary facilities; hence, they are easy to relocate. Therefore, their continuation in the city depends on local governments to make higher incentives (such as tax reductions or exemption from service fees) to keep them attractive, and this creates the peril of a race to the bottom in competition-based settings. Especially, big companies easily exploit these

---

[18] For instance, the creation of *départements* in France dates back to the Napoleonic era when the territorial boundaries are decided by a day's ride from the capital of the department. So, even in the case of impartial creation of administrative boundaries, technological advancements may outdate the purposefulness of the initial decision.

vulnerabilities. For instance, in 2017, Amazon has announced a public bidding for local governments to offer the best incentive for the location of their next headquarters in North America, which has attracted a widespread competition among interested cities.[19] Therefore, we can presume that post-industrial evolution made endogenous capacities of cities more susceptible to change.

Some recent studies even report the impact of administrative boundaries on economic growth of provincial counties and urban districts (see Zhang et al. 2017; Jovanović 2009). This means that administrative boundaries do not necessarily reflect the equal distribution of endogenous capacities but they may even enforce the creation of further inequalities within and across the jurisdictional borders.

Therefore, we can assume that there is a need for more adjustment between administrative boundaries, economic geographies, and public governance policies. One recent trend (especially in Northern Europe) is rescaling administrative boundaries with municipal amalgamations of neighboring town municipalities and district municipalities in order to improve service efficiency and economies of scale (see Kuhlman and Bouckaert 2016). However, administrative changes in municipalities are politically costly for elected representatives both at local and at central level. Especially, this is more challenging for bigger municipalities where local identities are more prevalent to allow extensive changes in administrative boundaries, yet the stakes are also higher as upper-tier municipalities reserve higher responsibilities in public services. Furthermore, municipal mergers and rescaling territories are only influential to adjust economies of scales within neighboring territories, but the divergence effect of global trade (see again Krugman 1991) is not limited within urban areas but also spreads out geographically across the country. In a nutshell, the presumption of the same tier of governments has equal opportunities to use their endogenous capacities is flawed as endogenous capacities are accumulated in specific territories separate from administrative boundaries, and rescaling practices are politically costly and only influential within territorially adjacent areas.

---

[19] In November 2017, the TV show 'Last Week Tonight with John Oliver' has aired a special coverage about this bidding process of local governments, among which a local government in the state of Georgia even offers to create a new town named 'Amazon'.

218   E. TAN

Consequently, there are in practice no perfect horizontal symmetries in local government. In every country, there are more prosperous and therefore more politically influential local governments, regardless of their equal administrative status with counterparts. For example, in Turkey, controlling the metropolitan municipality of Istanbul has broader implications for general elections by given its economic and demographic importance.[20] Likewise, as earlier shown in the cases of Mexico and China, prosperous regions have more political leverage and power over central government to stand against state predation and preserve their autonomies. On the other hand, less prosperous regions are more exposed and in a weaker position to stand against external influences of uneven markets and/or state predation. So, macroeconomic forces not only create asymmetries in the endogenous capacities of local governments, but they also influence their political powers and autonomies regardless of their administrative status.

At this juncture, it is important to question the effectiveness of constitutionally symmetrical decentralization policies to improve efficiency in public service deliveries. Symmetrical constitutional arrangements limit available policy instruments for central government into two available courses of action, either creating bigger size municipalities through mergers or amalgamations, or recentralization of certain autonomies to an upper-tier government. My argument is this is not only inefficient as a policy practice but also potentially ineffective in mitigating allocative and productive inefficiencies since endogenous capacities can change in time independent from spatial conditioning (for instance, by emigration or immigration). Although the functional advantage of asymmetric treatments over symmetrical arrangements has been acknowledged before, the challenge has been asymmetrical policies often provoke reactions for equal and symmetrical treatments and thus limits the efficacy of asymmetrical constitutional solutions (Watts 2010). Here, establishing theoretically and empirically the prevalence of socio-economic factors over government capabilities presents a new chance to reinvigorate the discussions on effective asymmetrical decentralization designs and on suitable policy instruments in alleviating certain risks contingent to asymmetrical treatments. I have earlier discussed some potential policy instruments in that regard; therefore, I will just give here the summary of key theoretical deductions and their policy implications:

---

[20] In an AKP consultation meeting in 2017, Erdoğan, who is also a former mayor of Istanbul, stated 'whoever loses Istanbul, loses Turkey' meaning that winning the local elections in Istanbul is crucial to win general elections. http://www.hurriyet.com.tr/yazarlar/abdulkadir-selvi/erdogan-istanbul-icin-hangi-uyarilarda-bulundu-40590320.

6 CONCLUSION: TOWARD AN ASYMMETRICAL DECENTRALIZATION DESIGN

Key Theoretical Deductions:

- Competition-based decentralization theories assume that same tier of government has similar endogenous capacities, thus through competition higher allocative and productive efficiency can be achieved. However, macroeconomic forces foster unequal distributions and divergence; therefore, endogenous capacities are skewed to certain spatial areas. Furthermore, economic differences create political asymmetries in the relationship with the central government as well. Therefore, under symmetrical arrangements, allocative efficiency through competition is harder to achieve.

- Information-based decentralization theories assume that the proximity of public service organizations to consumers promotes allocative and productive efficiency. This assumption is further enhanced under democratic governance conditions. In addition to this, governance theories predicate with higher citizen engagement in co-production and co-delivery of services, and co-sharing responsibilities with other societal actors higher productive efficiency can be attained. Nonetheless, the latter two assumptions are contingent on the socio-economic factors. Furthermore, psychosocial studies suggest that inequalities in society (or rather perception of inequalities) impair social capital, citizen ownership, and engagement. In the absence of these conditions, the advantage of local government over field agencies of central government in allocative and productive efficiency is limited. Thus, in juxtaposition with the previous point, systemic factors behind unequal distribution of endogenous capacities undermine the information-based assumptions of decentralization theories as well.

- These theoretical deductions are backed by empirical observations, primarily in developing and transition countries, where inequalities in wealth distribution and regional disparities are more severe and prevalent. Under these conditions, asymmetrical decentralization policies according to the socio-economic development parameters, both in design and operations, should improve the predictability and assumptions of decentralization theories in relation to better governance outcomes.

- A disadvantage of asymmetrical decentralization policies over symmetrical policies is that it does not necessarily coincide with the administrative hierarchy of government; therefore, it creates a systemic pressure on the legitimacy of the policy actions. In order to mitigate this risk, it is important to complement asymmetric decentralization policies with smart policy instruments.

220   E. TAN

In connection with these theoretical deductions, the asymmetric decentralization policies can have following policy implications in bringing better governance outcomes:

Policy Implications:
- An important advantage of asymmetric decentralization policies is on improving the efficient and effective allocation of resources and the effectiveness of income redistribution. Asymmetrical designs, where local governments with better socio-economic indicators have wider autonomies in public governance in relation to decision-making, revenue raising and public service responsibilities and less contribution from the general budget, allow central governments more efficiently allocate its resources to places where there is a need for further investments and improvements in areas affecting socio-economic parameters. Effective redistribution policies can mitigate the regional developmental disparities in the long run, thus creating better competition conditions among local governments and less volatility in endogenous capacities.
- Asymmetrical decentralization models can limit the destabilizing effect of decentralization policies on macroeconomic policies. By limiting the fiscal autonomy in public expenditures of local governments with less endogenous capacities, the risk of soft budget constraint can be confined.
- Local elite captures and externalities in public services can increase the transaction costs of public service and foster inefficiencies in public service delivery. Yardstick competition and comparative benchmarking can mitigate the impact of these factors.
- Flexible design in asymmetric arrangements with local governments is important to mitigate the undermining impact of asymmetric decentralization to administrative legitimacy and its vulnerability to blame politics. Here, the socio-economic development-based asymmetrical arrangement can bring to a certain extent impartiality and less resistance to asymmetric arrangements. Furthermore, comparative benchmarking methods can be also useful for citizens to objectively assess the performance of their local government and may neutralize passing-the-buck politics toward central government and blame-avoidance toward exogenous factors.
- Asymmetric decentralization policies can also improve the effectiveness of capacity building practices. Capacity building practices can focus more on community engagement in places with higher

income inequalities and exclusionist practices toward fringe communities, or it can focus more on organizational and technical dimensions in places where improvement of mobilization capacities brings higher returns in revenues.

CONCLUSION AND FINAL REMARKS

When does decentralization lead to better governance? This question stood out in every chapter of this book. By focusing on the relationship between governance capacity and decentralization, I tried to shed some light on this broad question. Accordingly, the findings in Turkey establish local capacity as an integral part of the design and evaluation of decentralization policies. The significant relationship observed between the local capacity, or local socio-economic development, and the fiscal autonomy of local government has been in congruence with the findings in other country cases and comparative studies. This primarily challenges certain theoretical assumptions of fiscal decentralization theory. The theory on fiscal decentralization argues that local government can monitor and act better on local needs; thus, the assignment of tax and expenditure authority to local government would create the conditions of higher accountability, efficiency, and effectiveness in governance. By setting the importance of local capacity on the outcomes of decentralization, my research suggests that the success in decentralization relies on socio-economic conditions instead of the local government's convenience to act on local needs. Furthermore, it is even possible to posit that the contradictory outcomes of decentralization policies, which are often observed in developing countries, can be associated with the socio-economic disparities among regions and provinces. Hence, in reference to the debate of whether certain capacities are preconditioned for the success of decentralization, or decentralization leads to improved capacities, I am inclined to lean on the former by considering the strong influence of local capacity on decentralization outcomes and also on organizational capacities.

In developing countries with disproportionate distribution of wealth and regional inequalities, decentralization is more likely to result in varying outcomes when a uniform and symmetrical decentralization reform is applied at the subnational level. For these countries, asymmetrical decentralization policies can lead to better public governance. Nonetheless, socio-economic disparities among regions are not exclusive to developing countries, and as the economic geography literature suggests that the forces of international trade foster spatial disparities. The basic idea with asymmetric decentralization is more capable local government should have less intervention from central government, and this way the central government can use its resources more efficiently to support lagging behind provinces. Although the idea of asymmetric decentralization is not something new, its applications in public administration literature have been limited. One likely reason for this limited attention could be ideas about asymmetrical arrangements take organizational capacities as the locus of furthering decentralization. These make asymmetrically decentralized systems relatively exposed to political instabilities. Moreover, the findings in Turkey suggest that the role of organizational capacities is limited in comparison with local capacity, and organizational capacities are determined to a certain extent by the socio-economic conditions. Therefore, asymmetrical arrangements hinged on organizational capacities are likely to produce equivocal outcomes. In conclusion chapter, several policy applications for asymmetrical decentralization have been discussed. One policy recommendation is clustering regions or provinces according to socio-economic development levels to match with varied fiscal and administrative discretions in public service delivery. Regions with higher indices can be authorized with levying taxes and higher self-financing responsibilities in expenditure assignments, whereas regions with lower indices can have a co-financing option and share of responsibility in public services with central government's agencies. Additionally, implementing a comparative benchmarking system and flexible arrangements can further enhance the stability of asymmetrical decentralization designs.

The field study was conducted in a single country case and on a specific tier of subnational government. Although this methodological choice enabled the controlled environment to address the research questions, only the fiscal accountability dimension of decentralization theories is tested in the analysis. About the political accountability dimension of decentralization theories in public governance, the confounding relationship between decision-making and local capacity suggests that socio-economically more advanced communities would likely to have further interests and capacities in participating effectively in local governance. Under these circumstances, elected representatives of the local government should be more responsive to local demands, and therefore, they may pursue more autonomous policies from the central government even in the presence of state predation or higher institutionalization of party politics. The examples from Mexico and China support this line of argumentation. However, it is also possible, elected representatives of socio-economically developed provinces may feel emboldened by governing a politically valuable local government, and thus, their political stance may reflect more on self-serving interests rather than the best interests of his/her electorates. In this scenario, political autonomy does not necessarily lead to better public governance. On the other hand, in socio-economically deprived areas, practices and regulations about citizen participation in governance may bring behavioral changes and create a sense of local ownership, and this can substitute the anticipated influence of local capacity on political responsiveness. Therefore, further studies are needed to better understand the influence of socio-economic conditions on public accountability assumptions of decentralization theories in public governance.

Finally, my argument on the relationship between decentralization and development is that decentralization can be a policy instrument to attain economic development as long as certain socio-economic conditions exist beforehand. In the lack of socio-economic parameters, the central government should be an active participant in investments and provide incentives for the private sector to engage in economic activities. Consequently, conflicting empirical results about decentralization and development can be partially explained by the corresponding socio-economic realities, rather than by the failure in the implementation of decentralization policies or by lacking capacities in the subnational governments. In that regard, the findings of this study also call for attention on the effectiveness of capacity building practices. Hitherto, the equivocal outcomes of decentralization practices, especially in developing countries, were largely addressed as part of 'management deficit' in governance, and various capacity building programs have been implemented by international donor organizations to educate managers, organizations, and even communities. Taking into account the socio-economic conditions before deciding on the right capacity building action can improve the effectiveness of interventions.

References

Acemoglu, D., & Robinson, J. (2012). *Why Nations Fail: The Origins of Power, Prosperity and Poverty*. New York: Crown.

Alibegovic, D. J. (2013). Less Is More: Decentralization in Croatia and Its Impact on Decentralization. In W. Bartlett, S. Malekovic, & V. Monastirioitis (Eds.), *Decentralization and Local Development in South East Europe* (pp. 51–67). Hampshire: Palgrave Macmillan.

Alonso, J. M., & Andrews, R. (2018). Fiscal Decentralization and Local Government Efficiency: Does Relative Deprivation Matter? *Environment and Planning C: Politics and Space.* Available online June 2018. https://doi.org/10.1177/2399654418784947.

Bardhan, P. (2002). Decentralization of Governance and Development. *Journal of Economic Perspective, 16*(4), 185–205.

Barrett, C. B., Mude, A. G., & Omiti, J. M. (2007). *Decentralization and Social Economics of Development-Lessons from Kenya.* Trowbridge: Cromwell Press.

Bartlett, W., Malekovic, S., & Monastiriotis, V. (2013). *Decentralization and Local Development in South East Europe.* Hampshire: Palgrave Macmillan.

Bartlett, W., Đulić, K., & Kmezić, S. (2018). *The Impact of Fiscal Decentralization on Local Economic Development in Serbia.* LSE Papers on Decentralization and Regional Policy (Research Paper No. 7).

Bauböck, R. (2001). *Multinational Federalism: Territorial or Cultural Autonomy?* Willy Brandt Series of Working Papers in International Migration and Ethnic Relations 2/0. ISSN 1650-5743/Online publication.

Besley, T., & Case, A. (1995). Incumbent Behavior: Vote-Seeking, Tax-Setting and Yardstick Competition. *American Economic Review, 85*(1), 25–45.

Bird, R. M., & Ebel, R. D. (2006). Fiscal Federalism and National Unity. In A. Ehtisham & G. Brosio (Eds.), *Handbook of Fiscal Federalism* (pp. 499–521). Cheltenham: Edward Elgar.

Birdsall, N., Ross, D., & Sabot, R. (1995). Inequality and Growth Reconsidered: Lesson from East Asia. *World Bank Economic Review, 9*(3), 477–508.

Bouckaert, G., Loretan, R., & Troupin, S. (2016). *Public Administration and the Sustainable Development Goals.* Written Statement by the International Institute of Administrative Sciences, Submitted to the 15th Session of the United Nations Committee of Experts in Public Administration.

Burns, J. P. (1987). China's Nomenklatura System. *Problems of Communism, 36,* 36–51.

Buser, W. (2011). The Impact of Fiscal Decentralization on Economics Performance in High-Income OECD Nations: An Institutional Approach. *Public Choice, 149*(1/2), 31–48.

Charbonneau, É., & Van Ryzin, G. G. (2015). Benchmarks and Citizen Judgments of Local Government Performance: Findings from a Survey Experiment. *Public Management Review, 17*(2), 288–304.

Chien, S. (2007). Institutional Innovations, Asymmetric Decentralization, and Local Economic Development: A Case Study of Kunshan, in Post-Mao China. *Environment and Planning C: Government and Policy, 25,* 269–290.

Chon, D. S. (2012). The Impact of Population Heterogeneity and Income Inequality on Homicide Rates: A Cross-National Assessment. *International Journal Offender Therapy and Comparative Criminology, 56*(5), 730–748.

6 CONCLUSION: TOWARD AN ASYMMETRICAL DECENTRALIZATION DESIGN 225

Daly, M., Wilson, M., & Vasdev, S. (2001). Income Inequality and Homicide Rates in Canada and United States. *Canadian Journal of Criminology, 43*(2), 219–236.

Deininger, K., & Squire, L. (1996). A New Data Set for Measuring Income Equality. *World Bank Economic Review, 10,* 565–591.

De la Fuente, M., & Vasquez, G. (2005). *Decentralización y derechos humanos en Bolivia. Los Casos de Mizque y Tiquipaya.* Geneva: International Council on Human Rights Policy.

Diaz-Cayeros, A., Magaloni, B., & Weingast, B. R. (2005). *Tragic Brilliance: Equilibrium Party Hegemony in Mexico* (Working Paper). Stanford: Hoover Institution, Stanford University.

Diaz-Serrano, L., & Rodríguez-Pose, A. (2015). Decentralization and the Welfare State: What Do Citizens Perceive? *Social Indicators Research, 120*(2), 411–435.

Elgar, F. J., & Aitken, N. (2010). Income Inequality, Trust and Homicide in 33 Countries. *European Journal of Public Health, 21*(2), 241–246.

Elgar, F. J., Craig, W., Boyce, W., Morgan, A., & Vella-Zarb, R. (2009). Income Inequality and School Bullying: Multilevel Study of Adolescents in 37 Countries. *Journal of Adolescent Health, 45,* 351–359.

Faguet, J.-P. (2001). *Does Decentralization Increase Responsiveness to Local Needs? Evidence from Bolivia.* Centre for Economic Performance and Development Studies Institute, London School of Economics.

Galasso, E., & Ravallion, M. (2001). *Decentralized Targeting of an Anti-Poverty Program.* Development Research Group Working Paper, World Bank.

Heilmann, S., & Kirchberger, S. (2000). *The Chinese Nomenklatura in Transition: A Study Based on Internal Cadre Statistics of the Central Organization Department of the Chinese Communist Party.* Trier: Trier University.

Hellman, J., Hofman, B., Kaise, K., & Schulze, G. G. (2003). *Decentralization, Governance, and Public Services: An Assessment of Indonesian Experience.* Jakarta: The World Bank.

Hermann, B., Thöni, C., & Gächter, S. (2008). Antisocial Punishment Across Societies. *Science, 319,* 1362–1367.

Hodge, A., Firth, S., Jimenez-Soto, E., & Trisnantoro, L. (2015). Linkages Between Decentralization and Inequalities in Neonatal Health: Evidence from Indonesia. *The Journal of Development Studies, 51*(12), 1634–1652.

Holzhacker, R. L., Wittek, R., & Woltjer, J. (2016). *Decentralization and Governance in Indonesia.* London: Springer.

Hsieh, C., & Pugh, M. (1993). Poverty, Income Inequality, and Violent Crime: A Meta-Analysis of Recent Aggregate Data Studies. *Criminal Justice Review, 18*(2), 182–202.

Huang, Y. (1996). *Inflation and Investment Control in China: The Political Economy of Central-Local Relations During the Reform Era*. New York, NY: Cambridge University Press.

Huang, Y. (2002). Managing Chinese Bureaucrats: an Institutional Economic Perspective. *Political Studies, 50*, 61–79.

Jin, H., Qian, Y., & Weingast, B. R. (2005). Regional Decentralization and Fiscal Incentives: Federalism, Chinese Style. *Journal of Public Economics, 89*, 1719–1742.

Jovanović, M. N. (2009). *Evolutionary Economic Geography: Location of Production and the European Union*. New York, NY: Routledge.

Knutsson, H., Ramberg, U., & Tagesson, T. (2012). Benchmarking Impact Through Municipal Benchmarking Networks. *Public Performance & Management Review, 36*(1), 102–123.

Krugman, P. R. (1991). *Geography and Trade*. Leuven: Leuven University Press.

Kuhlmann, S., & Bogumil, J. (2018). Performance Measurement and Benchmarking as "Reflexive Institutions" for Local Governments: Germany, Sweden and England Compared. *International Journal of Public Sector Management, 31*(4), 543–562.

Kuhlman, S., & Bouckaert, G. (2016). *Local Public Sector Reforms in Times of Crisis: National Trajectories and International Comparisons*. The Governance and Public Management Series. Basingstoke: Palgrave Macmillan.

Lessman, C. (2012). Regional Inequality and Decentralization: An Empirical Analysis. *Environment and Planning A, 44*, 1363–1388.

Ligthart, J. E., & Van Oudheusden, P. (2015). In Government We Trust: The Role Of Fiscal Decentralization. *European Journal of Political Economy, 37*, 116–128.

Lin, J. Y., & Liu, Z. (2000). Fiscal decentralization and Economic Growth in China. *Economic Development and Cultural Change, 49*(1), 1–21.

Litvack, J., Ahmad, J., & Bird, R. (1998). *Rethinking Decentralization in Developing Countries*. Washington, DC: The World Bank.

Ma, L. J. C., & Wu, F. (2005). Restructuring the Chinese City: Diverse Processes and Reconstituted Spaces. In L. J. C. Ma & F. Wu (Eds.), *Restructuring the Chinese City: Changing Society, Economy, and Space* (pp. 1–20). London: Routledge.

Martinez-Vazguez, J., & McNab, R. (1997). *Fiscal Decentralization, Economic Growth, and Democratic Governance*. International Studies Program (Working Paper 97-7). Washington, DC: USAID Conference on Economic Growth and Democratic Governance.

McGarry, J., & O'Leary, B. (2012). Territorial Pluralism: Its Forms, Flaws, and Virtues. In F. Requejo & M. C. Badia (Eds.), *Federalism, Plurinationality and Democratic Constitutionalism: Theory and Cases*. Abingdon and New York: Routledge.

6 CONCLUSION: TOWARD AN ASYMMETRICAL DECENTRALIZATION DESIGN

Montinola, G., Qian, Y., & Weingast, B. R. (1995). Federalism, Chinese Style: The Political Basis for Economic Success in China. *World Politics, 48,* 50–81.

Oates, W. (1993). Fiscal Decentralization and Economic Development. *National Tax Journal, 46*(2), 237–243.

Oi, J. (1992). Fiscal Reform and the Economic Foundations of Local State Corporatism in China. *World Politics, 45,* 99–126.

Oksenberg, M., & Tong, J. (1991). The Evolution of Central-Provincial Fiscal Relations in China, 1971–1984: The Formal System. *The China Quarterly, 125,* 1–32.

Persson, T., & Tabellini, G. (1994). Is Inequality Harmful for Growth? *American Economic Review, 84*(3), 600–621.

Qian, Y., & Weingast, B. R. (1997). Federalism as a Commitment to Preserving Market Incentives. *Journal of Economic Perspectives, 11*(4), 83–92.

Rodriguez, V. E. (1995). Municipal Autonomy and the Politics of Inter Governmental Finance: Is It Different for the Opposition? In V. E. Rodriguez & P. M. Ward (Eds.), *Opposition Government in Mexico.* Albuquerque: University of New Mexico Press.

Rodriguez-Pose, A., & Ezcurra, R. (2011). Is Fiscal Decentralization Harmful for Economic Growth? Evidence from the OECD Countries. *Journal of Economic Geography, 11,* 619–643.

Sapolsky, R. M. (2017). *Behave.* London: Penguin Books.

Schragger, R. C. (2010). Decentralization and Development. *Virginia Law Review, 96*(8), 1837–1910.

Seabright, P. (1996). Accountability and Decentralization in Government: An Incomplete Contracts Model. *European Economic Review, 40*(1), 61–89.

Shah, A. (1994). *The Reform of Intergovernmental Fiscal Relations in Developing and Emerging Market Economies.* World Bank Policy and Research Series No. 23. Washington, DC.

Shirk, S. (1993). *The Political Logic of Economic Reforms in China.* Berkeley: University of California Press.

Smoke, P. (2015). Managing Public Sector Decentralization in Developing Countries: Moving Beyond Conventional Recipes. *Public Administration and Development, 35,* 250–262.

Tarlton, C. D. (1965). Symmetry and Asymmetry as Elements of Federalism. *Journal of Politics, 27*(861), 874.

Thede, N. (2009). Decentralization, Democracy and Human Rights: A Human Rights-Based Analysis of the Impact of Local Democratic Reforms on Development. *Journal of Human Development and Capabilities, 10*(1), 103–123.

Treisman, D. (2002). *Defining and Measuring Decentralization: A Global Perspective.* Unpublished manuscript.

Warner, M. E. (2003). Competition Cooperation and Local Governance. In D. Brown & L. Swanson (Eds.), *Challenges for Rural America in the Twenty First Century* (pp. 252–262). University Park: Penn State University Press.

Watts, R. L. (2005). A Comparative Perspective on Asymmetry in Federations. *Asymmetry Series* (4), IIGR, Queen's University.

Watts, R. L. (2010). *Asymmetrical Decentralization: Functional or Dysfunctional*. Paper Presented at International Political Science Association. Québec City, Québec, Canada.

Wehner, J. H.-G. (2000). Asymmetrical Devolution. *Development Southern Africa, 17*(2), 249–262.

Weingast, B. R. (2014). Second Generation Fiscal Federalism: Political Aspects of Decentralization and Economic Development. *World Development, 53,* 14–25.

Wilkinson, R. (2000). *Mind the Gap: Hierarchies, Health and Human Evolution*. London: Weidenfeld and Nicolson.

Zhang, L.-Y. (1994). Location-Specific Advantages and Manufacturing Direct Foreign Investment in South China. *World Development, 22,* 45–53.

Zhang, T., & Zou, H. (1998). Fiscal Decentralization, Public Spending and Economic Growth. *Journal of Public Economics, 67*(2), 221–240.

Zhang, X., Li, C., Li, W., Song, J., & Yang, C. (2017). Do Administrative Boundaries Matter for Uneven Economic Development? A Case Study of China's Provincial Border Counties. *Growth and Change, 48*(4), 883–908.

APPENDICES

© The Editor(s) (if applicable) and The Author(s), under exclusive
license to Springer Nature Switzerland AG, part of Springer Nature 2019
E. Tan, *Decentralization and Governance Capacity*, Public Sector
Organizations, https://doi.org/10.1007/978-3-030-02047-7

230 APPENDICES

Functional allocation of municipal services in 2016 (Thousand TL)

	Salaries	Social security cont.	Purchasing	Interests	Current transfers	Capital expenses	Capital transfers	Loan	Total
Administrative services	5,150,917	805,620	12,279,815	1,949,798	2,213,026	2,176,283	791,429	2,289,640	27,656,528
Civil defense services	2706	439	24,959		7476	647			36,227
Public order and security services	1,828,314	278,451	1,397,550		14,358	582,406			4,101,079
Economic affairs and services	1,536,482	266,320	6,048,173		402,736	11,952,937	75,333		20,281,981
Environmental protection	851,347	148,277	7,393,319		11,191	1,182,777	1592		9,588,503
Housing and welfare services	1,855,404	304,556	4,430,682		27,265	12,950,328	42,191		19,610,426
Health services	249,735	40,555	717,231		36,477	26,855	57		1,070,910
Recreation, culture and religion services	675,937	105,876	5,184,115		239,065	687,132	23,183		6,915,308
Education services	14,996	2071	313,331		1801	46,255			378,454
Social security and social aid	124,382	18,425	690,037		768,008	29,693			1,630,545
Total	12,290,220	1,970,590	38,479,212	1,949,798	3,721,403	29,635,313	933,785	2,289,640	91,269,961

Data source Ministry of Finance

APPENDICES 231

The SEGE-11 Index and Scores

Demographic Indicators

1	Population density
2	Fertility rate (between 15 and 49)
3	Dependent young population rate (0–14 years old)
4	Net immigration rate
5	Urbanization rate

Education Indicators

6	Literacy rate
7	Literacy rate in woman population
8	Secondary education schooling rate
9	Vocational and technical schooling rate
10	Provincial YGS[a] success rate
11	Ratio of university or equivalent degree graduates in 22+years old population

Health Indicators

12	Number of hospital beds per 100.000 people
13	Number of doctors per 10.000 people
14	Number of dentists per 10.000 people
15	Number of pharmacies per 10.000 people
16	Ratio of green card[b] holders in the province

Employment Indicators

17	Unemployment rate
18	Labor force participation rate
19	Ratio of population in working age (15–64) to overall population
20	Ratio of manufacturing sector in social insured employment
21	Ratio of social insured employment to overall population
22	The average daily earning
23	The average daily earning- Woman
24	Employment rate

Competition and Innovation Capacity

25	Share of the province in Turkey's export
26	Export amount per person
27	Number of manufacturing companies (share in Turkey)
28	Ratio of registered companies in manufacturing sector
29	Electricity consumption per person in manufacturing sector
30	Number of production parcels in organized industry zones (share in Turkey)
31	Number of small enterprises (share in Turkey)
32	Total capital in the new enterprises (share in Turkey)
33	Foreign capital enterprises per 10.000 people

(continued)

232 APPENDICES

(continued)

34	Trademark application per 100.000 people
35	Patent application per 100.000 people
36	Rate of post-graduate and doctorate degree holders in 30+years old population
37	Agricultural production value per population living in rural area
38	Number of certified beds in touristic facilities (share in Turkey)
39	Amount of incentivized investments (share in Turkey)
Fiscal Capacity	
40	Bank credits in the province (share in Turkey)
41	Saving deposits in the province (share in Turkey)
42	Amount of bank deposits per person
43	Active online banking individual users per 1000 people
44	Active online banking business users per 1000 people
45	Budget revenues per person
46	Provincial tax revenues (share in Turkey)
Accessibility	
47	Asphalted road ratio in rural area
48	Distance of the province to the nearest airport
49	Broadband users per household
50	GSM subscribers per person
51	The value of the province in terms of goods per km on national highways
52	The ratio of total railway lines to land surface area
Quality of Life	
53	Rental total space in shopping malls per 1000 people
54	Rate of the population benefited from sewerage services to total population
55	Household electric consumption per person
56	Number of cars per 10.000 people
57	CO_2 average value
58	Particulate matter (smoke) average value
59	Ratio of population without social security coverage to overall population
60	Number of convicts per 100.000 people
61	Number of suicide cases per 100.000 people

[a]National university entry exam
[b]Green cards are distributed to those without any social security coverage to receive public health services free of charge

APPENDICES   233

SEGE-2011 Development Index of Provinces

Rank	Province	Index value	Rank	Province	Index value
1	İstanbul	4.5154	42	Malatya	−0.0785
2	Ankara	2.8384	43	Afyon	−0.0797
3	İzmir	1.9715	44	Artvin	−0.1046
4	Kocaeli	1.6592	45	Erzincan	−0.1056
5	Antalya	1.5026	46	Hatay	−0.1302
6	Bursa	1.3740	47	Kastamonu	−0.1471
7	Eskişehir	1.1671	48	Bartın	−0.1976
8	Muğla	1.0493	49	Sivas	−0.2208
9	Tekirdağ	0.9154	50	Çorum	−0.2405
10	Denizli	0.9122	51	Sinop	−0.2479
11	Bolu	0.6394	52	Giresun	−0.2564
12	Edirne	0.6383	53	Osmaniye	−0.2892
13	Yalova	0.6263	54	Çankırı	−0.3312
14	Çanakkale	0.5999	55	Aksaray	−0.3671
15	Kırklareli	0.5923	56	Niğde	−0.3761
16	Adana	0.5666	57	Tokat	−0.3821
17	Kayseri	0.5650	58	Tunceli	−0.3892
18	Sakarya	0.5641	59	Erzurum	−0.4327
19	Aydın	0.5597	60	Kahramanmaraş	−0.4677
20	Konya	0.5308	61	Ordu	−0.4810
21	Isparta	0.5272	62	Gümüşhane	−0.4814
22	Balıkesir	0.4764	63	Kilis	−0.5733
23	Manisa	0.4711	64	Bayburt	−0.5946
24	Mersin	0.4636	65	Yozgat	−0.6079
25	Uşak	0.3737	66	Adıyaman	−0.9602
26	Burdur	0.3684	67	Diyarbakır	−1.0014
27	Bilecik	0.3634	68	Kars	−1.0923
28	Karabük	0.2916	69	Iğdır	−1.1184
29	Zonguldak	0.2758	70	Batman	−1.1203
30	Gaziantep	0.2678	71	Ardahan	−1.1384
31	Trabzon	0.2218	72	Bingöl	−1.1920
32	Karaman	0.1864	73	Şanlıurfa	−1.2801
33	Samsun	0.1579	74	Mardin	−1.3591
34	Rize	0.1550	75	Van	−1.3783
35	Düzce	0.1056	76	Bitlis	−1.4003
36	Nevşehir	0.1029	77	Siirt	−1.4166
37	Amasya	0.0510	78	Şırnak	−1.4605
38	Kütahya	0.0198	79	Ağrı	−1.6366
39	Elazığ	−0.0103	80	Hakkari	−1.6961
40	Kırşehir	−0.0211	81	Muş	−1.7329
41	Kırıkkale	−0.0687			

Source Turkish Ministry of Development, 2013

List of Indicators
Capacity Indicators

	Code	Name	Clarification	Relevancy	Type	Instrument	Source of data	Measurement level	Unit of analysis
Mobilization capacity	MOB1	Property taxation	The ratio of collected taxes to overall registered residents	Capability in own-source revenues	Financial	Survey	Deputy mayor (q2)	Ratio	0–1
	MOB2	Utilization of immovable property	The ratio of the annual revenue generated from immovable to the overall value of the immovable owned by the municipality	Capability in own-source revenues	Financial	Survey	Deputy mayor (q1)	Ratio	0–1
	MOB3	Debt structure	The ratio of short-term debts to long-term debts	Sustainable debt level	Financial	Survey or municipality's own data	Deputy mayor or manager of financial department (q4)	Ratio	0–1
	MOB4	Adequacy of financial resources	The score on the adequacy of existing financial resources for municipal functions	Financial capacity	Financial	Survey	Mayor (q21)	Ordinal	1–5 scale
	MOB5	Purchasing power	The ratio of the expenditures on goods and services to the overall expenditures	Financial capability for purchasing	Material	Survey or municipality's own data	Deputy mayor or manager of the financial department	Ratio	0–1
	MOB6	Physical and technical adequacy	The mean score of 5 Likert items on adequacy in; (1) computer and computer hardware, (2) technical equipment and machinery, (3) internet connection and computer software, (4) physical conditions of civil servant's offices, (5) physical conditions of manager's offices	Material adequacy inside the municipality	Material	Survey	Deputy mayor (q7)	Interval	1–5

	Code	Name	Clarification	Relevancy	Type	Instrument	Source of data	Measurement level	Unit of analysis
	MOB7	Material adequacy in public services	The mean score of the adequacy of equipment in each service area	Material adequacy in terms of service areas	Material	Survey	Mayor (q18)	Interval	1–5
	MOB8	Public procurement	The mean score of 4 Likert-items, (1) swiftness of public procurement, (2) Sufficiency of public procurement to meet the municipality's needs, (3) competence of municipal personnel on public procurement processes, (4) adequacy in e-procurement options	Capacity in public procurement	Material	Survey	Deputy mayor (q11/1, 2, 4, 5)	Interval	1–5
Decision-making capacity	DM1	Success in strategic planning	The mean score of the mayor and deputy mayor's evaluation of the last strategic planning	Capability in strategic planning	Planning	Survey	Mayor (q 9, 1) and Deputy mayor (q36)	Interval	1–5
	DM2	Performance budgeting	The mean score of 7 Likert-item on performance budgeting; (1) timing in budget planning, (2) integration of budget plans with performance plans, (3) implementation of performance criteria on budget negotiations, (4) coherence with strategic planning, (5) integration of activity-based costing, feasibility analysis, risk assessment and cost accounting in budget plans, (6) adequacy of equipment to monitor and assess performances, and (7) adequacy of e-budget system	Capacity in performance budgeting	Planning	Survey	Deputy mayor (q37)	Interval	1–5

(continued)

(continued)

Code	Name	Clarification	Relevancy	Type	Instrument	Source of data	Measurement level	Unit of analysis
DM3	Importance of strategic plan and performance plans on actual decision-making	The mean score of 2 Likert items; (1) the importance of the strategic plan on implementation, (2) the importance of performance reports on high important political decisions	The actual impact of strategic and performance plans on decision-making	Planning	Survey	Mayor (q9/3, 4)	Interval	1–5
DM4	Intra-organizational communication	The mean score of 7 Likert items; (1) communication among departments, (2)communication between deputy mayors and directors, (3) share of information inside the municipality, (4) adequacy of IT systems, (5) storing of information, (6)division of work and collaboration among department, and (7) communication between civil servants and councillors	The capacity of intra-organizational communication	Communication	Survey	Deputy mayor (q27)	Interval	1–5
DM5	Importance of local representatives on decision-making	The mean score of the importance of Urban Council and muhtars on the formation of the municipal program	The relevance of representatives of citizens on decision-making	Communication	Survey	Mayor (q9/5, 6)	Interval	1–5
DM6	Datasheets	The number of datasheets spread in 2012	Collecting information on the characteristics of citizens	Communication	Survey	Deputy mayor (q34)	Ratio	Number
DM7	Citizen polls	The number of citizen polls took place in 2012	Collecting information on the expectations of citizens	Communication	Survey	Deputy mayor (q33)	Ratio	Number

Code	Name	Clarification	Relevancy	Type	Instrument	Source of data	Measurement level	Unit of analysis
DM8	E-government system	The mean score of dummy variables on online service available on the municipality's website. Each variable will be registered as 1 or 0. It comprises 8 services; (1) transaction with taxes, fees, etc., (2) business search, (3) reaching personal documents, (4) company registration, (5) statistical information, (6) applying for permits and licences, (7) personal statements on finances and taxes, and (8) information about zoning status	Collecting information on citizens via online services	Communication	Municipality website	Municipality website	Interval	0–1
DM9	E-participation system	The mean score of dummy variables on online e-participation means in municipality's website. Each variable is registered as 1 or 0. It comprises 7 variables; (1) announcement of municipal decisions, (2) announcement of projects, (3) announcement of plans, (4) broadcasting municipal sessions, (5) social media tools, (6) opinion polls, and (7) white desk	Collecting information about the opinion of citizens via online services	Communication	Municipality website	Municipality website	Interval	0–1
DM10	Visitors to the website	The ranking of the municipal website according to the Alexa traffic rank. Lesser numbers indicate higher ranks	The level of online communication with citizens	Communication	Alexa traffic ranking	Alexa's website www.alexa.com (6 August 2013)	Ratio	Number

(continued)

(continued)

	Code	Name	Clarification	Relevancy	Type	Instrument	Source of data	Measurement level	Unit of analysis
Implementation capacity	IMP1	Education level of the mayor	The level of education. Primary school-1; Junior High-2; High school-3; Undergrad-4; Postgraduation-5; Doctoral-6	The intellectual capacity of the mayor	Management	Survey	Mayor (q1)	Ordinal	1–6 scales
	IMP2	Years in office	The number of years in the office as mayor	Experience of the mayor	Management	Survey	Mayor (q1)	Nominal	Number
	IMP3	Initiative taking in management	The mean score of initiative-taking by the deputy mayors and directors	The level of initiative-taking in management	Management	Survey	Mayor (q12)	Interval	1–5
	IMP4	Collaboration in management	The mean score of collaboration between deputy mayors and directors, and deputy mayor and mayor	The level of collaboration in management	Management	Survey	Mayor (q13) and Deputy mayor (q24/3, 4)	Interval	1–5
	IMP5	Management practices (staff development)	The mean score of 3 Likert items; (1) practices to increase motivation among staff, (2) training on leadership and management, and (3) practices to increase initiative taking in directors and other personnel	The quality of management practices to increase organizational capacity	Management	Survey	Deputy mayor (q24/1, 2, 5)	Interval	1–5
	IMP6	Seniority in directors	A sum value indicating the years of occupation for directors. There are 5 ranges divided by 5 years scale. 0–5 years=1; 5–10 years=2; 10–15 years=3; 15–20 years=4; above 20−5 The number of personnel on each cluster will be multiplied by the corresponding number	Experience in management	Management	Survey	Deputy mayor (q14)	Interval	1–5

Code	Name	Clarification	Relevancy	Type	Instrument	Source of data	Measurement level	Unit of analysis
IMP7	Seniority in personnel	A sum value indicating the years of occupation for personnel. There are 5 ranges divided by 5 years scale. 0–5 years = 1; 5–10 years = 2; 10–15 years = 3; 15–20 years = 4; above 20 = 5. The number of personnel on each cluster will be multiplied by the corresponding number	Experience in personnel	Human resources	Survey	Deputy mayor (q15)	Interval	1–5
IMP8	Norm cadre	The norm cadre indicates the number of personnel required for municipal functions. The ratio of the number of norm cadre to the total number of employees	Sufficiency in number of personnel or overstaffing	Human resources	Survey	Deputy mayor (q12)	Ratio	Number
IMP9	Technical personnel	The ratio of technical personnel to the overall number of personnel	Capacity in technical personnel	Human resources	Survey	Deputy mayor (q13)	Ratio	0–1
IMP10	Specialized personnel	The ratio of personnel graduated postgrad or equivalent vocational training to overall personnel	Capacity in qualified personnel	Human resources	Survey	Deputy mayor (q13)	Ratio	0–1
IMP11	Personnel in municipal companies	The ratio of number of personnel employed in municipalities to the overall number of personnel	Sufficiency in number of personnel	Human resources	Survey	Deputy mayor (q12)	Ratio	Number

(continued)

(continued)

	Code	Name	Clarification	Relevancy	Type	Instrument	Source of data	Measurement level	Unit of analysis
	IMP12	HR management system	The mean score of 7 Likert items: (1) the functionality of HR management system (mayor), (2) the sufficiency of HR management system, (3) the coherence of the HR management plans with the municipality's needs, (4) competence of the HR department, (5) implementation of HR strategies, (6) monitoring and assessing the training need, and (7) trainings meet the municipality's needs	Capacity in HR management	Human resources	Survey	Mayor (q10) and deputy mayor (q19)	Interval	1–5
	IMP13	Employment policies	The mean score of 4 Likert items; (1) sufficiency in personnel number, (2) sufficiency in qualified personnel number, (3) efficiency of employment policies, and (4) match of new recruits the job criteria	The success in employment policies	Human resources	Survey	Deputy mayor (q20)	Interval	1–5
	IMP14	Formation	The average hour of occupation training per personnel who received training	HR quality	Human resources	Survey	Deputy mayor (q18)	Ratio	Number

Decentralization Indicator

	Code	Name	Clarification	Relevancy	Type	Instrument	Source of data	Measurement level	Unit of analysis
DEC		Decentralization	The ratio of own-source revenues (tax revenue + revenue from enterprise & properties + capital revenues + receivables) to overall revenues	Financial autonomy	Fiscal decentralization	Datasheet on local administration's revenue	http://www. bumko.gov.tr	Ratio	0–1

Control Variables

INF	Influence of central government	The mean score of 8 Likert-items for the influence of central government and its agencies on: (1) delivery of municipal services, (2) administrative activities, (3) decision-making about municipal services, (4) partnerships with other local administrations, private sector organizations and civil society organizations, (5) own-source revenues, (6) grants and aids, (7) debts and loans, and (8) investments	Influence of central government on local governance	External factor	Survey	Mayor (q24)	Interval	1–5
POP	Population	The rank of the province in terms of population. The lower the rank, the higher the population	Direct impact on financial capacity and local capacity	External factor	Union of Turkish municipality's database	http://www.tbb.gov.tr/storage/catalogs/2012-belediye-nufuslari.pdf	Interval	from 1 to 81
PolDiv	Political diversity	Municipalities which are not governed by the justice and development party (AKP) will be rated as 0, the rest will be rated as 1	The arbitrary stance of central government toward municipalities governed by opposition parties can affect decentralization and capacity	External factor	Local elections newsportal	http://secim.haberler.com/2009/il-sonuclari.asp	Ordinal	0 or 1
Party	Party affiliation	The percentage of votes of winning party in the municipality according to the 2009 local election. A lower percentage indicates less party affiliation among the management	Different party affiliation inside the municipality might affect capacity in local government	External factor	Local elections newsportal	http://secim.haberler.com/2009/il-sonuclari.asp	Ratio	0–1

Data List
Mobilization Capacity

Provinces	MOB1	MOB2	MOB3	MOB4	MOB5	MOB6	MOB7	MOB8
Adiyaman	0.54	0.009	0.189	2.00	0.310	4.20	3.86	3.25
Afyonkarahisar	0.85	0.051	0.000	4.00	0.365	4.60	4.79	4.25
Aksaray	0.77	0.21	0.700	3.00	0.341	–	4.64	–
Amasya	0.57	0.019	0.795	3.00	0.331	4.00	4.21	4.00
Ardahan	0.37	0.007	0.621	1.00	0.369	3.00	2.86	5.00
Artvin	0.73	0.034	0.000	4.00	0.334	–	4.64	4.50
Bilecik	0.70	–	0.000	2.00	0.340	5.00	3.64	2.75
Bitlis	0.33	0.017	0.030	–	0.287	3.80	–	4.75
Bolu	0.68	0.023	0.410	–	0.425	4.50	4.21	5.00
Burdur	0.51	0.01	0.077	3.00	0.460	4.00	4.14	3.50
Canakkale	0.64	0.02	0.176	5.00	0.362	3.80	4.07	3.00
Corum	–	–	–	4.00	0.419	–	4.14	–
Denizli	0.66	0.027	0.239	–	0.369	4.60	–	4.25
Giresun	0.65	–	–	4.00	0.415	–	4.86	–
Gumushane	–	–	–	3.00	0.391	–	3.83	–
Kahramanmaraş	0.78	0.024	0.450	3.50	0.400	5.00	4.64	4.00
Karabuk	0.76	0.0175	0.296	4.00	0.412	3.20	4.07	3.25
Karaman	0.77	0.0057	0.200	3.00	0.294	4.80	3.57	1.00
Kars	0.80	0.0131	0.000	3.00	0.381	3.40	3.64	3.50
Kastamonu	0.58	–	0.000	5.00	0.355	4.80	4.57	4.00
Kutahya	–	–	–	5.00	0.344	–	4.14	–
Manisa	0.84	–	0.300	5.00	0.413	4.60	4.93	4.50
Mardin	0.65	0.0027	0.000	1.00	0.346	4.20	4.21	4.75
Mugla	0.82	0.1395	0.195	3.00	0.414	4.60	5.00	4.00
Mus	0.68	–	0.000	1.00	0.307	4.40	4.00	4.50
Nigde	0.72	–	0.044	3.00	0.355	–	4.21	–

Provinces	MOB1	MOB2	MOB3	MOB4	MOB5	MOB6	MOB7	MOB8
Rize	0.74	0.0488	0.100	–	0.502	4.40	–	–
Sivas	0.70	0.0187	0.555	4.00	0.435	4.20	4.07	4.75
Tokat	–	–	–	5.00	0.384	–	4.29	–
Trabzon	0.60	0.0085	0.614	2.00	0.458	5.00	4.64	5.00
Usak	0.78	0.0723	0.400	4.00	0.333	–	4.43	3.25
Van	–	–	–	1.00	0.362	–	2.79	–
Yozgat	0.80	0.1271	0.089	3.00	0.411	4.20	4.36	3.50

Decision-Making Capacity

Provinces	DM1	DM2	DM3	DM4	DM5	DM6	DM7	DM8	DM9	DM10
Adiyaman	3.13	4.00	3.00	4.00	3.00	0.00	0.00	0.88	0.50	3449743.00
Afyonkarahisar	3.88	4.00	4.50	4.43	4.50	0.00	0.00	0.75	0.63	1,169,742.00
Aksaray	4.50	4.00	5.00	3.71	2.50	5.00	2.00	0.63	0.63	551612.00
Amasya	4.00	3.57	5.00	4.00	4.00	0.00	0.00	0.13	0.50	1961721.00
Ardahan	2.63	4.14	5.00	4.29	3.00	0.00	0.00	0.00	0.38	4914915.00
Artvin	5.00	5.00	5.00	5.00	2.50	0.00	0.00	0.75	0.50	2543869.00
Bilecik	3.63	3.71	3.50	3.57	2.00	4.00	2.00	0.38	0.25	966902.00
Bitlis	–	4.00	–	4.14	–	0.00	1.00	0.00	0.38	8373694.00
Bolu	4.38	3.50	4.00	–	3.50	1.00	1.00	0.75	0.50	569875.00
Burdur	4.38	4.29	4.00	4.00	3.50	0.00	0.00	0.88	0.50	2867540.00
Canakkale	4.00	3.14	4.00	4.29	4.00	12.00	1.00	0.75	0.63	448494.00
Corum	–	–	4.00	–	2.00	–	–	0.50	0.88	1484275.00
Denizli	–	4.00	–	4.57	–	12.00	1.00	0.75	0.50	319202.00
Giresun	–	–	5.00	–	4.00	–	–	0.00	0.50	1616509.00
Gumushane	–	–	–	–	3.00	–	–	0.25	0.38	3340409.00
Kahramanmaraş	5.00	5.00	5.00	4.71	5.00	2.00	2.00	0.50	0.75	362258.00

(continued)

244   APPENDICES

(continued)

Provinces	DM1	DM2	DM3	DM4	DM5	DM6	DM7	DM8	DM9	DM10
Karabuk	3.38	2.71	4.00	3.86	3.50	3.00	0.00	0.75	0.88	1685665.00
Karaman	3.88	4.00	5.00	2.43	3.50	4.00	1.00	0.88	0.50	1162660.00
Kars	3.00	2.86	4.00	3.29	3.00	0.00	0.00	0.00	0.25	3481300.00
Kastamonu	4.50	3.43	4.50	3.57	4.50	1.00	–	0.75	0.38	2942933.00
Kutahya	–	–	4.00	–	3.00	–	–	0.63	0.88	2550939.00
Manisa	4.63	5.00	5.00	4.14	4.50	–	2.00	0.63	0.75	467635.00
Mardin	3.50	3.14	5.00	4.29	5.00	0.00	0.00	0.00	0.50	1702479.00
Mugla	4.00	4.29	4.00	5.00	4.50	3.00	2.00	0.50	0.63	2604425.00
Mus	3.50	3.29	4.50	3.57	2.50	0.00	0.00	0.13	0.50	5949733.00
Nigde	4.00	4.71	3.00	4.43	3.00	1.00	1.00	0.83	0.63	795495.00
Rize	–	–	–	–	–	1.00	1.00	0.83	0.50	1568630.00
Sivas	4.50	3.14	5.00	3.29	5.00	0.00	0.00	0.75	0.83	388966.00
Tokat	–	–	–	–	1.50	–	–	0.50	0.38	2053151.00
Trabzon	4.88	3.57	5.00	4.57	4.00	1.00	1.00	0.83	0.63	453182.00
Usak	3.88	3.86	4.50	4.57	2.00	0.00	1.00	0.83	0.83	576835.00
Van	–	–	3.50	–	4.00	–	–	0.00	0.25	3113899.00
Yozgat	3.50	3.00	4.50	4.14	3.50	0.00	0.00	0.13	0.25	5514491.00

Implementation Capacity

Provinces	IMP1	IMP2	IMP3	IMP4	IMP5	IMP6	IMP7	IMP8	IMP9	IMP10	IMP11	IMP12	IMP13	IMP14
Adiyaman	4.00	9.00	4.00	3.33	3.33	3.41	1.62	1.17	0.09	0.10	0.00	3.14	3.25	32
Afyonkarahisar	4.00	4.00	4.00	4.67	4.33	3.34	4.35	1.30	0.21	0.12	0.00	3.43	4.50	86
Aksaray	4.00	9.00	4.00	4.00	2.67	3.49	2.41	1.75	0.13	0.02	0.00	3.14	4.00	9
Amasya	4.00	4.00	3.50	4.67	3.33	3.86	4	1.02	0.16	0.07	1.49	4.15	4.00	20
Ardahan	4.00	4.00	1.50	3.67	3.33	2.4	1.33	0.75	0.07	0.15	0.00	3.71	3.25	17
Artvin	4.00	14.00	5.00	4.67	3.33	3.28	3.75	0.87	0.16	0.24	0.84	4.14	4.00	7

Provinces	IMP1	IMP2	IMP3	IMP4	IMP5	IMP6	IMP7	IMP8	IMP9	IMP10	IMP11	IMP12	IMP13	IMP14
Bilecik	4.00	9.00	3.00	3.67	3.00	–	–	–	–	–	0.00	2.57	3.00	20
Bitlis	4.00	4.00	–	–	4.00	3.19	3.6	1.91	0.12	0.17	0.07	–	3.75	0
Bolu	4.00	9.00	3.50	–	–	3	3.92	1.09	0.08	0.03	0.74	–	–	5
Burdur	4.00	9.00	4.00	4.33	3.33	3.29	2.29	1.57	0.19	0.40	1.44	3.43	3.25	0
Canakkale	4.00	10.00	4.00	4.33	4.00	2.82	4.18	1.54	0.13	0.36	0.25	3.15	3.50	200
Corum	4.00	4.00	3.50	–	–	–	–	–	–	0.26	–	–	–	3
Denizli	4.00	2.00	–	–	4.67	2.86	4.05	1.32	0.20	0.02	0.00	–	3.75	147
Giresun	4.00	4.00	4.50	–	–	–	–	1.43	0.07	–	–	–	–	94
Gumushane	4.00	14.00	4.00	–	–	–	–	–	–	–	–	–	–	
Kahramanmaraş	4.00	10.00	4.00	4.67	4.67	3.05	3.92	1.84	0.15	0.21	3.17	4.57	3.75	32
Karabuk	3.00	4.00	4.50	4.67	1.67	2.03	4.18	1.55	0.10	0.02	1.88	4.71	5.00	–
Karaman	6.00	4.00	3.00	3.00	2.33	3.19	2.48	1.35	0.15	0.30	0.06	2.86	2.00	24
Kars	4.00	4.00	3.50	3.67	2.67	3.51	1.59	2.20	–	0.25	1.34	3.28	2.75	30
Kastamonu	4.00	14.00	4.50	4.00	4.00	3.08	2.75	–	0.09	0.15	1.04	3.57	3.75	16
Kutahya	5.00	9.00	3.50	–	–	–	–	2.26	0.25	0.14	1.82	2.43	–	–
Manisa	4.00	4.00	4.50	4.67	3.33	–	–	2.26	0.25	0.14	1.82	2.43	3.00	10
Mardin	4.00	4.00	3.50	4.33	4.33	3.44	1.47	2.11	0.21	0.11	1.46	4.43	4.00	20
Mugla	5.00	14.00	5.00	5.00	4.67	2.39	4.36	1.68	0.19	0.38	0.00	4.00	4.50	13
Mus	4.00	9.00	3.50	3.33	2.33	3.34	3.88	0.90	0.05	0.01	0.00	3.00	3.25	0
Nigde	3.00	4.00	4.50	3.67	3.67	2.83	4.6	2.14	0.20	0.48	0.00	3.15	4.00	0
Rize	4.00	9.00	–	–	–	2.59	3.35	2.54	0.28	0.23	1.82	–	4.00	104
Sivas	4.00	4.00	4.00	3.33	3.00	4.02	4.76	0.93	0.15	0.24	2.20	3.43	4.50	200
Tokat	6.00	9.00	3.00	–	–	–	–	–	–	–	–	–	–	–
Trabzon	6.00	4.00	4.00	4.67	4.00	3.43	4.27	1.40	0.00	0.02	1.26	4.86	3.50	37
Usak	4.00	9.00	3.00	4.33	3.33	2.84	1.3	1.34	0.13	0.45	–	3.71	4.50	78
Van	1.00	1.00	3.00	–	–	–	–	–	–	–	–	–	–	–
Yozgat	4.00	9.00	4.00	4.33	3.33	3.86	2.6	1.13	0.33	0.09	1.44	3.71	4.00	2

246 APPENDICES

Other Variables

Provinces	INF	POP	PolDiv	Party	Dev	INF
Adiyaman	2.625	217,463	1	0.49	−0.960	2.625
Afyonkarahisar	3.5	186,991	1	0.48	−0.080	3.5
Aksaray	3.25	186,599	1	0.58	−0.367	3.25
Amasya	3.5	91,874	1	0.40	0.051	3.5
Ardahan	2.125	19,075	1	0.37	−1.138	2.125
Artvin	2.571	25,771	0	0.44	−0.105	2.571
Bilecik	3.875	51,260	1	0.38	0.363	3.875
Bitlis	–	46,111	1	0.43	−1.400	–
Bolu	3.25	131,264	1	0.43	0.639	3.25
Burdur	3.75	72,377	1	0.40	0.368	3.75
Canakkale	3.25	111,137	0	0.39	0.600	3.25
Corum	1.875	231,146	1	0.46	−0.241	1.875
Denizli	–	525,497	1	0.40	0.912	–
Giresun	3.625	100,712	0	0.47	−0.256	3.625
Gumushane	2.750	32,444	0	0.42	−0.481	2.750
Kahramanmaraş	3.625	443,575	1	0.65	−0.468	3.625
Karabuk	2.000	110,537	0	0.31	0.292	2.000
Karaman	1.375	141,630	1	0.49	0.186	1.375
Kars	2.875	78,100	1	0.33	−1.092	2.875
Kastamonu	2.375	96,217	1	0.49	−0.147	2.375
Kutahya	3.750	224,898	1	0.62	0.020	3.750
Manisa	1.625	309,050	0	0.39	0.471	1.625
Mardin	2.250	86,948	1	0.45	−1.359	2.250
Mugla	1.250	64,706	0	0.46	1.049	1.250
Mus	3.125	81,764	1	0.51	−1.733	3.125
Nigde	3.875	118,186	1	0.40	−0.376	3.875
Rize	–	104,508	1	0.47	0.155	–
Sivas	3.000	312,587	0	0.51	−0.221	3.000
Tokat	2.125	132,437	1	0.50	−0.382	2.125
Trabzon	3.125	243,735	1	0.48	0.222	3.125
Usak	2.250	187,886	0	0.40	0.374	2.250
Van	2.250	370,190	0	0.54	−1.378	2.250
Yozgat	4.500	78,328	1	0.55	−0.608	4.500

APPENDICES   247

Translation of the Survey Questions
Survey I- For the Mayors

1. Below are some questions on your personal profile. Please fill in the required fields and provide an explanation if necessary.

> What is your last degree obtained? (elementary, junior high, high school, university, vocational school, masters, doctorate)
> For how many years are you a mayor?
> Did you work as a manager in a municipality before being elected as mayor?

2. Does your municipality have a communication plan? Please mark the appropriate response.

YES	NO	I DON'T KNOW

3. This purpose of this question is to learn the structure of the information pathways in your municipality. Please fill in the required fields and provide an explanation if necessary. For some question, you are asked to provide an approximate value. For these questions, please indicate a range which corresponds best to your answer.

> How many regular meetings do you have per month with the municipal committee?
> How many regular meetings do you have per month with the directors of departments?
> How many regular meetings do you have per month with the elected councilors?
> How many meetings do you have approximately per year with the representatives of the central government?
> How many meetings do you have approximately per year with the governor of your province?
> Approximately, how many petitions are you receiving per month from the elected councilors?
> Approximately, how many days do you need to respond to the petitions from the elected councilors?

APPENDICES

> How many regular meetings do you have per year with the Urban Council?
> How do you describe the approach of civil society organizations participating in the meetings with the Urban Council? (e.g. open to cooperation, critical, constructive, destructive ...etc.)
> How many meetings do you have approximately per year with muhtars?

4. Please indicate the importance of communication with the actors by providing a value between 1 and 5. Please circle the number that corresponds best with your judgment. The value 1 indicates 'the least important' and the value 5 indicates 'the most important'.

	Scale				
	Least important				*Most important*
1. Municipal Assembly	1	2	3	4	5
2. Urban Council	1	2	3	4	5
3. Representatives of central government	1	2	3	4	5
4. Private sector organizations in the locality	1	2	3	4	5
5. Muhtars	1	2	3	4	5
6. Unions of municipalities	1	2	3	4	5
7. Civil Society Organizations	1	2	3	4	5
8. Governor	1	2	3	4	5

5. Which channels do you use most on your communication with the representatives of the central government? Please circle the number that corresponds best with your judgment. The value 1 indicates 'the least' and the value 5 indicates 'the most'.

	Scale				
	Least				*Most*
1. Personal direct communication	1	2	3	4	5
2. Via the affiliated political party	1	2	3	4	5
3. Via the union of municipalities	1	2	3	4	5
4. Via the agents of central government in the province	1	2	3	4	5

6. This question is about the participants in strategic planning and their methods of participation. Please, mark the boxes with 'X' to indicate the actors who participated in strategic planning and their methods of participation. It is possible to mark more than one box for each actor. Empty boxes will be interpreted as the corresponding participation did not take place in strategic planning.

Participants	Method of participation			
	Face to face meeting	Group meetings	Survey	Other (please specify)
Elected Councilors				
Municipal Committee				
Deputy Mayors				
Directors				
Non-executive municipal personnel				
Members of Urban Council				
Muhtars				
Residents/Citizens				

7. Did you receive any consultancy services during the preparation of the strategic plan? Please mark the appropriate answer. If your answer is 'Yes', please state the extent of the consultancy service.

YES (please explain)	NO

8. Did you conduct citizen polls or surveys to realize citizen participation in strategic planning? Please mark the appropriate answer.

YES	NO	I DON'T KNOW

9. This question is about your evaluation of the planning structure of your municipality. Please circle the number that corresponds

250 APPENDICES

best with your judgment. The value 1 indicates 'weak or least' and the value 5 indicates 'perfect or most'.

| | *Scale* | | | | |
	Weak				*Perfect*
1. The success of your last strategic planning process	1	2	3	4	5
2. The adequacy of current guidelines on strategic planning	1	2	3	4	5
3. The importance of the strategic plan on the municipality's functioning	1	2	3	4	5
4. The importance of performance reports on political decisions of high importance (i.e. investments, appointment in high ranking positions, decisions on budget limits)	1	2	3	4	5
5. The importance of Urban Council's proposals on designating the municipal program	1	2	3	4	5
6. The importance of muhtars' proposals on designating the municipal program	1	2	3	4	5

10. Do you have a human resource management system in your municipality? If yes please rate the effectiveness of this system by giving a value between 1 and 5 to evaluate. The value 1 indicates 'the least effective' and the value 5 indicates 'the most effective'.

YES (please give a number between 1 and 5)   NO

11. Did the head of departments and/or other managers receive an occupational training during your presidency? If yes, how many occupational trainings took place last year?

12. Do your directors and deputy mayors take enough initiatives? Please give a value between 1 and 5 to evaluate. The value 1 indicates 'weak' and the value 5 indicates 'perfect'.

Deputy Mayors
Directors

13. How do you assess the level of cooperation among your departments? Please give a value between 1 and 5 to evaluate. The value 1 indicates 'the least' and the value 5 indicates 'the most'. If you think, the level of cooperation is insufficient, please indicate the reasons.

14. Is there an awarding system for your municipality personnel? If yes, please explain briefly this system.

252 APPENDICES

15. Are there regular staff satisfaction surveys in your municipality? If yes, how often do you conduct satisfaction surveys?

16. Are there occasional social events organized for your personnel? If yes, how often do you organize?

17. Which of these sources do you use to supply your municipality's material needs? Please mark with 'X' the sources that you use.

State supply office
Municipal enterprises
Other municipalities
Private sector organizations

18. Please rate the adequacy of equipment on the public service areas given below. Please circle the number that corresponds best with your judgment. The value 1 indicates 'weak' and the value 5 indicates 'perfect'.

	Scale				
	Weak				Perfect
1. Construction	1	2	3	4	5
2. Water and sanitation services	1	2	3	4	5
3. Transport	1	2	3	4	5
4. Environment and environmental health, waste collection, and hygiene	1	2	3	4	5
5. Police, fire service, emergency, rescue and ambulance services	1	2	3	4	5

APPENDICES   253

	Scale				
	Weak				Perfect
6. Urban traffic	1	2	3	4	5
7. Burial and cemetery services	1	2	3	4	5
8. Parks and recreation	1	2	3	4	5
9. Housing	1	2	3	4	5
10. Culture and art	1	2	3	4	5
11. Tourism	1	2	3	4	5
12. Sports and youth activities	1	2	3	4	5
13. Social aids and services	1	2	3	4	5
14. Promotion of local economy and trade activities	1	2	3	4	5

19. Please rate the importance of the sources given below on meeting the material needs of your municipality. Please circle the number that corresponds best with your judgment. The value 1 indicates 'least important' and the value 5 indicates 'most important'.

	Scale				
	Least important				Most important
1. State supply office	1	2	3	4	5
2. Municipal enterprises	1	2	3	4	5
3. Other municipalities	1	2	3	4	5
4. Private sector organizations	1	2	3	4	5

20. Do you have unofficial partnerships with other municipalities? Please mark the appropriate answer.

YES	NO	I DON'T KNOW

21. How sufficient are your financial resources to cover the municipal services? Please give a value between 1 and 5 to evaluate. The value 1 indicates 'least sufficient' and the value 5 indicates 'most sufficient'.

254 APPENDICES

22. How important are the sources given below on the debt acquisition of your municipality? Please circle the number that corresponds best with your judgment. The value 1 indicates 'the least important' and the value 5 indicates 'the most important'.

	Scale				
	Least important				Most important
1. Central government	1	2	3	4	5
2. Municipal enterprises	1	2	3	4	5
3. Private sector organizations	1	2	3	4	5
4. Bank of provinces	1	2	3	4	5
5. National and international banks	1	2	3	4	5
6. Other municipalities	1	2	3	4	5

23. If you have an additional 1 Million Turkish Lira to spend freely on the municipal services, how would you allocate this amount to the municipal services? Please fill in the amount for the service areas that you wish to allocate money, without exceeding the total sum of 1 Million Turkish Lira.

Service areas	Amount (TL)
Administrative & general	
Economical activities	
Construction	
Environment preservation	
Education	
Sports, culture, entertainments	
Religion	
Public security & order	
Health	
Social Aid	

24. This question aims to learn the influence of central government and/or its provincial organizations on your municipality. Please circle the number that corresponds best with your judgment.

The value 1 indicates 'the least important' and the value 5 indicates 'the most important'.

	Scale Minimum				Maximum
1. The influence on the delivery of municipal services	1	2	3	4	5
2. The influence on administrative activities	1	2	3	4	5
3. The influence on decision-making about municipal services	1	2	3	4	5
4. The influence on partnerships with other local administrations, the private sector organizations, and civil society organizations	1	2	3	4	5
5. The influence on own-source revenues	1	2	3	4	5
6. The influence on grants and aids for your municipality	1	2	3	4	5
7. The influence on the debts and loans of your municipality	1	2	3	4	5
8. The influence on the municipality's investments	1	2	3	4	5

25. This is an open-ended question about your assessment on the adequacy of your municipality's capacity. Please state below your opinion about the adequacy of your municipality's capacity.

256   APPENDICES

Survey II- For the Deputy Mayors

1. This question is about the value of the municipality's immovable. Please, fill in the value of immovable according to 2012 numbers.

	Amount (TL)
The total value of immovable owned by the municipality	
The revenue earned from immovable in 2012	

2. What is the rate of property tax collection in 2012? Please state the percentage of property tax collection on registered residents in your municipality according to 2012 data.

3. According to the last budget report, what is the amount of the municipality's revenue and expenditure? Please fill in.

	Amount (TL)
Total revenue	
Total expenditure	

4. This question is about the debt structure of your municipality. Please fill in according to 2012 data.

	Amount (TL)
Total debt owned by the municipality	
Total debt with a due date in a year	

5. For which expense items are you utilizing the municipal debts? Please mark with 'X' the appropriate responses.

Administrative costs
The current expense of public services
Infrastructure investments

Superstructure investments
Financial investments to raise revenues

6. This question is about the structure of your municipal enterprises. Please fill in and provide an explanation if necessary.

   The number of municipal enterprises

   The total value of your municipal enterprises (in case you don't have actual numbers, please indicate an approximate value)

7. This question is about the adequacy of the physical conditions and equipment in your municipality. Please circle the number that corresponds best with your judgment. The value 1 indicates 'weak or least' and the value 5 indicates 'perfect or most'.

	Scale				
	Weak				Perfect
1. Computers and computer hardware	1	2	3	4	5
2. Technical equipment and machinery	1	2	3	4	5
3. Internet connection and computer software	1	2	3	4	5
4. Physical conditions of civil servant's offices	1	2	3	4	5
5. Physical conditions of the manager's offices	1	2	3	4	5

8. How many public bid opening did you have since January 2012 for public procurement? What is the total value of the public bids?

   Number of public bid opening in 2012

   The total value of public bids in TL

9. Do you have a municipal partnership established to meet the material needs of your municipality? If your answer is yes, please circle the appropriate value which best presents your judgment on the importance of these partnerships in meeting the material needs. The value 1 indicates 'the least important' and the value 5 indicates 'the most important'.

YES					NO	I DON'T KNOW
1	2	3	4	5		

258 APPENDICES

10. What are the reasons for avoiding the partnerships with other municipalities? Please mark the options which correspond to your opinion.

Current law is not clear about municipal partnerships	☐
No adequate personnel capacity to contribute to municipal partnerships	☐
No adequate budget for municipal partnerships	☐
No municipality on the area where we want partnerships	☐
Not avoiding from municipal partnerships	☐
Other (please specify)	

11. This question is about the effectiveness of public procurement processes. Please circle the number that corresponds best with your judgment. The value 1 indicates 'weak or least' and the value 5 indicates 'perfect or most'.

	Scale				
	Weak				Perfect
1. The swiftness of public procurement	1	2	3	4	5
2. Sufficiency of public procurement to meet the municipality's needs	1	2	3	4	5
3. Adequacy of current legislation	1	2	3	4	5
4. Competence of municipal personnel on public procurement processes	1	2	3	4	5
5. Competence in e-procurement options	1	2	3	4	5

12. This question is about the personnel structure in your municipality. Please fill in and provide an explanation if necessary.

Total number of municipal personnel
Number of civil servants
Number of contracted personnel
Number of workers
Number of norm cadre personnel
Number of municipal personnel employed in municipal enterprises

13. This question is about the attribute of the municipal personnel. Please fill in and provide an explanation if necessary.

Total number of permanent and contracted personnel in technical services
Number of personnel with a postgrad degree or an equivalent degree from a vocational school
Number of women personnel
Number of women managers (i.e. deputy mayors and directors)

14. This question is about the experience of your personnel in occupation. Please indicate the number of personnel for each range of years in employment.

Total number of years in employment	Number of personnel
0–5 years	
5–10 years	
10–15 years	
15–20 years	
20+ years	

15. This question is about the experience of your directors in occupation. Please indicate the number of personnel for each range of years in employment.

Total number of years in employment	Number of personnel
0–5 years	
5–10 years	
10–15 years	
15–20 years	
20+ years	

16. Is there a particular unit in the municipality responsible to monitor the training needs? Please mark the appropriate response.

YES	NO	I DON'T KNOW

260 APPENDICES

17. Do you have a municipal training program for your personnel? Please mark the appropriate response.

YES	NO	I DON'T KNOW

18. What is the total amount of training provided to municipal personnel in 2012? What is the total number of participants in the training?

Total hours of training
Total number of participants

19. This question is about your evaluation of the human resource management in your municipality. Please circle the number that corresponds best with your judgment. The value 1 indicates 'weak or least' and the value 5 indicates 'perfect or most'.

	Scale				
	Weak				Perfect
1. Sufficiency of the HR management system	1	2	3	4	5
2. The coherence of the HR management plans with the municipality's needs	1	2	3	4	5
3. Competence of the HR department	1	2	3	4	5
4. Implementation of HR strategies	1	2	3	4	5
5. Monitoring and assessing the training need	1	2	3	4	5
6. Training meet the municipality's needs	1	2	3	4	5

20. This question is about your evaluation of employment policies in your municipality. Please circle the number that corresponds best with your judgment. The value 1 indicates 'weak or least' and the value 5 indicates 'perfect or most'.

	Scale				
	Weak				Perfect
1. Sufficiency in personnel number	1	2	3	4	5
2. Sufficiency in qualified personnel number	1	2	3	4	5
3. The efficiency of employment policies	1	2	3	4	5
4. Match of new recruits the job criteria	1	2	3	4	5

21. Do you have a specific budget allocated for personnel training? If your answer is yes, please indicate the amount allocated.

Yes (please indicate the amount allocated)   No

22. Do you adopt performance criteria in your municipality? If your answer is yes, please mark the options where you adopt performance criteria.

Salary payment
Promotion decision
Contract renewal
Performance criteria are not used

23. Is there a term of reference for departments to avoid duplication of work? Please mark the appropriate response.

YES   **NO**   **I DON'T KNOW**

24. This question is about your evaluation of the management systems in your municipality. Please circle the number that corresponds best with your judgment. The value 1 indicates 'weak or least' and the value 5 indicates 'perfect or most'.

| | *Scale* | | | | |
	Weak				*Perfect*
1. Practices to increase motivation among staff	1	2	3	4	5
2. Training on leadership and management	1	2	3	4	5
3. Collaboration and harmony between deputy mayors and directors	1	2	3	4	5
4. Collaboration and harmony between mayor and deputy mayors	1	2	3	4	5
5. Practices to increase initiative taking in directors and other personnel	1	2	3	4	5

262   APPENDICES

25. Is there a particular unit in the municipality responsible for interdepartmental communication? Please mark the appropriate response.

YES	NO	I DON'T KNOW

26. Do you have an information sharing system in your municipality? If yes, please indicate who can reach this system.

Mayor
Deputy Mayors
Directors
Civil servants

27. This question is about your evaluation of the communication systems in your municipality. Please circle the number that corresponds best with your judgment. The value 1 indicates 'weak or least' and the value 5 indicates 'perfect or most'.

	Scale				
	Weak				*Perfect*
1. Communication among departments	1	2	3	4	5
2. Communication between deputy mayors and directors	1	2	3	4	5
3. The share of information inside the municipality	1	2	3	4	5
4. Adequacy of IT systems	1	2	3	4	5
5. Storing of information	1	2	3	4	5
6. Division of work and collaboration among departments	1	2	3	4	5
7. Communication between civil servants and councilors	1	2	3	4	5

28. How many meetings do you organize per month with directors? Please provide explanations if necessary.

29. Do you have guidelines or training for the elected councilors on how to engage in communication with municipal personnel? Please mark the appropriate response.

| YES | NO | I DON'T KNOW |

30. Do you have guidelines or training for the elected councilors on how to engage in communication with citizens? Please mark the appropriate response.

| YES | NO | I DON'T KNOW |

31. Is there a desk for citizens to appeal their complaints and requests? Please mark the appropriate response.

| YES | NO | I DON'T KNOW |

32. Is there an electronic registry system to store the complaints received from citizens? Please mark the appropriate response.

| YES | NO | I DON'T KNOW |

33. How many citizen polls did you undertake in 2012?

34. How many spreadsheets did you disperse in 2012 via your website or on hand?

264 APPENDICES

35. Did you allocate a specific amount for 'Information and Technology' on your last budget? If your answer is yes, please indicate the amount allocated.

YES (please indicate the amount allocated)	NO

36. This question is about your evaluation of the strategic planning process. Please circle the number that corresponds best with your judgment. The value 1 indicates 'weak or least' and the value 5 indicates 'perfect or most'.

	Scale				
	Weak				Perfect
1. Describing the vision, mission and strategic goals	1	2	3	4	5
2. Identifying measurable outputs and performance indicators for goals	1	2	3	4	5
3. Monitoring the implementation of the strategic plan	1	2	3	4	5
4. Evaluation of the implementation of the strategic plan	1	2	3	4	5

37. This question is about your evaluation of the budget planning process. Please circle the number that corresponds best with your judgment. The value 1 indicates 'weak or least' and the value 5 indicates 'perfect or most'.

	Scale				
	Weak				Perfect
1. Timing in budget planning	1	2	3	4	5
2. Integration of budget plans with performance plans	1	2	3	4	5
3. Implementation of performance criteria on budget negotiations	1	2	3	4	5
4. Coherence with strategic planning	1	2	3	4	5
5. Integration of activity-based costing, feasibility analysis, risk assessment and cost accounting in budget plans	1	2	3	4	5
6. Adequacy of equipment to monitor and assess performances	1	2	3	4	5
7. Adequacy of e-budget system	1	2	3	4	5

Index

A
Accountability, 11
Administrative boundaries, 216
Administrative decentralization, 40
Administrative discretion, 103
Allocative efficiency, 44
Asymmetrical decentralization, 194
Asymmetrical federalism, 203
Asymmetric decentralization design, 215

B
Bank of Provinces, 112
bestuurskracht, 51
Better governance, 43
Black box, 54

C
Capability, 54
Capacity building, 13
Capacity development, 50
Capital revenues, 129
Centralization, 5

Citizen participation, 113, 194
Civil society organizations, 118
Clientelistic arrangements, 198
Co-creation, 36, 193
Communication capabilities, 67
Communitarian governance, 30
Comparative benchmarking system, 210
Competence, 54
Conditional grants, 209
Co-production, 36, 193
Corporate governance, 31
Corporatist governance, 31
Corruption, 12
Co-sharing, 211
Councilors, 138

D
Decentralization, in China, 213
Decentralization reforms, 2, 13
Decentralization theorem, 7
Decentralized governance, 2
Decision-making capacity, 68
Deconcentration, 40

© The Editor(s) (if applicable) and The Author(s), under exclusive license to Springer Nature Switzerland AG, part of Springer Nature 2019
E. Tan, *Decentralization and Governance Capacity*, Public Sector Organizations, https://doi.org/10.1007/978-3-030-02047-7

266 INDEX

Delegation, 40
Deliberative democracy, 8
Democratic accountability, 44
Democratic governance, 9, 193
Democratization, 8
département system, 81
Deprivation levels, 199
Developing countries, 9, 194
Development studies, 13
Devolution, 40
Dubois, H.F., 38

E
Economic development, 200
Economic geographies, 217
Economic growth, 8, 195
e-Devlet gateway, 142
Efficiency in public services, 7
e-governance, 141
e-government, 134
e-Government Benchmark Report, 134
e-government services, 142
Elite captures, 198
Endogenous capacities, 216
e-participation, 141
European Charter of Local Self-Government, 86
Eurostat Information Society Indicators, 140
Exploratory factor analysis, 179
Externalities, 220

F
Fattore, G., 38
Fees, 129
Fesler, J.W., 38
Financial capabilities, 67
Fiscal decentralization, 42

Fiscal decentralization theorem, 197
Fiscal discretion, 111
Fiscal federalism, 42
Flexible design, 220
Franks, T., 54

G
Galan [1990], 3
Globalization, 24
Good governance, 26
Governability, 63
Governance capacity, 49
Governance perspective, 22
Gözler (2003:125), 81

H
Hierarchical governance, 29
Holding governance, 31
Horizontal equity, 47
Human resource capabilities, 67
Human resources management (HRM), 150

I
ICT infrastructure, 137
Implementation capacity, 68
Income inequality, 202
Income redistribution, 8
Influence of central government, 172
Information capital, 62
Innovation, 8
Institutional capabilities, 67
Institutional capacity, 56
Institutions, 198
Intergovernmental transfer shares, 128
Interjurisdictional competition, 47
Interjurisdictional competitiveness, 214

I

Intermunicipal partnerships, 136
Intra-organizational communication,
137

J

Justice and Development Party, 88

K

Krugman, P.R., 216
Kuhlmann, S., 35

L

LAR II, 137
Leviathan hypothesis, 7
Likert-scale items, 165
Local Agenda 21 program, 114
Local capacity, 68
Local governance, 13
Local government, 4, 33

M

Macroeconomic stability, 8
Management, 56
Management sciences, 13
Managerial capabilities, 67
Managerial governance, 31
Managerial' capacity, 56
Market governance, 30
Market liberalization, 6
Material capabilities, 67
Mayors, 138
Metagovernance, 62
Mintzberg, H., 39
Mobilization capacity, 68
muhtar, 81
Municipal administrations
district, 80

metropolitan, 80
metropolitan district, 80
provincial, 80
town, 80
Municipal amalgamations, 217
Municipal enterprises, 102
Municipal taxations, 129

N

'Napoleonic' administrative tradition,
79
Neo-institutionalists, 30
Network governance, 28
New public governance (NPG), 33
New Public Management (NPM), 22,
27
New Trade Theory, 216
'Norm cadre' system, 152

O

OECD countries, 112
OECD Fiscal Decentralization
Database, 166
OLS regressions, 182
Organizational capacity, 56
Organizational learning, 61
Own-source revenues, 129
Oxhorn, P., 38

P

Party affiliation, 172
Performance, 55
Performance budgeting., 143
Performance programming, 145
Political accountability, 211
Political decentralization, 41
Political discretion, 108
Political diversity, 172

Political economy, 195
Political parties, 175
Political sciences, 13
Polychoric correlation, 178
Population, 172
Post-industrial evolution, 216
Prince Sabahaddin, 82
Privatization, 6
Proctor, T., 62
Productive efficiency, 44
Pro-growth governance, 31
Provincial protectionism, 12
Prud'homme, R., 38
Public administration, 13
Public administration reform, 91
Public choice theory, 7
Public economics, 13
Public governance, 27
Public-private partnerships (PPPs), 29, 116
Public procurements, 134
Public service efficiency, 127
Public service governance, 31

Q
Quality of governance, 8
Quantitative research design, 160

R
Recentralization, 218
Regional development agencies (RDA), 97
Regional inequality, 197
Relational capital, 64

S
SIGMA assessment report, 151

Size of government, 8
Social capital, 65
Socio-economic development, 189
Socio-Economic Development Ranking Survey of Provinces and Regions (SEGE-2011), 167
Special provincial administrations (SPAs), 80
Spillover effect, 11
State -economic enterprises (SEE), 81
State predation, 218
State Supply Office, 134
Strategic planning, 143
Suprastructure governance, 31
Surveys, 161
Symmetric decentralization design, 215
Systemic capacity, 56
Systemic governance, 31

T
Tiebout, 7
Total Survey Error (TSE) method, 162
Trafford, S., 62
Tragic brilliance, 211
Training, 148
Transition countries, 194
Turkey, 4
Turkish local government, 159
Turkish public administration, 4, 79
Tutelage relationship, 79

U
Uneven markets, 202
Union of Turkish Municipalities, 148
Unions of Local Governments, 96

V
Variable geometry, 204
Variable speeds, 204
Village administrations, 80

W
Welfare governance, 31

Why Nations Fail?, 198
Wollmann, H., 35

Y
Yardstick competition, 210